CRIMES UNSPOKEN

Crimes Unspoken

The Rape of German Women at the End of the Second World War

Miriam Gebhardt

Translated by Nick Somers

polity

First published in German as *Als die Soldaten kamen. Die Vergewaltigung deutscher Frauen am Ende des Zweiten Weltkriegs*, © Deutsche Verlags-Anstalt, a division of Verlagsgruppe Random House GmbH, Munich, Germany, 2015

Polity Press
65 Bridge Street
Cambridge CB2 1UR, UK

Polity Press
350 Main Street
Malden, MA 02148, USA

ISBN-13: 978–1–5095–1120–4

A catalogue record for this book is available from the British Library.

Library of Congress Cataloging-in-Publication Data

Names: Gebhardt, Miriam, author.
Title: Crimes unspoken : the rape of German women at the end of the Second
   World War / Miriam Gebhardt.
Other titles: Als die Soldaten kamen. English | Rape of German women at the
   end of the Second World War
Description: Cambridge, UK, Malden, MA : Polity Press, [2016] | Includes
   bibliographical references and index.
Identifiers: LCCN 2016021691 (print) | LCCN 2016022335 (ebook) | ISBN
   9781509511204 (hardback) | ISBN 9781509511228 (Mobi) | ISBN 9781509511235
   (Epub)
Subjects: LCSH: World War, 1939–1945--Women--Germany. |
   Rape--Germany--History--20th century. | Rape
   victims--Germany--History--20th century. | Soldiers--Sexual
   behaviour--History--20th century. | Women--Crimes
   against--Germany--History--20th century. | Single mothers--Germany--Social
   conditions--20th century. | Soviet Union--Armed Forces--Germany (East) |
   United States--Armed Forces--Foreign service--Germany--History--20th
   century. | France--Armed Forces--Germany--History--20th century. |
   Germany--History--1945–1955.
Classification: LCC D810.W7 G3913 2016 (print) | LCC D810.W7 (ebook) | DDC
   940.53082/0943--dc23
LC record available at https://lccn.loc.gov/2016021691

Typeset in 10.75 on 14 pt Adobe Janson by
Servis Filmsetting Ltd, Stockport, Cheshire
Printed and bound by Clays Ltd, St Ives PLC

For further information on Polity, visit our website:
politybooks.com

CONTENTS

ACKNOWLEDGEMENTS

I am grateful for the assistance provided to me while researching this book from Martina Böhmer, an expert in dealing with traumatized rape victims in geriatric care, and Jürgen Klöckler, city archivist in Konstanz. My thanks go also to the staff of the archives mentioned in this book, particularly Gerhard Fürmetz from the Bayerisches Hauptstaatsarchiv. The discussion and essays by students who attended my course at the University of Konstanz in the summer semester 2013 were a great inspiration.

I thank the Deutsche Verlags-Anstalt for suggesting and handling this book, particularly Thomas Rathnow and Karen Guddas, and my agent Rebekka Goepfert and social media adviser Oliver Rehbinder.

Finally, I should like to mention my husband Anthony Kauders, to whom this book is dedicated, for his personal encouragement and professional support during the burdening research work.

The author can be contacted through www.miriamgebhardt.de and www.facebook.com/gebhardt.autorin.

INTRODUCTION

A book project on the rape of German women at the end of the Second World War and during the occupation has first to confront certain prejudices. It is as if a single frame in a film has been frozen in our collective memory. It shows a Russian with Asiatic features yelling 'Urri, Urri', but demanding not only the watch but also the woman. We have all seen it on television: blonde woman, played by Nina Hoss, amid the rubble, with a slavering Mongol waiting in the shadows. Is there still anything important to say on this subject? The war is long over, the victims are very old or dead, and later generations find the war stories from Hollywood or Babelsberg more exciting. And then rape – is that not a relic, an archaic crime that always proceeds along much the same lines whether in Germany then, or in Iraq, Syria or South Sudan today? At best the subject offers a cheap platform for the eternal moralists and nationalists with their clear ideas about good and evil. Then it was the Russians who were the wrongdoers; today it is others – in any event, evil men once again.

While working on this book, I frequently asked myself why the wartime rape of German women was still of interest to me today, more than seventy years later. The simple and half-true answer is that the lens through which we look at this time is in urgent need of cleaning.

We historians neatly talk of a 'gap in research' when we find very little reliable information about a topic. But the historians' demand for full accountability is not a sufficient argument for me. There must be more important reasons for descending into such a dark valley.

One such reason could be the demand for fair treatment. The legitimacy of the recollection of the events that took place after the arrival of the Allies is still questioned. There are still voices that say that the investigation of the mass rape of German women is inevitably designed to make up for the crimes committed against victims of German aggression and hence to relativize the Holocaust.[1] Others contest the relevance of the subject itself, claiming that German society is just deluding itself into thinking that it has a blind spot in this regard. It is a pseudo-taboo, they say, that is repeatedly broken so that it can be erected again.[2] And there are those who doubt the credibility of the victims, as the recent discussion of the diary by 'Anonymous' entitled *A Woman in Berlin* has shown.[3]

But for me the main reason for addressing this fundamental mistrust is that a considerable number of those affected have never been recognized as victims. According to my calculations, at least 860,000 women (and a good number of men) were raped after the war. At least 190,000 of them, perhaps even more, were assaulted by US soldiers, others by British, Belgian or French. Nothing has ever been said about these victims. Just as the misdeeds of 'big brother' were swept under the carpet in East Germany, West German society also kept silent about the attacks by its democratic liberators. The women raped by Russian soldiers were at least afforded some recognition, even if it was manipulated for ideological ends, being used to point a finger in the East–West conflict. The women violated by GIs, British and French soldiers, by contrast, were, if anything, punished with contempt. Under the Sword of Damocles of the public condemnation of 'fraternizing women' – i.e. women who allegedly prostituted themselves to the 'enemy' and thus stabbed their own nation in the back – it was practically impossible for the victims of Western sexual aggression to have their stories told. The same applied to the women in the Soviet occupied zone and East Germany. In those cases, too, the experience of violence, if mentioned at all, was put down to their own character weakness.

There have been only two books to date that have reached a

wider audience: the diary by 'Anonymous' mentioned earlier, which was made into a film in 2008, and the first study by the feminist and film-maker Helke Sander in 1992. Both projects had the same setting – Berlin – and the same perpetrators – members of the Red Army. However worthy these two studies were, they reinforced the belief of most Germans that the wartime sexual violence was a problem of the Soviet soldiers, whereas the other Allies had rather to be protected from lovelorn German women. Thus Sander and 'Anonymous', and also the journalist Erich Kuby with his series 'The Russians in Berlin', which appeared in the German news magazine *Der Spiegel* in the 1960s, helped confirm the stereotype. As a consequence, the way people recall the mass rape at the end of the Second World War has become a right–left question: on the one hand, the revisionists and right-wing functionaries representing the German refugees from Eastern Europe, for whom the suffering of women was part of the dream of a Greater Germany, and, on the other hand, the left-wingers, who wanted to defend the reputation of the Soviet 'liberators' by playing down the rape by the Soviet army. This remains the greatest prejudice in dealing with this subject today.

But ignoring the crimes does not make them go away. There are still women (and possibly men as well) living in old people's and nursing homes who remain haunted by their painful memories. They only need to hear a word in English or to be washed roughly by their carers for the memory to return. For that reason, Martina Böhmer, a specialist in geriatric care and trauma therapist, has been touring Germany for years in an attempt to raise the awareness of the staff of those institutions that they might be dealing in their daily work with victims of traumatizing wartime sexual violence.[4]

Even if this problem will soon cease to exist because the last victims will have died, will it have been resolved? Psychologists have discovered that Germany's history still has an impact, generations later. This is easy to understand in the case of women and men who as children were witnesses, or even the product, of the rape of their mothers. But it is also important for their children to be aware of what happened and of the fate of the victims, and to form an idea of the wounds that many of the supposedly sturdy and resolute 'Trümmerfrauen' ('rubble women'), today's grandmothers and great-grandmothers, carried with them from

the war. It is also essential to look again at the moral and sexist prejudices that women were confronted with at the time. They were denied
any recognition not only because what they had suffered was considered shameful, but also because female sexuality was basically viewed
with suspicion. They are accused of somehow having asked for it.

In the beginning, they probably kept quiet because of numbness and
shock, and the inability to put their experience into words. Then other
things became more important – above all, the economic and social
reconstruction of the country and the re-establishment of the conven-
tional patriarchal family model. Then, their own painful experiences
had to take second place to political considerations and to the desire
to take advantage of the assistance offered by the Allies. There was
also the justified priority of dealing with the crimes committed by the
Germans. But at some point, the reasons for continuing to ignore the
mass rape dry up.

Even today there is an impenetrable barrier of silence, the social
opprobrium, moral condescension, political instrumentalization, official chicanery, patronizing compensation, feminist partiality and lack
of recognition causing raped women (and men) to be repeatedly hurt,
humiliated, ignored or preached to. Experts give the name 'secondary
victimization' to this cruel experience on the part of the victims of violence, who then become victims of social exclusion.

One further aim of this book is to show the degree to which raped
women after 1945 were made into victims again by doctors who arbi-
trarily approved or refused abortions, by social workers who declared
pregnant women to be 'wayward' and put them in reformatories, by
neighbours who self-righteously gossiped about the supposedly bad
reputation of these women, and by unfeeling jurists who refused compensation because they didn't believe the women's statements.

Many detailed studies will still be required to make a complete reconstruction of the post-war rapes – in other words, to do justice to all of
the circumstances inside and outside East and West Germany, to the
legal and administrative consequences in all four occupied zones, and
to communications between the Allied armed forces and the German
authorities, and to follow up the traces of the fathers of the children of
raped women throughout the world. For the British occupation zone
in particular, I found only very few sources. Were the British soldiers

the only ones to behave decently at the time? Many questions remain to be answered. Nevertheless, the sources I was able to study provided such concurring and convincing answers that some of the crassest misconceptions about wartime sexual violence against German women can be refuted:

- it was mostly Russians who attacked fleeing German women in particular, so as to take revenge for their own suffering;
- the Western Allied soldiers did not need to use force as they got everything they wanted for a Lucky Strike;
- the rape victims got over the experience 'incredibly quickly' because they formed part of a community in which everyone had suffered the same fate;
- when they returned from the war or imprisonment, the husbands of the raped women rejected their 'dishonoured' wives and children;
- the women raped by Russian or black soldiers aborted as quickly as possible for racist reasons;
- the rape problem was suppressed after 1949 on account of injured male vanity, and reinterpreted as a metaphor for the rape of the nation as a whole.

These are all misconceptions and generalizations that this book would like to dispel. My aim is to cast a new light on this difficult subject and to untangle the half-truths and traditional prejudices. Above all, I would like to correct the image of monstrous Asiatic Russian or Moroccan rapists as compared with white Western liberators, who, as has now become clear, followed precisely the same script of plunder and rape. Fantasy, prejudices and reality can be quickly separated if we reconstruct the events of the time from the victims' perspective, rather than turning them into malleable material for the rewriting of history as both conservative and liberal representations have tended to do in the past. It is time for the victims themselves to speak and for them to be rehabilitated, without their being exonerated from the crimes committed by the Germans under the Nazi regime. It is important to recognize the ambiguity of the victim and perpetrator roles in order to provide relief to their children and grandchildren from the traumatic after-effects of what their mothers and grandmothers experienced seventy years ago. This can be done by continuing to heighten the awareness of our own history that has been gradually developing in Germany in the last few years.

1

SEVENTY YEARS TOO LATE

In Bamberg

That evening, the engineer's wife Betty K. was roused by loud knocking at the corridor door. When she opened the door, her eighteen-month-old child in her arms, she was confronted by two huge negro soldiers, who pushed her aside and entered the apartment. After they had turned all the rooms upside down, they assaulted the woman and, according to her own statement, raped her three times. The woman's father was restrained the whole time by one of the negroes and then shot to death.

Rudolf Albart, author of a war diary[1]

In a village near Magdeburg

The officer had begun to speak, when a German man came from the neighbouring village and through an interpreter said that a Russian soldier had raped his twelve-year-old daughter. The man pointed to the soldier. I then witnessed for the first and hopefully the last time a man being beaten to death. The high-ranking officer kicked and trampled the man to death entirely on his own.

Liselotte M. recalls the Red Army victory celebrations on
8 May 1945[2]

WRONG VICTIMS?

At least 860,000 German women and young girls, and also men and boys, were raped at the end of the war and in the post-war period by Allied soldiers and members of the occupying forces. It took place everywhere – in the north-eastern corner of the Reich territory by the advancing Red Army, in the south-western corner of the Reich territory with the advance of the French, in the southernmost corner at the edge of the Alps during the occupation by the French and Americans, and in the western part by the British. The perpetrators' uniforms differed, but the acts were the same. GIs and Red Army soldiers, British and French, Belgians, Poles, Czechs and Serbs took advantage of the conquest and occupation of Germany first to plunder and then to rape. They repeated, albeit to a different degree, what the Wehrmacht had done earlier to Germany's wartime opponents.[3]

The question of friend or foe was secondary. On their way to Germany, the Americans raped the wives of allied British and French, and also freed slave labourers and concentration camp inmates – just like the Soviets, who had already inflicted a wave of raping on the countries liberated by them.

War-related rape is a global and traditional problem connected with patriarchal gender roles, in which women (and also men) are seen as the spoils of war. During the Second World War, all armies committed this war crime, and all populations suffered in differing degrees; French women were raped by German and American soldiers, Polish women by German and Soviet soldiers, and so on. It is part of the warrior myth that the victor savours his triumph with a sexual conquest. The Japanese army in the Second World War was a particularly notorious example, enslaving as many as 300,000 women from China and Korea, from other occupied territories in Indonesia, Malaysia, the Philippines and Taiwan, and even from the Netherlands and Australia. It took Japan over seventy years to acknowledge that the so-called 'comfort women' had a right to compensation. Even if we extend the time horizon and consider later events, such as the mass rapes in Yugoslavia with up to 20,000 victims, or those in Rwanda with as many as 500,000, the mass rape of German women, although it is difficult to obtain precise figures, remains a historically unique phenomenon.

And yet, even today, these crimes are not talked about, and the women concerned are not officially regarded as victims of the Second World War. They have no memorials, no commemorative rituals, no public recognition, let alone an apology – a state of affairs attacked by Monika Hauser, founder of the women's rights organization medica mondiale and alternative Nobel Prize-winner.[4] Commemorating the rape victims appears to be even more problematic than dealing with the suffering of refugees and those expelled from the East. As many women were raped while in flight and in the context of these expulsions, they suffered from this silence twice over – as displaced persons and refugees, and as rape victims. At the same time, women from the smallest villages in Bavaria, in south-west Germany, in the Palatinate and in Westphalia suffered the same fate, only at the hands of Western soldiers. These victims also kept silent about what happened then.

How can this long silence be explained? Evidently, the German women raped as a consequence of the Second World War were the wrong victims – because they were not men and did not belong to the ranks of those who had been killed, crippled or traumatized; because they were not the victims of the Nazi regime but, on the contrary, might well have been implicated in the Nazi crimes; because they were subject to violence by the victorious powers as an ersatz for the criminal Nazi Germany; and because they were the unheroic victims of a morally charged crime that they were often accused of having brought upon themselves. Those who were not demonstrably 'innocent' – virgins if possible – those who did not defend themselves vigorously even when faced with a weapon, were regarded as 'Yank lovers', 'Veronika Dankeschön' (for venereal disease), who threw themselves at the occupiers for a bar of chocolate or a pair of stockings.

The victims naturally had good reason to remain silent. First of all there were the Cold War alliances. In the East, where many refugee women were stranded and subject to sexual aggression at the hands of Soviet soldiers, the atrocities committed by 'big brother' could not be mentioned. In the West, where there were also many refugees, and where women were subject to attacks by American, French and, in isolated cases, British occupiers, the process of westernization or Americanization was an obstacle to dealing with the other side of post-war experiences.[5] As the historian Walter Ziegler writes, the subject of rape by Americans 'was marginalized, like the numerous shootings, because of the later close friendship with the USA and the atrocities committed by the Soviets'.[6] The Russians raped, the Americans distributed candy – this was the preconception that prevails to this day. The stories of individual groups of German victims, particularly displaced persons and German prisoners of war held captive by the Soviets, became a central focus in the 1950s in the formation of an identity by the German nationalists and refugee associations,[7] but the individual experience of the women victims was appropriated and placed in the service of politics.

There were, of course, women and men who campaigned for the victims of war-related rape and their children, but the motives of these few parliamentarians or veteran association officials were not primarily reparation or compensation, but a criticism of Communism and the reinstatement of the traditional family model. It was for the paternal state to come to the aid of the children of these rapes and to grant these women special status compared with other mothers of illegitimate children.

Apart from the political reasons for the long silence regarding the rapes at the end of the war, i.e. the need to defer to post-war Allies, we can also identify social reasons. For a long time, it was mainly men who dealt with rape victims and their problems, be they members of the administration, charity organizations and parties, doctors or historians. At a time when efforts were being made to restore the traditional family in the 1950s, they had little reason to make the obvious point – that men had not been able to protect their women at the end of the war and that women's bodies became public property. As society sought to reassert its masculinity, it was not an opportune moment to bring up the question of whether a son or daughter might have been conceived by the enemy.

The years after 1945 were characterized by feelings of moral panic, fear and insecurity. Not only was Germany confronted by the task of economic and political reconstruction, the Germans were haunted by ghosts and spectres reminding them of their loss of self-determination and the prospect of being at the mercy of foreign powers. This was symbolized by the metaphor of the rape of their own nation, specifically their own women, something that society emphatically rejected.[8]

In summary, it was not so much the individual silence of the women after the war concerning the subject of mass rape as the embarrassed silence of a nation whose basic convictions about sex and society had been shaken and who wished to expunge from memory the inherent structural violence against women by re-establishing the traditional patriarchal family ideal.[9]

It was only decades later, after the reunification of Germany, that this frozen posture slowly thawed. The two main works recalling the mass rapes, Helke Sander's *BeFreier und Befreite*, and the German reprint and filming of *A Woman in Berlin*, were products of the 1990s and 2000s. They were still not completely successful in overcoming the reluctance by society to confront this topic. Sander was angrily accused by historians of falsifying history, and through her calculations of relativizing the number of Holocaust victims. There was still evidently an image of heroic victims of the air raids, imprisonment, expulsion and fatherless children as opposed to the disgrace of sexual subjugation. The discussion that flared up following the republication of *A Woman in Berlin* in 2003 took a different tack. The book was a bestseller, but the credibility of the author, who had described her experiences in spring and summer 1945 and did not wish to be named, was disputed, an all too common pattern in dealing with rape victims, and this was then followed by the indiscreet revelation of her true identity.

Historians did not cover themselves with glory either in their treatment of rape victims. Professional chroniclers were unable to summon up sympathy for the victims, and their concerns were reserved for those symbolically associated with the male aspects of warfare. The sons of soldiers who grew up without a father, in particular, succeeded in attracting the attention of scholars and the public to their fate.[10] Historical studies still shy away from dealing with the rapes at the end of the war. The new *Oxford Companion to World War II*, a work of over 1,000 pages claiming to be a comprehensive summary, does not even devote a chapter to this topic. The latest books on German history in the twentieth century also devote a paragraph at best to the experience of hundreds of thousands of women. Rape appears still to be tacitly regarded as a by-product of the 'legitimate' use of force in wars. And it was only due to public pressure that the exhibition 'Kriegsende und Vergangenheitspolitik in Deutschland' at the Haus der deutschen

Geschichte in 2005, sixty years after the capitulation, displayed a single exhibit on the subject. The accompanying studies made no mention of rape.[11]

Academics and society have both failed utterly in dealing with this topic. A small research project at the University of Greifswald on post-traumatic stress in rape victims is a comparatively insignificant effort by society on behalf of the 860,000 women who, on my conservative estimate, were raped by Allied soldiers between 1944 and 1955.[12] And even if the 'unheroic' and usually female victims of violence are finally accorded some recognition today, it is unfortunately too late for most of them. They are no longer alive to experience it.

HOW MANY WERE AFFECTED

To determine how many women were raped as a result of the war, it is necessary first of all to define the timeframe. When do we stop counting? Which rapes were associated with the war and which were 'merely' rapes by occupying soldiers in peacetime? I have restricted my study to the time from the fighting during the advance of the Allies on Germany to the end of the occupation period.[13] My account begins in autumn 1944, when the Red Army reached the eastern border of the German Reich, setting off the mass flight westwards. It contin-ues in Berlin, when rape was so common in spring 1945 that women are said merely to have asked one another, 'How many times have they done you?' Moreover, the rapes did not end after the fighting had stopped. We then move on to Upper Bavaria, to a self-contained and traditionally rural area, in which priests reported numerous sexual assaults by the French and, above all, the Americans. In Bavaria, as well, the problem was not over in summer 1945. The locals continued to complain of 'breaches of the peace by US soldiers and the failure by the German authorities to respond'. In considering the consequences for the victims, we move to south-west Germany, where places like Freudenstadt and Stuttgart achieved sad notoriety on account of mass rapes by the French army. We can study these crimes through a par-ticularly disturbing source describing the efforts by raped women to obtain compensation from the authorities for unwanted children.

The current book cannot and does not offer a comprehensive

overview of the events after the end of the war but looks at the incidents and their consequences on the basis of individual fates and regions and the problems raised by them. As there is practically no mention in the records of the British as occupying forces, and as the information to be gained from sparse material in archives like the Hamburg State Archive does not differ from that relating to the other occupying powers, British involvement in war crimes receives scant attention in this book.[14]

We know, however, that members of the British armed forces also committed rape, albeit probably to a lesser extent. Although the civilian population under British and Belgian occupation was greater than in the American or Soviet zones,[15] there are far fewer recorded cases in the archives. One known incident took place in Soltau on the Lüneberger Heide. The town was captured on 17 April 1945 after a stubborn rearguard action by the Germans. On the first night, the British soldiers combed all houses for soldiers and arms, and stole watches and other valuables. Rumour had it that the town was to be punished for its stiff resistance. In the first two days of occupation, there were several rapes in Soltau and the surrounding rural communities, one of them committed by an officer.[16]

The criminologist Clive Emsley also found very few crimes of this nature in the British military history archives and wondered whether the absence of corresponding judicial files was significant. It could be, he mused, that civilian victims remained silent out of shame, and that in any case there was little chance of an investigation of crimes committed by the occupying power, which was generally reckoned to be highly disciplined. Moreover, the victims would have had difficulty in identifying uniformed men, and the soldiers in question could in any case have easily presented alibis for one another. Two British soldiers, for example, were accused in summer 1945 of raping two women near Lübeck and stealing their bicycles. Their superior officer gave them an alibi for the time of the incident, although they were clearly in possession of the women's bicycles, and the officer had even signed leave passes for them. The bicycles were returned to the two women and they were sent home in tears.[17] Cases like this indicate that the British occupiers also have skeletons in their closet and that further research is needed.

The legal situation in post-war Germany made it almost impossible for the German police to investigate rape and prosecute the perpetrators. In the first years of the occupation, a German policeman would not have been able to report anything even if he had burst in on an American gang rape. He could not have intervened, let alone arrested the soldiers, because the military police were responsible for crimes against the German population. Nor, incidentally, would German civilians have been entitled to come to the aid of the victims, as the Germans were forbidden from attacking members of the occupying forces or proceeding against them in any other form. The occupying power had sole responsibility for charges and investigations involving its soldiers, with the result that in most cases no charges were ever brought in the first place. The perpetrators could also not be arraigned before a German court. Here, too, the military courts had jurisdiction.

In 1955, the Paris Agreements came into force, ending the Federal Republic of Germany's status as an occupied country, even if state sovereignty still remained restricted until German reunification in 1990 and the entry into force of the Two Plus Four Agreement in March 1991. In the East, the Soviet Military Administration in Germany was the effective supervisory and command structure in the Soviet occupied zone until 1949, making way then for the Soviet Control Commission in the newly formed German Democratic Republic. In September 1955, a treaty between the GDR and the USSR formally established the sovereignty of East Germany. The official end of the occupation period set the seal on a gradual easing and calming of relations between Germany and its former enemies. From then on, the Allies were less interested in settling accounts with the German aggressor and more concerned to protect their respective allies in the East–West conflict that was now raging. This changed not only the relationship between the occupiers and the occupied but also the symbolic significance of sexual aggression by Allied soldiers against the civilian population.

The victims of rapes after 1955 – at least on paper – were not part of a population that had just lost the war but the female citizens of an alliance partner (the FRG joined NATO in 1955). These rapes were no longer excesses arising out of a collective group conflict but the isolated acts of individuals. The rapes, committed by men in uniform in peacetime, could now also be better investigated and prosecuted by the

German authorities, at least in theory. By 1955, the drawn-out political process regarding the legal status of the rape victims had ended.

In this ten-year period from 1945 to 1955, it is important to visualize the dramaturgy of the events. Without a doubt, most of the rapes took place as the Allies were advancing, no doubt on account of the atmosphere of violence and conquest, but also because of the numbers involved. At the end of the war there were 3 million US soldiers in Europe. By early 1946, there were only 600,000. Criminal acts against the civilian population by the US Army levelled out in 1947 and 1948, although there was a surge every time new troops were stationed, particularly in 1950/51.[18] In the early 1950s in particular, Bavarian communities like Würzburg or Aschaffenburg had frequent cause to complain about sexual aggression by US soldiers. The number of British soldiers stationed in Germany also fluctuated. In the closing phases of the Second World War, there were 400,000. Two years later, only 100,000 were stationed there. In 1951 the number rose to 250,000, and in 1952 to 300,000. The number of Soviet soldiers in Germany dropped by the end of 1947 from 1.5 million to 350,000. After 1949 this largest occupying army increased again to 500,000 or 600,000 soldiers. Added to this were over 200,000 civilians and family members.

With the transition from conquest to ordered occupation, not only the army personnel but also the nature of the rapes changed. This new quality can be seen in the case of an American soldier, who in 1945 went on a rampage of violence, possibly as a result of a war-related psychosis. By contrast, the actions of a group of drunken French soldiers, who in early 1951 attacked an elderly woman in broad daylight, dragged her into a military vehicle and brutally abused her, are more in the nature of a demonstration of power.

Apart from fluctuations in the military personnel, the living conditions of the soldiers, from billeting in private houses to the construction of dedicated housing for soldiers and their families, were also a factor in the risk of rape. The victorious powers pursued different policies in this regard. While US troops were encouraged to bring over their families, the Red Army housed its soldiers in barracks on the outskirts of towns and, for much longer than the Americans, forbade them from fraternizing with the civilian population, let alone marrying. The

French billeted their soldiers in private houses, resulting in a particularly precarious situation for rape victims, as they had difficulty in proving that they had not provoked the attack themselves on account of the close contact with the perpetrator. Like the Americans, the British attempted to prohibit fraternization – with just as little success – and soon had a reputation in the population for being less casual than the GIs, but more respectful and disciplined.[19]

Apart from the attitudes of the former enemies, the structure and discipline of the units, and the likelihood of prosecution and punishment, we should also take account of the soldiers' own political and personal motivation. Their own perception, and that of outsiders, of their status as conquerors, liberators, occupiers and protectors (from the other great occupying power) had an effect on the specific encounters between individual soldiers and the German population and on the crime rate as a whole, as we shall discuss later.

Having established the timeframe, it should be pointed out from the start that it is impossible to obtain even a rough idea of the number of rape victims from the available source material and research. None of the occupying powers has investigated the matter systematically to date, despite some serious initial attempts by American researchers. The Moscow archives continue to protect the reputation of veterans, and little is known as well about the British and French involvement in mass rapes. We are thus reliant on estimates, which in this war, as in all wars, vary considerably. It is in the interests of former enemies to magnify the crimes of the other side. The individual victims and their families, however, often prefer to remain silent.

It is in any case impossible to identify incidents that would be considered sexualized or sexual aggression by today's standards.[20] In 1945 and the following years, rape was defined only as the direct physical overpowering of the woman's resistance (in some cases at gunpoint) with vaginal penetration and credible opposition by the victim, to the exclusion of all other forms of sexual aggression. Women with even the slightest reputation for easy virtue were not generally recognized as rape victims, and 'innocent' girls and respectable wives were more readily believed than young, single women.

The difficulty in estimating numbers is well illustrated by the differences in the estimates. Some put the number of rapes at 11,000 by

Americans (J. Robert Lilly); others say there were 2 million by the
Soviets (Helke Sander), or 2 to 2.5 million during flight and expulsion
(Ingeborg Jacobs).[21] Even as the incidents were occurring, there were
different figures in circulation. In the battle for Berlin alone, anything
from 20,000 to 100,000 women were said to have been raped.[22] One
eyewitness, the resistance fighter Ruth Andreas-Friedrich, was so overwhelmed by the acts of aggression she saw that she reckoned that one
in two women in Berlin were victims. Doctors who treated the victims
also cited large numbers, particularly in Berlin, where events were particularly fraught and where rumours spread like wildfire on account of
the panic inspired by the Red Army.

In my opinion, the most serious estimate can be obtained by looking
at the number of 'occupation children' fathered by occupying soldiers.
In doing so, I combine two approaches. One is based on the assumption that around 5 per cent of the children of occupying soldiers were
conceived as a result of an act of aggression. The other is based on the
estimate that one in ten rapes resulted in pregnancy, and that of these
pregnancies one in ten was brought to term.[23] Obviously, both assumptions leave plenty of scope for error. The incidence of rape was higher
among refugees in flight, and the number of abortions lower in rural
regions. The official number of rape children is also approximate, as
not all mothers admit that their children were conceived in that way,
and others claimed rape in the case of consensual sex. Moreover, many
of the babies died, particularly while their mothers were in flight, and
were thus never registered. Not included in these figures are also rape
victims who were too young or too old to become pregnant. There are
repeated reports of the rape of prepubescent children, such as a ten-
year-old girl in Kitzingen in summer 1946, who was sexually abused
by an American soldier.[24] The idea that it was mostly women of child-
bearing age who were raped is also a misconception.

Now to my estimates: according to information from the Federal
Statistics Office of 10 October 1956, there were 68,000 illegitimate
occupation children in care in the Federal Republic including West
Berlin. This figure is known on account of the multiple surveys that
have been carried out. One reason the statistics were obtained was for
use as an argument in political discussion, not only in connection with
financial reparations for women with unwanted pregnancies but also as

a kind of moral quid pro quo. The question of whether an unwanted pregnancy could be considered 'occupation damage' was discussed for over ten years, both publicly and in parliament. These discussions, which I shall also come back to in detail, have not been studied at all to date.

Of the 68,000 illegitimate occupation children in the West, 55 per cent were fathered by Americans, 15 per cent by French, 13 per cent by British, 5 per cent by Soviets, 3 per cent by Belgians and 10 per cent by other nationalities. According to the mothers, 3,200 children were the result of rape.[25] This is approximately 5 per cent. This proportion is also similar for the individual federal states.[26]

This is not yet the baseline figure for computing the number of rapes. It does not include the children whose mothers were married to Germans but who were made pregnant by a member of the occupying army – in other words, the children of rape within an existing marriage, who were legitimized by the husband. If the figures by the American Provost Marshal for rapes between March and September 1945 are correct, a quarter of the victims were married.[27] This would add 1,100 children to the total. The figure also fails to take account of children under personal rather than state guardianship, which I am ignoring in my calculation.

According to this calculation, we have around 4,300 'rape children'. These are only the figures for the west and future Federal Republic of Germany, however. As far as the Soviet zone and future German Democratic Republic are concerned, we can only conjecture. As a third of the refugees and displaced persons from the former German eastern territories affected by rape lived in the GDR in 1950, and as there were frequent cases of rape under Soviet occupation and in the future GDR, I assume that at least the same number of cases occurred there, bringing us to a total of 8,600 children. Extrapolating by a factor of 100, we arrive at a total of 860,000 victims of rape. This figure refers to women considered German citizens in 1955 and who had been raped by soldiers or other members of the Allied armies while in flight, in the last stage of the fighting or during occupation until 1955. As many women were raped more than once, the total number of cases is much higher.

My estimate is on the low side. In the latest survey of German history in the twentieth century, the number of rapes in the entire Reich territory by the Red Army alone is put at 1 million, although without new calculations having been made.[28] The standard work by Norman M. Naimark, *Die Russen in Deutschland*, and Helke Sander's working group both assume up to 2 million victims of the Red Army.[29] The American criminologist J. Robert Lilly, who speaks of only 11,000 rapes by the US Army, takes the proceedings before American military courts as the basis and multiplies it by a factor of 20, on the principle that only 5 per cent of cases led to criminal proceedings.[30] This 5 per cent quota also applies to rapes following the landing of Americans in Great Britain and France, which appears high compared with Germany, where there were fewer scruples and no organized criminal prosecution during the occupation of the enemy country. Lilly also quotes only the period until September 1945. If we extrapolate his findings, the discrepancy between his estimate of the number of American perpetrators and mine is in fact quite small.

Helke Sander, who was the first person to study systematically the subject of mass rape by the Red Army takes a much broader view. With the aid of the demographer Gerhard Reichling in the 1990s, she put the number of rapes in Berlin alone at 110,000, with a further 1.9 million in the Soviet occupied zone, the former German eastern territories, and during flight and expulsion. This makes 2 million German women victims of war-related rape by the Soviets.[31] As the figures by Sander and Reichling for a long time remained the first and only estimate, this assumption has since been accepted as fact. It is constantly cited, usually accompanied by the comment that exact figures are unavailable.[32]

Helke Sander's working group, with Ingrid Schmidt-Harzbach, Barbara Johr and Gerhard Reichling, based its calculations on the following assumptions: 20 per cent of the raped women became pregnant, of whom 90 per cent aborted, and around 5 per cent of the children born in Berlin between the end of 1945 and summer 1946 were fathered by Russians. On this basis, arrived at through random samples in Berlin hospitals and taking the figure of 1.4 million women living in Berlin at the time, it determined that around 110,000 women, or 7 per cent, had been raped by Red Army soldiers in early summer and autumn 1945.[33] Of these, 10,000 had died or became seriously ill with gonorrhoea – which often made them infertile – or syphilis.

One seeming discrepancy compared with my estimates is the rate

SEVENTY YEARS TOO LATE

of pregnancy as a result of rape. More recent studies have shown that in the USA, where contraception and the morning-after pill are available, 5 per cent of the rapes of young women result in pregnancies, whereas in studies in countries like Mexico or Ethiopia, where these contraceptive methods and the possibility of abortion are less available, the figure is around 17 per cent. The rate therefore appears to be correlated with contraception and the age of the victims (and the number of rapes per woman). As there was no Pill in 1945 and the perpetrators are unlikely to have used contraception, but also as many non-fertile girls and women were raped, I have taken a generally accepted mean conception rate of 10 per cent, which would make my estimate of the total rapes higher than Sander's.

The main difference between Sander's and my estimate, however, is the underlying number of rape children. Sander's estimates are based on random samples from just two Berlin hospitals, without knowing whether they were representative or whether only certain cases of raped women were treated there. I would venture that these patients were probably women who had been severely mistreated, injured or infected with an STD, or whose menstruation had stopped after the rape. Even in a large city like Berlin, it was by no means a matter of course at the time for people to go to a hospital.

Gerhard Reichling estimates a somewhat higher rape quota of 7.5 per cent for German refugees, displaced persons, deportees and inhabitants left behind in the East. He claims that they were raped more frequently because they had less protection outside the cities. Based on this assumption, he arrives at a total of 1.9 million rapes.[34] The obvious problem here too is that Reichling, unlike us today, had no official figures for the number of occupation and rape children. Moreover, his supposition that rape was more frequent in the East than in Berlin, where women also had scant protection in the bombed-out houses, is tenuous. Above all, an extrapolation on the base of a fixed rate has the disadvantage that it does not reflect the dynamics of war and flight. The war situation meant that different numbers of soldiers were on the move at different times and were in varying mental and material states.

In my opinion, the excessive figures in the project by Helke Sander, Barbara Johr and Gerhard Reichling are due to the still-existent latent bias in the East–West conflict and the impetus of the initial revelation and scandal surrounding the mass rape of German women. Sander's approach in the early 1990s in particular was still influenced directly by the feminist struggle against sexual aggression by men, which since the mid-1970s had given great stimulus to the movement. Before Sander, no one had bothered to research this topic systematically. She deserves recognition for this. Nevertheless, I consider my estimate of 860,000 rape victims to be more realistic – once again pointing out, however, that these are only cases of vaginal penetration. In the absence of data and source material, other forms of sexual aggression, including acts perpetrated on male victims, cannot be included.

I cannot even speculate on the relative weighting that should be given to the individual occupying armies. I should like nevertheless to mention one way of estimating the ratio. If we assume a 5 per cent quota for the American occupation zone, we arrive at around 5,000 rape children among the 37,000 occupation children. This would suggest that around 190,000 women living in the Federal Republic were raped by Americans, 50,000 women by French, 45,000 by British, 15,000 by Soviet and 10,000 by Belgian occupiers. This estimate would only be anything like accurate if the 5 per cent quota applied equally to all occupying armies.

The difficulties with estimating the number of victims are undeniable. The crimes could not be recorded and investigated by the German authorities at the time. This is why I have had to make do with estimates. It is understandable that the reliability of my proposed figures should be questioned. However, I am occasionally criticized for basing my figures 'only' on reports by the victims themselves. It is the word 'only' that disturbs me. Of course, there might have been the occasional false accusation. But this fundamental suspicion is not only a further form of disrespect for the victims and their suffering but also a reflection of the old patriarchal idea that the word of rape victims should be doubted in principle.

This book answers this criticism by detailing the insurmountable barriers faced by victims when they attempted to talk about the violence inflicted on them: their own personal sense of shame, society's moral values, and fear of how their husbands and families might react. If a woman gave birth to a child, she had to deal with the dilemma of whether to speak out and tell the truth or to keep silent and protect her child's welfare. Many women preferred not to tell their children how they were conceived. Women who ventured to speak about the violence faced grave social consequences. Rape victims were generally suspected of having provoked or even desired the intercourse, particularly when the attacker was a white Western soldier. Understandably, the victims usually didn't want to risk having their honour and dignity violated again. Given the fact that rape victims very often had to remain silent for decades because they knew that no one would believe them, I cannot accept the criticism that the statements and reports were 'only' those of the victims.

SEXUAL AGGRESSION AGAINST MEN

Sexual aggression against boys and men is also absent from my calculations because of the lack of data. The fact that not only girls and women are raped in wartime is easily overlooked. Rarely is sexual aggression against men studied, with few exceptions such as the Bangladesh war in 1971 between West Pakistani groups and Bengali Moslems, or more recently the disturbing images of Abu Ghraib prison in Iraq, where female soldiers were also involved in abuse and sexual aggression.

Sexual assaults against men are played down or reinterpreted by the victims themselves more frequently than attacks on women. In post-war Germany, aggression against 'defenceless" women could be exploited politically, whereas male victims of sexual aggression fell outside the binary patriarchal framework of heroic men and passive women victims.[35] Isolated references to the rape of men and boys can be found nevertheless in source material and are striking. The biographer of the actor Horst Buchholz, for example, relates that, while the twelve-year-old Buchholz was in flight from Silesia to Berlin, he arrived in a Red Cross camp near Magdeburg, where he had to harvest onions with other boys. One of the supervisors is said to have indecently assaulted them several times.[36]

The State Ministry of the Interior reported on 19 June 1946 on the abuse of two boys by two American soldiers in Upper Franconia. The GIs had forced the thirteen-year-olds to perform oral sex. The offence was listed in the files as 'sexual offence with children' and not as 'rape'.[37]

Adult men were also victims. A 48-year-old dentist from Bad

Kissingen was invited by four American soldiers in the night of 4–5 December 1951 to join them in a round of schnapps. They then offered to drive him home. On the way they stopped to relieve themselves. The dentist, A. P., also got out of the car. One of the soldiers grabbed his head and forced him down with the words 'Du leck!' ('Suck me!'). A second soldier attempted the same thing. A. P. struggled and was beaten up. With a bleeding head he walked 2 kilometres to the next village. The police chief, who forwarded the case to the regional authority of Lower Franconia, concluded his report with the explicit remark that nothing adverse was known about the victim (meaning homosexuality) and that his statement appeared credible.[38]

In my research in the Freiburg State Archive, I found a particularly disturbing case of a further male rape victim. W. H., a shoemaker from Haslach, made the following report to the Inland Revenue Office in Freiburg in February 1960, fifteen years after the event.[39] In summer 1945 he visited a Moroccan barracks with a friend, who knew some of the colonial soldiers. While he was conversing with the soldiers, one of the men persuaded him to enter a side room, locked the door, took him by the throat, pulled his trousers down and raped him. Because he had no physical injuries, he only told his friend about it, but not his parents or his sister, 'because I was ashamed', as he wrote. The reason he reported it after all, fifteen years later, and requested compensation was that he now had 'third-degree syphilis (cerebral palsy)'.

The Inland Revenue Office, which could only approve compensation where there were witnesses or other evidence, attempted to locate the friend, who was now living in North America, and received the following written confirmation of the story: 'W. could not defend himself because he was absolutely unprepared for the attack and the Moroccan was three times as strong as he was and threatened him with a knife when he tried to resist. W. showed me the bruises and scratches on his arms and neck.' The friend also explained why the victim had not reported the affair earlier:

First, a fifteen-year-old growing up under the influence of the Third Reich knew nothing about homosexuality or venereal disease, topics not taught at school. Second, he was ashamed to report it to his parents because he simply didn't know about the risk of infection. Third, he couldn't go to the German police for help, because in those chaotic times there were only a few police officers in our town and they had no authority whatsoever over the occupying troops.

As in most other cases, the claim for compensation was refused for lack of evidence.

These examples tell us nothing about how frequently men were victims of sexual aggression in the post-war period. It is nevertheless unquestionable that there were also male victims of such attacks and that they suffered extremely as a result.

A WORD ABOUT METHOD

Research into the mass rape of German women began too late for oral history methods to be used – in other words, the systematic evaluation of eyewitness interviews. But, apart from biological reasons and the considerable problems of critically analysing biographical recollections that are so far in the past that they have been revised many times and reshaped by the media, I have another reason for not interviewing the victims. As modern psychological findings tell us that the recollection of such events can lead to a new trauma, I believed that in this particular case the interview method would be too risky.

This topic also called for a careful approach to the sources for another reason. There are inevitably few official records of these sexual aggressions. The German authorities had no leverage, and the military authorities were not informed, as far as possible, as the acts were strictly forbidden and in some cases severely punished, even with the death penalty. When such incidents were nevertheless brought to the attention of the military authorities, the court proceedings followed their own self-serving rules, which were not necessarily in the interests of the victims, as we shall see later. Military court files are therefore of limited value as sources. Descriptions by the perpetrators themselves are rare, and in any case highly biased.

The experience of the victims, who are the focus here, has not been studied satisfactorily either. A few testimonies have been published, exclusively from the Soviet occupation zone. It is no coincidence that the only personal testimonies are from the East. The descriptions were a logical follow-up to Goebbels' horror stories about the inferiority of the Soviets and made use of the same stereotypes. In addition, they are firmly anchored in the post-war consciousness as examples of the experience of flight and expulsion and emphasis on the war crimes of the enemy. This applies in particular to a frequently cited collection of refugee stories compiled by the Federal Ministry for Displaced Persons, Refugees and War Victims in the 1950s. The use of the word 'enemy' alone is indication of the lack of objectivity of these documents.

To find personal testimony by women (or men) raped by Western Allies, we are reliant on chance findings in diary archives and claims for compensation by the victims.[40] These and all other personal testimonies also need to be treated with caution as they were often written to seek exoneration and were coloured by the narrative conventions of the time. A particularly opaque form of personal testimony is to be found in the applications by women seeking an abortion to the Health Department in Neukölln. They were written so as to have the best possible chance of being accepted by the authorities and doctors and cannot therefore be considered as the authentic voices of the women concerned. The same holds true of women applying for compensation after becoming pregnant as a result of rape; they are also tailored to the putative values of the authorities concerned so as to increase their chances of being accepted.

The perspective of politicians, clergymen and employees of the authorities, police officers, military judges, psychiatrists and doctors is no more reliable. They are all men who were not only subject to constraints and political priorities but were also influenced in their judgement by the ideas of morality and gender roles and characteristics of the time.

The fragmentary and unreliable sources are an obstacle to the scientific demand for comprehensive documentation and make it necessary for us to fill in the gaps ourselves. We can only attempt to make a virtue out of necessity and to use the shortcomings in the sources positively. For the period of expulsion and flight, there are printed autobiographical testimonies, which also give us an idea of the way the victims dealt with their situation; for the victims raped by Americans, we have for the most part only third-party documentation – from clergymen and political representatives – which, apart from the incidents themselves, also give us an indication of the social values at the time, particularly with regard to single women, foreigners and the socially disadvantaged. As far as women raped by the French are concerned, applications by women who became pregnant as a result provide eloquent testimony – but also demonstrate the lack of sympathy by the authorities in south-west Germany in the 1950s and 1960s. We have only a few isolated cases concerning the British, which nevertheless confirm the general picture.

We must also bear in mind the degree to which the initial research has been influenced by these methodological imponderables. The preconceptions regarding these rape victims still exist today, not least because of the uncritical and less than rigorous consideration of the sources. This will be discussed in greater detail in the last chapter of the book.

2

BERLIN AND THE EAST – CHRONICLE OF A CALAMITY FORETOLD

Many people think consciously of the things they themselves saw or had to carry out and which have to be set against what is allegedly taking place now. 'We are guilty ourselves, we've earned it' – that's the bitter recognition that many struggle through to.

Diary of Corporal Heinrich V., 10 April 1945[1]

The fear and despair did not develop overnight. Everything gradually built up until it suddenly became unbearable . . . After we had been in no-man's land for three weeks, the Russians arrived, and we had hoped so much that it would be the Americans.

Liselotte S., in a village near Magdeburg[2]

It is my secret, tantalizing dream, to see Berlin just once more, to feel Berlin, not as a blazing city at the front, but as a giant recovered somewhat after the war, who had been shamed and humiliated by its inhabitants and was now bowing servilely to foreigners and opening up its gates to the Soviet people, the Russian warriors, from the Brandenburg Gate to the very outskirts of the city.

Vladimir Gelfand, Red Army soldier, August 1945[3]

THE GREAT FEAR

At the start of 1945, most Germans had ominous presentiments about occupation by the Allied troops. They knew or at least had an idea of what German troops had done elsewhere and feared retribution. News at the end of the war had become scarcer and had never in any case been objective, and there were no newspapers whatsoever, so they were reliant on military reports and hearsay as sources of information as to what awaited them. All that the population heard *ad nauseam* was war propaganda containing horror stories about the advancing enemy troops. Leaflets announced that the 'murderous Bolshevist rabble' would 'defile' and 'butcher' women and girls if the German soldiers did not push them back in a last effort.[4]

As the Red Army advanced inexorably through Silesia and East Prussia towards Berlin, Hitler himself told his Gauleiter on 24 February 1945:

> What our women, children and men have suffered at the hands of this Jewish pestilence is the most cruel fate that a human mind could possibly conceive. There is only one way of responding to this Jewish–Bolshevist genocide and to its Western European and American whoremasters: with the utmost fanaticism and dogged determination to summon up the last strength that a merciful god enables people to find at a time when their lives are at stake. Those who become weak and fail should and will go under.[5]

Nazi propaganda had been filled for years with warnings of the ferocious revenge that the enemy would exact, particularly the so-called 'Jewish' revenge, often equated with the 'Bolshevist' threat. In his diary in summer 1941, propaganda minister Goebbels noted the words of his Führer, referring to the planned attack on the Soviet Union: 'In any case we have so much to answer for that we must win because otherwise our entire nation, with us at its head, will be eradicated along with everything that is dear to us. So let's get to work!'[6] Hitler's view that, if Germany were to lose the war, the German people, starting with the women, would also be lost, was repeatedly circulated.

When the war did enter its final phase and the Allied troops set foot on German soil, it was not at all clear right up to the last moment in many regions which of the victorious powers would arrive to become the new occupiers. Rumours abounded, but one thing was evident: the first encounters would be between young Allied soldiers on the one hand, and German women and children, old men and those unfit for service on the other. Of the German population awaiting the arrival of the Allied troops, 60 per cent were women and children and men under sixteen or over forty years of age.[7]

Fears waxed and waned, depending on the military situation. The mood improved if British or American troops were to be expected. On 10 April, the chaplain Oswald Kullmann from Kleinbartloff in Thuringia rejoiced: 'The Americans are coming! Excitement but no panic; excitement fluctuating between fear and joy, but tending more to joy.' In June, he wrote: 'Soon the Russians will be coming. They are preceded by rumours of atrocities, filling the population with new dread.' Thirty inhabitants fled – with good reason, as it turned out. At the end of June, the Americans handed over Kleinbartloff to the Soviets, and in early July there were reports that nine Russians and Poles had broken into a farm at Ober-Orschel and raped the women living there.[8]

Soviet soldiers held the most fear for the Germans. They were regarded as being unpredictable and so brutalized that they would not stop short of defiling children, old people and nuns, or even their own compatriots, such as the Soviet women working as slave labourers. The greatest fear was inspired by the 'Mongols' or 'Asiatics', soldiers from the eastern regions of the Soviet Union. They were followed by the French, particularly the dark-skinned colonial troops from Algeria, Tunisia and Morocco, who had a notorious reputation, recalling the mood after the First World War and the 'Black Shame' on the Rhine.[9] Among the Americans, the blacks or 'negroes' instilled fear and terror long before their arrival. The darker the skin and the more unfamiliar the physiognomy, the more threatening the soldiers appeared. This racial prejudice applied particularly to Africans and Mongols, who were reputed to be brutal rapists and generally regarded as being uncivilized with uncontrollable urges.

Feeding on the mixture of racial prejudice and propaganda, stories and rumours of atrocities committed by German troops in the East further exacerbated the fears within the civilian population. The greatest fear was that the Red Army would retaliate by committing similar atrocities. It prompted people in the East to abandon house and home, livestock and most of their possessions to escape from the approaching Soviets. But in Berlin as well, and everywhere else where the Russians were coming, Nazi propaganda and the fear of Communism meant that the spectre of bloodthirsty Soviet beasts, Asiatic hordes and Russian barbarians spread like wildfire.

The external appearance of these foreigners was already enough to cause anxiety. The occupiers came from all over the Soviet Union and spoke so many languages and dialects that even the officers sometimes had difficulty in communicating with their units. They were Russians, Byelorussians, Ukrainians, Caucasians, Georgians and Kazakhs, Armenians and Azerbaijanis, Bashkirs, Moldovans, Tatars, inhabitants of Irkutsk, Uzbeks and more, but in the perception of the indoctrinated German society this ethnic mosaic was reduced to 'Mongols', 'Cossacks' and 'Asiatics'. They were considered to be much less civilized than the Germans, and also Germany's other enemies. The first impression tended to confirm this belief. Unlike the Americans in their trucks and jeeps, the Soviets arrived by means of transport that were anything but impressive: motorcycles, horses, carts or simply on foot.

Escape through suicide

A particularly radical consequence of this ideologically fomented panic is illustrated by a story from Holzendorf-Mümmeldorf, a hitherto insignificant village halfway between Brüel and Criwitz in Mecklenburg. It had two farmsteads and a tenant farm owned by the church, with a lake to the west. When the first Red Army soldiers were sighted near the village on 4 May 1945 and reports began to circulate that some women had been raped, three inhabitants – the shepherd Martin Bründel from Müsseldorf, his father-in-law Christian Kunst and the tenant of the farm owned by the church – decided that they would not suffer the same fate. On 6 May, Bründel took his family down to the lake, where he cut the throat first of his twelve-year-old daughter Hannelore and then of his wife. The ten-year-old son Herbert and six-year-old daughter Helga, who tried to run away, were held back by their grandparents.

Their father beat them to death with a club and then proceeded to drown the two-year-old Hans. Then Kunst beat his wife to death. The two men abandoned their original plan of committing suicide themselves. Instead they made it look as if the women and children had been brutally raped and murdered by the Soviets. And it didn't end there: on the same afternoon the tenant shot his wife, daughter-in-law and himself. Bründel remarried after the war and became a member of the SED (East German Communist party). The deception was not discovered until 1962. Bründel and Kunst admitted that they had attempted to place the blame for the murders on the Soviets. They were both sentenced to death and executed.[10]

Even if this is a particularly drastic example of the panic and ideological delusion of the Germans, there are eyewitness reports hinting at large-scale suicides, even a 'suicide epidemic'.[11] Women in particular committed suicide to escape the feared rape and shame of falling victim to foreign soldiers. Even practising Christians were convinced that suicide was preferable to 'defilement' – by 'subhumans' into the bargain.[12]

The Führer and his entourage had already set the example of committing suicide for fear of falling into the hands of the enemy. Among the high-up Nazis, and also in the population at large, it took on epidemic proportions. The women close to Hitler – Eva Braun and Magda Goebbels – led the way. Goebbels' wife is thought to have killed her six youngest children herself as the only honourable end to the Nazi regime. It is therefore highly probable that many normal Germans also committed suicide, not only from fear of the Soviets but also because a life without National Socialism had no more meaning for them. Added to that was the idea of capitulation and the shame it represented, both individually and collectively. In the eyes of staunch Nazis, capitulation and flight were the worst disgrace. And what would be a more obvious symbol of capitulation than rape by a Red Army soldier?

Hitler had demanded total defeat and the complete destruction of Germany. He believed that it was more honourable to die a 'soldier's death' than to negotiate for peace, much less to surrender. The Nero Decree of 19 March 1945 ordered the destruction of the infrastructure in the belief that the enemy would in any case be completely ruthless. Seen in this way, suicide was an act not of cowardice but of self-sacrifice to thwart the enemy one last time.

Many women carried cyanide capsules and razor blades in their hand-bags. In April 1945, suicides in Berlin peaked at 3,881 cases, or 242.7 per 100,000 inhabitants, five times higher than in the years before. In 1945, there were 7,057 officially recorded cases of suicide for the whole of Germany; in reality the figure was probably higher. There were 42 cases in the devoutly Catholic region of Upper Bavaria between April and May 1945, compared with just 3 to 5 in previous years.[13]

Some figures are hard to believe. Although the source is dubious, a document reporting the flight and expulsion from a Pomeranian town describes the mass suicide of 600 people in an attempt to escape from the Red Army.[14] Even before the taking of Berlin, some 500 inhabitants of Schönlanke in Pomerania are said to have taken their lives 'for fear of the monsters from the East'. And in Demmin, Western Pomerania, between 700 and 1,000 people are reported to have committed suicide just before the arrival of the Red Army.[15] In the Berlin district of Pankow alone, there were 215 reported cases of suicide, mostly women, in a three-week period. Some women filled their pockets with bricks and jumped into the Havel. Others were victims of group suicides, being killed by their own parents or partners.

Nemmersdorf – a blueprint for what was to come

The massacre in Nemmersdorf was exploited for propaganda purposes to illustrate what awaited the Germans when the Red Army arrived. It was used by propaganda minister Goebbels to incite fear of the Russians and strengthen the determination of the population.

On 18 October 1944, the Soviets entered German territory for the first time and penetrated 60 kilometres into the German Reich along a 150-kilometre front. On 21 October, the Red Army reached Nemmersdorf, close to Königsberg (now Mayakovskoye in the Russian territory of Kaliningrad), a village with just under 700 inhabitants. The German Wehrmacht managed to retake the village on 23 October. The events that occurred in the forty-eight hours in between have still not been fully clarified today. Historians reckon that between nine-teen and thirty people were killed in the two days, including thirteen civilians caught between the fronts. The Nazi regime used the occasion for propaganda, sending emissaries to report on the atrocities.

They claimed that seventy-two people had been killed, others had been tortured and crucified on barns and, above all, that all of the women and girls had been raped. Another reporter, by contrast, spoke of just two cases of rape and twenty-six people shot in the back of the head. Nemmersdorf was nevertheless chosen as the deterrent example of what would happen if the Germans were defeated.[16] The newsreels showed horrifying pictures, probably staged, of dead women and children, whose skirts had been pushed up and their underwear removed. In the following months, Goebbels formed a pseudo-objective committee consisting of representatives of occupied and allied states to investigate the crimes committed by the Red Army. Witnesses of the events in Nemmersdorf were intimidated and put under pressure.

The Nemmersdorf massacre was instrumentalized until well into the post-war period as a rhetorical weapon against the 'Red Peril' from the East. The reports or rumours of villagers being nailed to barn doors or raped by Red Army soldiers were expanded to include gruesome details of castration and crucifixion. At some point, it was even claimed that there had been only one man among the victims, and that the seventy-two deaths were almost exclusively women and children. The photos by Goebbels' propaganda people were taken at face value. It was not until the 1990s that new eyewitness accounts put the exaggerated reports into perspective. What really happened in autumn 1944 will probably never be finally cleared up.

Hope and fear

Fear was therefore the prevailing sentiment in the last months of the war, at least in Berlin and the eastern territories of the German Reich. The attitude to the Western occupiers was generally more neutral. The focus in the last two years of the war had been on preventing the advance of the 'Red Peril', and it had been hoped that after the war it would be possible to pick up on the points of similarity that had existed earlier with the Western Allies, and perhaps even to unite in facing up to the Bolshevists.

Many south Germans positively welcomed the occupation and, in view of Hitler's call for total war, sought peace at any price. Even if the consequences of war were much easier to bear in the rural regions of

Bavaria than in the bombed cities, the inhabitants there were nevertheless acutely affected by the situation that prevailed in the last weeks
and months. Their own workers had been conscripted into the armed
forces or were working for the war economy, and the relationship with
foreign slave labourers and prisoners of war was problematic, to put it
mildly. In addition, evacuees from northern Germany and Munich who
were billeted in the smallest villages were regarded with considerable
suspicion by the rural population on account of their supposed aversion to work and soft lifestyle (they slept in so late in the morning!).
Alongside the stream of refugees and evacuees, who doubled the population of some villages, came straggling and undisciplined returning
German soldiers. Summary courts sentenced deserters to death, and
the men enlisted into the Volkssturm dug foxholes and requisitioned
rooms at random in private houses. Nazi functionaries, mostly members of the SS, set about destroying vital transport routes, especially
bridges, to slow down the enemy.

Practically no one believed in a miracle any more. On the contrary,
they feared that any additional military resistance would simply enrage
the enemy even further, and that the civilian population would have
to bear the brunt. But fanatical Nazis continued to terrorize the war-
weary citizens. Those who expressed doubts about the final victory
were still likely to be court-martialled and shot, even in the last hours
before the capitulation. Most Bavarians therefore preferred to face up
to the inevitable, keeping their white flags at hand in the hope that it
would be the Americans who arrived first. Instead of wishing their own
soldiers luck, they supported the enemy and longed for the German
Wehrmacht to make itself scarce. It was often women who dismantled
the anti-tank barriers to make it easier for the Allied soldiers.

Even in Berlin, there were many who failed to share the general hysteria and awaited liberation with black humour and defeatism, or even
with anticipation. Margret Boveri, for example, suggests that the divergent expectations might be explained by the refusal of some people to
give credence to the Nazi propaganda, and their personal experience
through contact with other nations. Boveri herself had travelled as a
foreign correspondent before and during the war, and in 1940 crossed
the Soviet Union on the Trans-Siberian railway. This experience
and, as she claimed, her upbringing in southern Germany meant that

she was not so pessimistic about occupation by the Red Army. 'The people of southern Germany, who have never come into contact with Russians, are much less prejudiced against them than the East Elbians, who have been fighting wars of succession with them for centuries. We are not afraid', she wrote in her diary-like letters shortly before the fall of Berlin.[17] This would soon change.

THE RED ARMY COMES

On 21 August 1942, the Wehrmacht hoisted the German flag on the highest mountain in the Caucasus. Shortly afterwards, the German offensive came to a standstill, and the course of the war shifted, with the paradigmatic turning point in Stalingrad in early 1943 transforming a war of conquest of *Lebensraum* in the East into a retreat and a war to defend against Bolshevism. In Africa at the same time, the victorious progress against the British and Americans came to an end, and in May 1943 the German and Italian troops surrendered in North Africa. The German U-boats lost the Battle of the Atlantic, the British bombed the Ruhr and destroyed vital munitions production, and the great tank battle near Kursk turned into a debacle. Shortly afterwards, the Americans and British landed in Sicily, and in September arrived on the Italian mainland. From then until the battle of Berlin in April 1945, the Wehrmacht was in retreat and engaged in defending lost positions. And with destruction. The soldiers were ordered to fight to the last man and, if territory had to be ceded to the enemy, to destroy everything. Protection of the civilian population was not an objective. In the conquest of East Prussia in early 1945 alone, hundreds of thousands on both sides lost their lives.[18]

Between April and December 1944, the Allies reached the frontiers of the German Reich. By the end of July, the Red Army had recaptured practically all of the territory lost since 1941 and had traversed eastern Poland as far as the Vistula, overrun Lithuania and approached the borders of East Prussia. In early October, it broke through to the Baltic coast north of the city of Memel. In the West, the Ardennes offensive delayed the advance of the Allied troops, giving the Soviet army a decisive advantage in the race to occupy as much territory as possible in the German Reich. The Red Army winter offensive began in January 1945, with 570,000 men on the German side against 1.5 million Soviets. The Soviet soldiers advanced 300 kilometres in just two weeks.

As soon as the Red Army approached, German civilians fled towards the Reich. During the war, the East had not only been a settlement area and colony but also a huge evacuation area for city dwellers in the West to escape from the air raids. In early 1944, 825,000 west Germans had escaped there. The new arrivals and the established German population were now fleeing westwards, from East and West Prussia, from Danzig, Pomerania, eastern Brandenburg and Silesia, but also from Slovakia, Croatia, Yugoslavia and Romania. Between January and May 1945 alone, 7 million people were on the move, marking the start of an end-less and drawn-out exodus with as many as 2 million deaths on the way.

For a long time, this flight and expulsion was the only stable point of reference in the accounts of mass rape. The refugees, with no home anymore and an uncertain future, the defenceless par excellence, became the iconic characters in this scenario. There are two reasons for this. The prophecy that German women would suffer when the 'Russians' arrived had been long prepared by the Nazi propagandists. The first to feel it were the fleeing women. The mass rapes during the flight and expulsion from the East were indeed partly to do with being overrun by an army that still had the atrocities committed by the German Wehrmacht and SS fresh in their mind. In addition, however, the Nazis exploited them in the interests of the propaganda of survival. The prophecy, based on old prejudices, racial ideology and the ideo-logical struggle, was fulfilled in a tragic fashion.

The other reason that the image of the refugee women as victims of rape has remained frozen in the collective memory is in the narra-tive itself. We have few institutional sources about the events at the time, but instead countless eyewitness accounts by victims, collected by groups representing the refugees and by the Federal Ministry for Displaced Persons, Refugees and War Victims, for private or academic purposes. This documentation has been used repeatedly since then as a source of literature on the crimes committed during this mass movement; thus, reports about refugee women were better known than reports about rapes in Bavaria or in the French-occupied south-west.

However, it is not only a question of the quantity but also of the quality of the narrative. The fleeing women were usually vulnerable and

left to their own devices. They had often abandoned everything, while
the remaining men were enlisted into the last lines of defence. Their
families were frequently torn apart, and they lost touch with relatives
and even with their own children. When the flight came to a standstill,
they often found themselves in claustrophobic, camp-like situations.
They hid in barns and shelters surrounded by battling troops, where
they had to hold out for weeks in agonizing fear without food and even
the most rudimentary facilities. And it was in these circumstances that
the rapes were committed. The women caught in hiding were singled
out by the soldiers, denounced by fellow sufferers and abused in front
of their children. The most harrowing aspect for these fleeing and
expelled women was that the sexual aggression was committed at a time
when they had been torn out of their social surroundings and were particularly exposed as a result.

They were people on the run, who had often had to leave with practically no preparation or time to pack, who had been left in the lurch
by the German authorities, who had ignored the calls for evacuation far
too long, and who were now hunted down by the Polish and Soviet soldiers who were brutally cleansing the captured territories of Germans.
At the same time there was desperate fighting down to the last man
and senseless fortifications after the decision had been made in summer
1944 to turn all of Germany into a fortress, with 400 kilometres of
defensive positions in Pomerania and 120 kilometres around Breslau
[Wrocław] alone. Wherever the earthworks, entrenchments and fortifications held up the Red Army for a few weeks, it merely meant that
the number of victims was higher. Soon there was nothing left to eat,
and people, especially small children, began to die *en masse*. Those who
survived the hunger and the first wave of violence had in some cases to
hold out until they were officially expelled from 1946 onwards, and in
the meantime they had to contend with slave labour, imprisonment in
camps and deportation.

But even those who had managed to get moving in time, with their
handcarts or on foot, often failed to escape. Death was everywhere:
corpses lay on the roads, dead animals in the fields, the most terrible
spectacle all around. Countless tragedies occurred in the race to escape
on boats, trains or foot marches; mothers were forced to look on help-
lessly as their babies and small children died of disease or starvation, or

to abandon frail parents. There were cases of women throwing their children off a boat into the icy water. And all the time the danger of aerial attacks, bombs, street fighting, being shot by friend and foe alike, robbery and murder by liberated slave labourers, concentration camp inmates and even criminals taking advantage of the situation. Boats sank, trains burned, vehicles were involved in accidents. There was no fat, no warm shelter or clothing, and countless people lost their lives through cold, damp, hunger, thirst and disease. And, on top of it all, the all-pervading fear of the enemy and what they would do to the women. An eyewitness on a flight from East Prussia to Schleswig-Holstein summed up the general mood she experienced in this inferno in one word: 'panic'.[19]

Trapped

We now know that in many German territories in the East, the Party functionaries delayed flight as long as possible and then ordered immediate departure. In Breslau [Wrocław], which Hitler had designated in 1944 as a 'fortress', the evacuation was ordered hurriedly and far too late. 'Hundreds of thousands of people now had to leave the crowded Silesian capital in icy cold weather in a few hours', eyewitnesses recall the flight in early 1945.[20] It was −10° Celsius; some were lucky enough to get a train, but the vast majority had to leave on foot. Of the 60,000 women and children who left Breslau, almost a third froze to death. Those who could not get away fast enough, including many evacuees from Berlin and the Rhineland, were trapped in the city. The fighting continued for twelve weeks; the city became a war zone and the women the spoils of war.

Leonie Biallas was almost fifteen when she saw the first Russian soldiers. A Soviet officer assured her: 'Russian soldiers don't kill women and children. That's just your Nazi propaganda.' But he warned: 'You have nothing to fear from us. But when the other troops come, no one can help you. We have four years of war behind us, and no one has had any leave. The men have been promised German women as trophies of war. That spurred them on to fight.'[21]

The Russian officer's warning turned out to be true. In her memoirs, Leonie Biallas graphically describes what happened to her trapped in the city and paints a terrible picture of the encounter between a naïvely innocent girl in pigtails and a fearful Red Army soldier with a black beard, bushy eyebrows and a fur hat:

> He grabbed hold of me and dragged me towards a door. I tried to escape, struggled desperately. My mother attempted to come to my aid and pull me from him. He pushed her away and opened the door. It led to the bathroom. Mother tried to come in as well. He slammed the door shut and bolted it. He was out of his mind and tried to pull my trousers down but couldn't undo the fastening. He pulled out a knife. I screamed. Now he's going to stab you, I thought. Mother hammered on the door from outside and also screamed. The soldier cut the belt with the knife and pulled off my trousers and underwear. Then he forced me down onto the stone floor. I hit my head. He threw himself on top of me. I was frozen and didn't even scream any more. But mother continued to moan all the time behind the door. I don't think it lasted very long. He stood up and left the bathroom and house without a word. I squatted on the cold floor and just wanted to crawl away into a corner. Mother came in, took me in her arms and comforted me. We were both crying.[22]

This was just the beginning of the torment suffered by Leonie, her mother and her aunt Gertrud, who was over 60 years old, along with the nuns in the nearby nunnery, or a 16-year-old girl who bled to death as a result of the rapes. Some women deliberately stuck to officers so as to escape the 'stinking lice-ridden' ordinary soldiers. Such was the case with the mother of Ruth Irmgard Frettlöh. The girl saw her leave a shed with a commandant – smiling. The picture remained etched in her memory and for decades clouded her relationship with her mother. It was only much later that she discovered that her mother had only been so nice to the rapist so as to protect her daughter.[23]

This behaviour is a feature of many of the descriptions of rape while in flight: mothers sacrificing themselves for their daughters, daughters for their mothers or fathers. The violent acts produced a tangled web of lifelong family guilt. We read in the sources of cases in which elder siblings, from one moment to the next, had to look after the younger ones because their mothers were regularly taken away by Soviet soldiers both for sexual services and also for work of all kinds. They also had to provide information about the whereabouts of their husbands if the Soviets suspected them of being Nazis or war criminals. It doesn't take much to imagine the moral dilemma of these women, who were exposed not only to sexual aggression but also to the threat of deportation.

One in five Germans has a refugee or deportation story in the family.[24] The richest source of information about the situation at the time, the main official outlet for speaking and providing written testimony afterwards was the documentation produced by the Federal Ministry for Displaced Persons, Refugees and War Victims, which appeared from 1954. Today it forms an impressive and contemporary source of memories comparatively close to the time the events took place. Caution is nevertheless required in interpreting the reports. The aim of the documentation was to institutionalize the memory of flight and expulsion in order 'to provide posterity with an authentic record of the terrible events in Eastern Europe at the end of the Second World War', as it says in the introduction to the record.[25] This 'historically motivated official government task' was directed by a high-level academic commission led by Theodor Schieder, who like his colleague Werner Conze was a highly respected historian of the time, but who has since been discredited on account of his Nazi sympathies. In the absence of other sources, the historians relied mainly on subjective recollections by the victims in their efforts to 'raise the personal experiences of 'flight and expulsion' to the level of public memory culture'.[26]

The commission studied the sources critically and, according to its own statement, devised a process for verifying the refugees' statements. Those who look at the thick volumes today, however, will quickly note that they are a product of their time. In selecting eyewitnesses, no consideration was given to their earlier functions in the Nazi state. The texts are full of ideological stereotypes, with 'Asiatic hordes' and 'monsters', and German compatriots who remained faithful to the bitter end. Among the attitudes typical of the time was the condescension towards Poles and Russians. There are repeated references to 'Polackenweiber' and 'hideous diabolical Mongol faces'.[27] We must therefore take these stories with a pinch of salt. The documentation is nevertheless a terrible chapter in the history of women at the end of the Second World War.

Josefine S.[28] from the district of Osterod [Ostróda] in East Prussia, now Poland, was surprised when she saw the first Soviet soldiers at the end of January 1945. She had been told that the enemy was nearly starved to death and was badly dressed, and yet she was confronted by strong and powerful young men and women soldiers bursting with health, all with good uniforms, felt boots and fur hats. And they all seemed to have joyful expressions on their faces. 'They waved at us and called "Hitler kaput", and for the first time I heard the rough and for us ugly sounding Russian language. We also saw the repellent faces of the functionaries.'[29]

One of the vehicles in the convoy stopped. Three tall soldiers got out, grabbed Josefine S. and threw her onto the vehicle. Her cries for help went unheard in the snowstorm. The car moved off again, and the icy wind blew around her. 'One of the youths, who was lying wrapped in blankets, grinned as he observed me and asked "Cold?"' The vehicle slowed down, and Josefine S. jumped out, but she was immediately grabbed again and lifted back onto it. There followed 'the most degrading moments' of her life.

At some point she managed to get away. She was up to her calves in soft snow. Help me, please God, was all she could think. Then she decided to accept 'the fate she had been abandoned to' and headed for a cow stall, where she found around 100 other people. Soldiers entered from time to time, including officers, and hauled out girls and young women. Crying and pleading were to no avail. The Red Army soldiers pointed revolvers at the women, grabbed them by the wrist and dragged them away. One father who tried to protect his daughter was taken out to the courtyard and shot. Then the girl was raped. 'She came back towards dawn with fear in her child's eyes. She had aged overnight. As her body was no longer capable of expressing her emotions, she sank down into the straw.' Josefine S. heard a man saying that he wished he had poison to kill himself, his wife and his daughters.

In the jaws of hell

This description is typical of the events taking place during flight and expulsion. Women often found themselves in a kind of camp situation.

Explosions and the fear of aerial attacks meant that the refugees had to find places to shelter on their way. They sat together in cellars, sheds or other shelters, waiting lethargically, often for days and weeks, while the war raged around them.

In Elbing [Elblag] in West Prussia, for example, 200 mostly elderly women and men were sheltering in a primary school and could not even leave the room to answer nature's call. The building was bombarded and burnt to the ground.[30] The 39-year-old E. O., with her 15-month-old daughter and 7-year-old son, had a terrible experience on 29 January 1945 as they watched a 15-year-old girl being repeatedly raped, and her mother, who tried to protect her, killed. The Soviets set up special rooms for the rapes. They hauled out women twice a day. This went on for a week. For E. O., the seventh day was the worst. She had to spend the whole night in the 'jaws of hell'. There was nothing to eat, only alcohol and cigarettes. By the next morning, she was severely injured and could hardly walk or lie down. Leading her two children by the hand, she was driven with other women on foot to a town 21 kilometres away. They were still given nothing to eat and believed they would all die on this death march. When the procession was broken up two weeks later, only 200 of the 800 women and a few old men were still alive. The dead were left by the side of the road.

'I was a physical and mental wreck and was thus spared these atrocities. Once they wanted to take my son Horst away; to prevent this I was used once more. Then the order was given that women were not to be raped. We were then able to defend ourselves, but it was too late. Thousands of women like myself are ruined and there is no one to help us', she said six years later for the official documentation. She walked as far as the British zone, where the soldiers proved to be 'good people'. She nevertheless attempted to commit suicide shortly before she reached safety. Someone pulled her unconscious out of the river Lahn.[31]

In February 1945, Rössel [Reszel] in East Prussia became a garrison town. The soldiers looted day and night. There was no end to the raping. If a Russian appeared at the door, the women and girls escaped through the windows. Then men surrounded the houses to capture their 'booty'. Many women attempted to obtain poison, but the doctor in the local hospital refused to help. One girl drank vinegar essence

and died a painful death. Among the abused victims were 13-year-old
children. One girl was so badly injured during a rape that she could no
longer walk and remained sick for a long time. Another girl hanged
herself.[32]

In Jastrow [Jastrowie] in the district of Wirsitz [Wyrzysk] in West
Prussia, H. H. and her children found themselves shelter on a farm.
Soon the first soldiers arrived, taking a break on the farm and drinking
alcohol. They forced the doors open, broke the windows and selected
their victims. It went on like this day and night, and had it not been for
her child H. H. would have preferred them to shoot her. She didn't
want to abandon it 'alone in a foreign world', so she had to put up with
'this most terrible humiliation'. One day a Russian soldier shot another
one. After this, the commanding officers became stricter.[33]

In Woldenberg [Dobiegniew] in the district of Friedberg in
Pomerania, now Lebus in Poland, Otto H. experienced the first terrible night: 'My niece was raped by fourteen Russian officers in the next
room. My wife was dragged into a barn by a Russian and also raped.
Then she was locked in the stable and at 5 a.m. next morning raped
again at pistol-point. When the troops left, we found my wife under a
pile of straw, where she had hidden in fear.'

A Russian appeared and picked out a 13-year-old girl. The child
screamed and struggled. The soldier loaded his pistol, had everyone
assembled and threatened to shoot them if they didn't bring the girl
into the next room within five minutes. 'We knew that he would use
the weapon and were forced to comply with his wishes. When he discovered that the girl was too weak, he gave her to another comrade. He
himself appeared in the room and we had to assemble again. This time
he took the mother, who was the youngest of the women. The mother
was raped in the bed while her daughter was assaulted on the floor next
to the bed by the other Russian. The mother was pregnant.'

Abuse and rape increased from one day to the next, with the result
that more and more locals and refugees sought shelter in the former
farm. Every night the Russians came, fired their weapons through the
windows, battered down the bolted doors and raped women and girls
in the presence of the children. Some of the victims were over sixty.
Sometimes vehicles drove up to the farm, took women and girls to
other places, where they were raped again. The following day they had

to walk back 20 or 25 kilometres.[34] The reports repeatedly describe systematic rape for several days in one place with different women. Contrary to what people thought in their panic at the time, however, there was never a military order in the Soviet Army to rape German women.

In Zietlow [Sidłowo], M. M. found shelter with other refugees in a sheep pen. Soviets kept on coming into the pen. At first they were looking for watches, then they took the boots from the Germans, then they drove all of the men except M. M.'s husband from the pen. They lined up the women and girls and pointed their loaded machine guns at them. M. M. thought they were all going to be shot, but the soldiers fired into the ceiling, where they suspected that German soldiers were still hiding. Next they took women and girls as they pleased. More and more Soviets pushed their way into the pen. Some women, some unfortunate girls were raped five or even ten times in that seemingly endless night.[35]

It is interesting to note how often the eyewitnesses mention the wide range in the ages of the victims. Many old and very young women, frail, sick, pregnant and even dying refugee women had personal experience of the later claim by feminists that it was not only young or attractive women who were raped and that the act was not sexually motivated but rather a demonstration of power. 'For weeks and months our women and girls went through hell on earth. I later visited an 82-year-old woman who never recovered from her experiences. Schoolgirls and confirmands suffered the same fate. I know of several women who were killed for trying to resist. One young woman and mother, a former confirmand of mine, had her skull bashed in after having tried to prevent a Russian soldier from having his way', reports the former pastor of Muttrin [Motarazyn] and Damen [Stare Dębno] in the district of Belgard [Białogard] in Pomerania.[36]

Another striking feature is the numerous gang rapes reported in the source documentation. In Lauenburg [Lebork] in Pomerania, Red Army soldiers stood in line in front of every house. One German woman was raped by as many as forty-five men, despite the fact that she was half-dead by the end. Victims included 78-year-old women and 9-year-old children. The Russian soldiers said that their wives and sisters had been treated far worse by the German soldiers. When leaving the village, B. met a farmer who told him that his 13-year-old daughter had been 'taken' for the fifth time that morning.[37]

Many rapes ended in death. E. H. from Luggewiese [Lubowidz] in the district of Lauenburg [Lebork] watched as her sister, paralyzed with fear, was shot by Red Army soldiers. With her mother, two children and 25-year-old sister Käte, E. H. fled on 9 March to the neighbouring village of Damerkow [Dąbrówka]. The next day, the Russians also attacked this village. At least thirty people were crowded together in a single room. The first soldiers demanded watches and other valuables. Then a tall Russian came into the room, looked around and pointed to Käte. 'He just gestured once with his finger. When she failed to get up immediately, he went up close to her and held his machine gun up against her chin. Everybody was screaming, but my sister remained silent, unable to move. Then the shot fired. Her head fell to the side, and blood streamed out. She was dead on the spot without a sound coming from her.'[38]

There are reports in the documentation about women being shot or shot at or committing collective suicide. Others went mad. The acts were usually done in a group, very often in public, which may be seen as further evidence that the rapes were also a demonstration of power. They were organized, and the men arranged the matters themselves, which meant that the women couldn't escape and that their suffering lasted a long time. Many women were abused for days on end.

F. V. from Dambitzen, a brickworks in the district of Elbing [Elbląg] in West Prussia, describes how she escaped in a vehicle. A farmer's daughter who was travelling with her was shot in the back because she resisted being raped. The mother of the severely wounded woman was shot in the hand. The daughter-in-law and wife of a Danzig businessman, who were also sitting in the vehicle, were raped many times during the journey by young soldiers who jumped on them, all in the presence of the dying woman. The refugees were given shelter by a forester, his wife and two married daughters with their children. The Russians appeared every evening, took a number of women and girls and raped them several times over. Sixty-two people from the farm and village of Occalitz [Okalice] drowned themselves in the lake, asked the forester to shoot them or took poison.[39]

Behaviour of the victims

Recollections are of limited value as sources for understanding the behaviour of the victims themselves. They say more about how they wanted to be seen than about their actual behaviour at the time. That said, the contemporary reports frequently mention resistance by the victims. Self-defence, presence of mind and ingenious escape strategies are emphasized. In her recollection of the end of the war, Gela Volkmann-Steinhardt speaks not only of the usual attempts to hide or escape to the forest, sleeping every night in a different place and making herself unattractive, but also of a feisty and fearless aristocratic aunt, who, with the 'concentrated wrath of her righteous ancestors', stuck a full chamber pot on the head of a young assailant. 'The helmet wouldn't budge in spite of the vain attempts by the drenched soldier to get it off. His two comrades were so doubled up with laughter that for this one evening the entire group escaped without the usual sacrifices.'

The author herself also thought up countless strategies. She used her anger, pretended to be fearless and resisted to the utmost. She showed her injuries, begged, pleaded and humbled herself if necessary: 'I once kissed the hand of a Kalmuck, begging for mercy like a submissive Anyushka. He was touched enough to withdraw.' Or she would show a photo of a fictitious husband, or gather her sons around her, who would scream the place down like savages if they sensed danger. All the same, these defensive strategies were of no avail in the long run: 'Hunters will eventually track down all the hiding places – even if the beast thinks out more and more sophisticated ones every night. They dragged out their trembling prey from the straw, from the cow troughs, from the dove-cots and the baking ovens.'[40] When Gela Volkmann-Steinhardt felt ashamed to face her children the next day, she discovered with amazement that the world had remained unchanged in spite of her action: 'The boys needed breakfast. And lunch. And water and wood. Until another day began – exactly the same as the day before, and another day with thousands of obligations.'[41]

It is anyone's guess whether descriptions of personal courage are really reliable. We will return later to the question of descriptions of self-efficacy or agency as motifs in autobiographical literature of the time, part of a gender discourse in which women were also capable of soldierly virtues like bravery, imperviousness to pain and willingness to make sacrifices. The metaphors used in the reports are also interesting. The perpetrators are often described as hunters and the women as prey who were first herded together and then isolated from the community. The men creep up, stalk, negotiate windows and stairs silently like cats, as if their moves are choreographed. All of the countless cases in the documentation of expulsion are very similar in this regard. The convergence in the interpretation of what happened can be explained by the way in which the victims came to terms with their experiences and also perhaps by the way they were interviewed and their reports edited. I assume that the documentation from the 1950s, which had a political subplot, influenced the descriptions. The impression is given of a communal or collective experience by resisting German women who, when they lost their homeland, flocked together like lambs and never had a chance of resisting the 'bestial' Soviet enemy in the role of the wicked wolf.

Alone in a crowd

Autobiographical reports that were not part of the politically motivated documentation but published individually show that the events can be perceived and interpreted in a different way. They emphasize the isolation and helplessness of the victims and are not uncritical of their male and female compatriots. Gabi Köpp describes how she was betrayed several times by women while she was in flight. First, her mother sent her away without any explanation of what she might expect; after that her fellow sufferers betrayed her to Russian soldiers:

> The women trembled with fear that they could be the ones to suffer. I literally felt, without being able to see it, that they were searching for me. . . . The women should go themselves, if they are so afraid of being shot. But then Frau W. says: "Where is little Gabi?" I hear it again and again. She won't stop until they've dragged me out from under the table. I think bitterly: "They can do this to me because I'm alone and don't have anyone to protect me.'"

For a long time afterwards, Gabi Köpp was troubled by the traumatic experience of being left in the lurch by her own people.

I would use stronger words today to describe what I called 'meanness' on the part of those women six decades ago. With ice-cold selfishness, their treachery sent a 15-year-old girl to her doom, fully aware of what they were doing to me. . . . I feel hate rising in me. Hate for these women who, if I had been their daughter, they would have kept silent.[42]

The betrayal to the Russians, the lack of solidarity among the women, are recurrent features of the autobiographical testimonies of the mass rape, notably in the well-known Berlin examples of Anonymous and Margret Boveri, which we shall return to separately.

But the Soviet sources also mention cowardice and the lack of solidarity among the Germans, saying that the abandoned German population were capable of anything in their fear of the Red Army. People hid in cellars and would not come out onto the street. When they encountered Soviet soldiers and officers, many threw their arms up in the air as if pleading for mercy. White flags flew from many buildings to indicate that the soldiers would meet no resistance and that the occupants were willing to follow all orders. Many Germans claimed to be Poles or Jews so that they would be spared, or pretended to be Communists and revolutionaries, with pictures of Stalin hanging on the walls.[43] It would almost seem as if the inglorious behaviour of the Germans – the struggle to hold out as ordered by the regime, the habit of obeying, the state terror that brutally nipped any signs of premature surrender in the bud, the vain attempts to hole up in the fortified towns, the ongoing panic – offered fertile soil for the aggressive behaviour of the Red Army soldiers. Social psychologists have described the phenomenon in which expectant behaviour fosters the corresponding reaction. At the same time, this is not to say that the Germans could have averted the calamity by acting differently.

The demographer Gerhard Reichling, who collected statistics in the 1950s on flight and expulsion, calculates that 1.9 million women and girls were raped by Red Army soldiers as they advanced on Berlin, 1.4 million of them while fleeing from the former German territories

in the East and 500,000 in the Soviet occupied zone. He further estimates that 292,000 children were born as a result of these rapes. This
would mean that a quarter of the women became pregnant after having
been raped and did not abort, which sounds implausible in the light
of other research and my own findings. As mentioned earlier, my own
estimates differ considerably from Reichling's. At all events, the data
on occupation and children born of rape in West Germany point to a
much smaller number of victims and a much higher abortion rate. My
calculations nevertheless put the number of victims in the hundreds of
thousands. While it is true that most of the mass rapes typically took
place during flight and expulsion from the East, there were nevertheless hundreds of thousands of German women for whom the danger
was yet to come.

BERLIN

The sound was unlike anything Berliners had heard before, unlike the
whistle of falling bombs, or the crack and thud of anti-aircraft fire.
Puzzled, the shoppers who were queued up outside Karstadt department store on Hermannplatz listened: it was a low keening coming
from somewhere off in the distance, but now it rose rapidly to a terrible piercing scream. For an instant the shoppers seemed mesmerized.
Then suddenly the lines of people broke and scattered. But it was too
late. Artillery shells, the first to reach the city, burst all over the square.
Bits of bodies splashed against the boarded-up store front. Men and
women lay in the street screaming and writhing in agony. It was exactly
11.30 a.m., Saturday, April 21. Berlin had become the front line.[44]

In his popular war book *The Last Battle*, the Irish-American journalist and writer Cornelius Ryan gives a vivid account of the start
of the battle for Berlin, which lasted until 2 May and was to lead to
house-to-house fighting and more civilian casualties than the air raids
on the city. These weeks are also symbolic in terms of the mass rapes.
Nowhere else are there so many well-known accounts of what happened to the Germans at the end of the war and afterwards: Barbara
Noack, Hildegard Knef, Margret Boveri, Bert Brecht, Leon Uris and
Erich Kuby, to mention but a few, have all written about it. For our

discussion of the mass rapes in Berlin, however, the most important is the description by a woman who wanted to remain anonymous, and whose book, *A Woman in Berlin*, was to cause a sensation decades later and, because a film was made out of it, has left the most intense trace in our visual memory. The (subsequently destroyed) anonymity of the author was one decisive reason why her story became the collectively perceived version. We would like for that reason to concentrate first on other cases.

The significance of Berlin has to do with the magnitude of the events but even more so with the fact that the rapes by the Soviets (other perpetrators are hardly mentioned) also stand as symbols for the overthrow of the German Reich. The raping of the women of Berlin is part of the narrative of the downfall of a proud Prussian German city, one where the 'greatest general of all times' had recently withdrawn into his bunker and prepared to commit suicide, a city that would in future be the pawn in the East–West conflict.

Let us allow Cornelius Ryan once again to set the scene: the Brandenburg Gate, Unter den Linden, the Reichstag building and the Royal Palace are in flames. People are running along the Kurfürstendamm, dropping briefcases and packages, bobbing frantically from doorway to doorway. At the Tiergarten a stable of riding horses receives a direct hit. The screams of the animals mingle with the cries and shouts of men and women; an instant later the horses stampede out of the inferno and dash down the Kurfürstendamm, their manes and tails blazing.

Within this inferno, Ryan is a great storyteller, weaving descriptions of the last days of the war in Berlin with the fate of the women who were raped. His book, which is still used by academics as a reference, speaks of Gotthard Carl, an air force captain, who believed until the end in the final victory. He hurried home and ordered his wife to go down to the cellar and stay there, sitting right opposite the cellar entrance. Gerda was amazed but her husband was insistent: he had heard that in other cities the Russians entered the cellars with flamethrowers and most people were burnt alive. 'I want you to sit directly before the cellar door so that you will be killed first. You won't have to sit and wait your turn.'[45] Gerda numbly did as she was told. For the first time since their marriage she didn't include Gotthard in her prayers. In the afternoon, she disobeyed his orders and returned to the apartment. She never saw her husband again.

First encounters

The truncated impression we have today, thanks to the historical films of the fall of Berlin, is of a sudden invasion by dark powers of a hitherto unsuspecting city. The violence did not explode all of a sudden, however, but gradually increased and smouldered for months and years. At first the Soviet soldiers wanted above all to put an end to the fighting. They were not looking for women but for German soldiers and members of the Volkssturm in hiding. They shared their rations and sweets with children on the streets. One anecdote in Ryan's book is of two women, one a widow and the other the wife of a major, who were sitting in a cellar when a huge shadow appeared on the wall. In the shadow's hands was a gun. To them the apparition appeared like a cannon being held in the paws of a gorilla, and the soldier's head seemed huge and deformed. They were unable to breathe. The Russian came into view, followed by another, and ordered them out of the cellar. 'Now it is going to take place', they thought. The two women were led outdoors, where the Russians handed them brooms and pointed to the debris and broken glass that littered the walk. Their surprise and relief were so obvious that the Russians burst out laughing.[46]

Much to the surprise of the Germans, many of the Soviets were highly disciplined. When they discovered that someone was an opponent of the Nazi regime or had been persecuted, they were usually courteous. Helena Boese came face to face with a Red Army trooper on her cellar steps. He was young, handsome and wearing an immaculately clean uniform. He just looked at her when she came out of the cellar and then, gesturing to indicate good will, gave her a stick with a white handkerchief tied to it as a sign of capitulation. Ilse Antz was asleep in the basement of her apartment house when the first Russian entered. She started in terror at the young, dark-haired trooper. He just smiled and said: 'Why afraid? Everything all right now. Go to sleep.'[47]

The Communists, the few resistance fighters and the hidden Jews of Berlin, like the 20-year-old Hans Rosenthal, who was later to become a popular television talk-show host, felt relief at the first sight of the

Russians. Rosenthal had spent twenty-eight long months hidden in a small allotment garden. For him the arrival of the Red Army was obviously liberating. There were embraces, scenes of fraternization with the Red Army soldiers, who were happy for their part that the fighting was finally over and that they had survived.

Ruth Andreas-Friedrich belonged to a resistance group and distributed flyers until the end urging the people of Berlin to surrender. It was the werewolves – a handful of Germans who continued to resist long after the Red Army had taken Berlin – not the Russians, who were the enemy. Her initial feeling when the Red Army arrived was one of incredible relief. She and her fellow resisters joyfully welcomed the Soviets, attempted to communicate with them in broken Russian and to show them the way so as help them put an end to the Nazi regime once and for all.

Berlin fell little by little. Some districts, like Weissensee, which had a large Communist population, surrendered immediately, with red flags hanging from the windows. Pankow and Wedding put up resistance for several more days. Hitler Youth, Heimatschutz, police and fire brigade members fought in the hope that they could turn the tables one last time. In Wilmersdorf and Schöneberg, the Soviets had to fight from house to house and clear their path with rocket launchers. In Grunewald and Tegel, it was possible to read the newspaper at night by the light of the flares. SS men continued to patrol the streets executing anyone in uniform who looked as if he had deserted, blowing up bridges and destroying as much infrastructure as possible to delay the conquest of Berlin.

In the perception of many eyewitnesses, the first line of Soviet conquerors consisted of disciplined and well-mannered soldiers who did not harm women. But then the others arrived, not with sweets but demanding the rights due to the conquerors: the women of the conquered.[48] I doubt if it was really like that. The difference between civilized and aggressive soldiers can also have had to do with the internal hierarchy and the different values in societies at war. It was a question of protecting the honour of the true warriors who were the first to reach Berlin as opposed to the units that arrived afterwards. I therefore believe that once again it was more the dynamic of interaction between Germans and Soviets that caused things to spin increasingly out of control.

Ryan describes the torment of Ursula K. in Zehlendorf, mother of 6-year-old twin daughters and a 7-month-old son, who, after having been raped in the night by four Russian soldiers, was set upon again in the morning by two Soviets with knives in their boots and fur caps. She ran out of the house into a building across the street, where she found a bathtub. Turning it upside down, she crawled in with her children. Or the 18-year-old Juliane B., who blackened her face and blond hair and hid under the sofa. In the adjoining cellar were two old people. Suddenly one of them shouted: 'She's there! There! Under the sofa.' While a young, neat-looking soldier began to disrobe her, she used various strategies to defend herself. First she cried and pleaded, then told him firmly and politely to behave himself. The soldier began to look annoyed. Finally she cried at him: 'I simply don't love you! There's no point in this! I simply don't love you!' That was enough for the soldier. He swore and dashed out of the cellar.[49]

Her friend and the friend's mother were not so lucky. They swallowed poison after they had been raped. Even the maternity home Haus Dahlem was not spared. The Ukrainian cook was shot at during an attempted rape, pregnant women and ones who had recently given birth were abused. The longer the fighting continued and the soldiers were in danger, the greater their rage. Alcohol, which was suddenly readily available, did the rest.[50]

The Soviets did not only assault German women. They also raped the Soviet slave labourers, Jews recently released from concentration camps and opponents of the Nazi regime. Ruth Andreas-Friedrich, the pro-Russian resistance fighter, wrote in horror in her diary on 6 May 1945:

For four years Goebbels told us that the Russians would rape us. That they defile and plunder, murder and burn. Propaganda, we said appalled, and looked forward to the arrival of Allied liberators. We didn't want to be disappointed now. We couldn't have stood it if Goebbels had been right. We had been in opposition for twelve years and now for once we wanted to be on the right side.

But this wish was not to come true. She could not possibly be in favour of what was happening now.

She was dismayed and bewildered. Wherever she went, she found the same misery: theft, looting, violence.

The victorious army set upon the women of Berlin with uninhibited avidity. We visited Hannelore Thiele, Heike's friend and classmate. She was huddled up on her couch. She barely looked up as we entered the room. 'I want to kill myself', she wept. 'I can't live like this.' 'Was it really so bad?' I asked cautiously. She looked at me miserably. 'Seven', she grimaced. 'Seven in succession. Like animals.'

In Klein-Machnow, Ruth Andreas-Friedrich met Inge Zaun, an 18-year-old who had been completely innocent in sexual matters:

Now I know everything. Sixteen times over. 'How can you defend yourself', she mused dully and indifferently, 'when they hammer on the door and fire off their rifles indiscriminately? New ones, different ones every night. When they took me for the first time and forced father to watch, I thought I would die. Later . . .' she makes a weary gesture with her hand. 'Since their captain has had a relationship with me, he's the only one, thank goodness. He listens to me and helps to ensure that the other girls are left alone.'

The disappointment felt by this opponent of Hitler is great. 'They defile our daughters, rape our women', say the men. There is no other talking point in the city. The girls are hidden in the roof timbers or buried in coal bunkers or wrapped up like old women. Almost no one sleeps in their own home.' Ruth Andreas-Friedrich hears a perturbed father say:

'Honour gone, everything gone.' [He] gives his daughter, who has been defiled twelve times, a rope. She takes it obediently and hangs herself on the nearest mullion. 'If you are defiled, there's nothing left but death', said the teacher of a girls' class two days before the collapse. More than half of the pupils drew their own conclusions and drowned themselves in the nearest lake. Honour gone, everything gone.[51]

Soon Ruth Andreas-Friedrich was also to be a witness to the consequences of the mass rapes. On 18 August 1945, she noted that the official doctors were talking about relaxing the abortion laws: 'The seed that our victors sowed in the first weeks of May has now started to sprout. Another six months and thousands of children will see the light of day without knowing who their father is, conceived in fear and born into a grey world. Should they be allowed to live?'

We know today that it was not thousands. The Secretary of Finance in Berlin reckoned in 1956 that around 200 'Russian children' had been conceived in violence.[52] But the official doctors were meeting because there was a great medical demand: 10 per cent of the women of Berlin had venereal diseases. The black market price for treatment with Salvarsan was two pounds of coffee, or 100 marks per injection. Hoechst launched this organic arsenic compound in 1914 as the first effective remedy for syphilis. It was now in huge demand. Sulphonamides were in short supply.

> Those who have the misfortune to contract a 'Mongol' syphilis are beyond help. Penicillin? Perhaps. But there's no penicillin for us. The Allies are the only ones allowed to have it. Girls and women sit distraught in the doctors' waiting rooms. 'Will I die?' ask some. 'Do I have to carry it to term? Do I really have to bring it into the world?' ask others anxiously.

The doctors did not show much sympathy or understanding. This aspect will be discussed later. Paragraph 218 of the Criminal Code, which prohibited abortion, remained in force but was unofficially ignored. It was a time of complete arbitrariness. Not everyone saw it in the same way as one of Ruth Andreas-Friedrich's friends:

> 'Of course we agree with the indication', said Frank with the conviction of a true believer. 'Children conceived through violence are a violation of human dignity. Women also have a right to self-determination. It is high time for us to abandon the depressing attitude that they are nothing more than baby machines. A means to an end. Demographic dairy cows. Humanity will not become extinct if Paragraph 218 is abolished.'[53]

A point of view that remains controversial even today.

ONE YEAR ON

When we think of the mass rapes in Berlin, we see pictures of any number of frightened women being pulled out of cellar hiding places after the arrival of the Red Army in early 1945. However vivid these pictures might be, they fail to tell the whole story. The situation didn't change with the occupation of the city. In 1946, police stations in the different zones continued to report incidents with members of the occupying forces.

The police reports are almost always about women who have been victims of aggravated robbery, bodily harm, murder and rape, or who committed suicide after such acts. The perpetrators were members of the armed forces, not only Soviets. The police reports are very restrained in their tone. The Soviet or other uniformed perpetrators are exonerated and the word 'allegedly' is almost ever-present. The number of reports between July and December 1946 alone is impressive. They convey an impression of the daily horror of a crime committed in homes, but frequently also on the open street. Women were the indiscriminate victims, the perpetrators soldiers from all four occupying powers.[54] The fear, as a child or woman, of encountering someone alone on the street or of being out at night persisted long after this time.

Extracts from police reports

> At around 5 a.m. on 23 July 1946, a special BVG bus was proceeding along Neuendorfer Str. in Spandau. The vehicle stopped suddenly next to a police car. A woman's cries for help were heard from inside the bus, and the police officer observed two men, one in the uniform of the Soviet navy, holding a woman. When the police officer attempted to approach, he was threatened with a pistol by the men. He managed, however, to rescue the woman from the bus, which then continued on its way.

> At around 10 p.m. on 26 July 1946, Gerda H. . . . was assaulted in Klosterbüschen, approx. 200 m to the east of the Brandenwerder level crossing by two persons in Soviet uniforms. The attackers attempted

unsuccessfully to rape H. They then manhandled the victim, and when she cried for help they were able to get away without identification.

At around 11 p.m. on 28 July 1946, the sentry Peter L., . . . in Spandau, am Bunker, was attacked by two persons in Soviet uniforms. L. attempted to come to the aid of two women, who were being molested by the attackers. He suffered serious injuries and had to be admitted to Spandau Hospital. A police car sent to the scene ascertained that the two attackers had been arrested by two members of the British occupying power.

At around 11.30 p.m. on 8 August 1946, Erna A., née B., born 7 June 1907, living at Berlin SW 61, Tempelhofer Ufer 16, was rescued alive from the Landwehr Canal by a police cadet and two civilians. According to A., she had been thrown into the canal by two members of the Red Army after a drinking bout. A. was released and allowed to go home.

At around 2.15 a.m. on 9 August 1946, Ilse M. . . . was allegedly attacked and raped on the corner of Reinickendorferstrasse and Iranischestrasse by two persons in Soviet uniforms.

At around 1.00 a.m. on 11 August 1946, the tram driver Otto H., . . . living in Berlin-Neukölln, appeared at police station 220 and reported that a Soviet civilian known to him had entered his apartment with the intention of raping his granddaughter. A police cadet arrived at the scene with an American MP but the perpetrator had already left. His car was seized.

At around 10 p.m. on 16 August 1946, a person in Soviet uniform forced his way into an apartment in Kieler Str. 18 and allegedly raped Elisabeth L., . . ., living in Berlin, who was visiting at the time. The attacker was able to get away without identification. The Soviet commandant's office was informed.

At around 2.15 a.m. on 26 August 1946, the 50-year-old Emma K. and the 41-year-old Anni O., Berlin N20, . . . were attacked in K.'s apartment in Berlin-Lichtenrade by several allegedly Russian-speaking persons. O. was raped at gunpoint. The following were stolen: clothing, food ration cards, ID papers, a radio and around RM 950 in cash.

At around 10.15 p.m. on 31 August 1946, the 28-year-old building worker Hedwig K. was allegedly attacked and raped in Schönefeld by five persons in Soviet uniforms. The relevant commandant's office and criminal police were informed.

At around 10.15 p.m. on 4 September 1946, Mrs Helene S. . . ., while crossing the bridge at Heesestrasse, was forced at gunpoint by a person in Soviet uniform to get into a car that had stopped next to her. The perpetrator then set off in the direction of Wuhlheide station, stopped on a farm track in Karlshorst and raped S. allegedly once in the car and a second time on the street. When a car approached, the attacker abandoned S. and escaped in his car.

On 5 September 1946, Soviet soldiers forced their way into an apartment in Württembergallee, Charlottenburg, and threw the housekeeper out of the window, killing her immediately.

In the night of 8 September 1946, a woman, who was pulling a handcart in Reinickendorf-West, was stopped by several persons in French uniforms, choked, searched and abused. When a man came to the woman's aid, the attackers let her go and assaulted the man, who was left lying on the ground allegedly bleeding heavily. The French MPs were informed.

At around 11 p.m. on 9 September 1946 the gardener Erika E. (...) was attacked in Lichterfelde-West. She was allegedly disrobed completely, and the attackers urinated in her face and mouth. When E. managed to escape and call for help, the attackers fled in the direction of Neuchatellerstrasse, taking all of E.'s clothing with them. The American MPs were informed of the incident.

At around 10.30 p.m. on 14 September, the commercial clerk Marianne V., born 14 September 1925, was attacked by six persons in American uniforms and allegedly raped. The attackers escaped without identification in a jeep no. 43318. The American MPs were informed of the incident.

On 18 September 1946, Waltraud P. . . . was allegedly molested on Gartenplatz by an inebriated person in Soviet uniform and raped by him in the ruins of Gartenplatz 4. The French gendarmerie were informed but the perpetrator could not be identified.

At around 10.30 p.m. on 24 September 1946, the schoolgirl Ilse J., born 8 April 1933, was taken by an American MP vehicle to their station. According to her, she had been allegedly stopped in Thielallee by a soldier in Russian uniform, taken to the Russian guardhouse and raped there. She was admitted to Stubenrauch Hospital.

On 28 September 1946, Gertrud G., born 23 August 1922, was found in the entrance to a building with a serious bullet wound in the chest. According to investigations to date, the Soviet citizen Alex C. gave himself up to the Russian commandant's office in Pankow as the alleged attacker. A report by the criminal police was sent to the Red Army public prosecutor.

On 26 September 1946, Mrs Christel O., born 1914, was found with serious head injuries and admitted to the Berlin-Steglitz Municipal Hospital. She had allegedly been attacked by a person in American uniform.

At around 11 p.m. on 2 October 1946, the domestic servant Ingeborg R. . . . was asked the way to Kaiserallee by two persons in American uniform, who had stopped their car on the Kurfürstendamm. She was allegedly asked to get into the vehicle to show them the way. The car travelled in the direction of Grunewald, however. There she was pulled out of the car by one of the occupants and raped. Her handbag with RM 450 in cash, food ration cards and ID papers were stolen.

At around 11 p.m. on 3 October 1946, Marlies P. . . ., living with her parents, was allegedly raped in Röderstrasse by two persons in Soviet uniform. P. was admitted to hospital.

At around 0.15 a.m. on 20 October 1946, Mrs Gerda K., born 1920, and Mrs Hedwig L., born 1919, travelling from Stendal to Mohrenstrasse, were attacked by two persons in Soviet uniform and raped at gunpoint.

At around 5 p.m. on 25 October 1946, an inebriated person in Soviet officer's uniform allegedly attempted to rape Anna M., born 1890, the cleaner at the restaurant Habsburger Hof, in the restaurant. The waiter there at the time was threatened with a pistol. The American MPs, who were alerted immediately, were able to arrest the perpetrator.

At around 9.30 p.m. on 25 November 1946, the kitchen help Emma W. . . . was attacked and allegedly raped in Zinnowitzer Str. by two persons in Soviet uniform. Her ID papers and approx. RM 130 in cash were stolen.

At around 4 a.m. on 9 December 1946, two persons, allegedly in Soviet uniforms, and three persons in civilian clothing speaking broken German, forced their way into the apartment of the fitter Will W., born 1904, allegedly raped his wife and stole all their linen, clothing and spirit ration. The attackers were able to get away without identification.

At around 6.30 a.m. on 18 December 1946, Willi P. reported to the police station that he had found his girlfriend, Frieda L. . . . dead in the apartment. The doctor ascertained that she had been strangled and found scratches on her. The investigations to date indicate that L. had taken a Soviet soldier into the apartment to spend the night.

We don't know the stories behind these police reports, but the grim and laconic descriptions give an idea of the dangers that Berlin women were exposed to every day by Allied troops long after the war had ended. How many more sexual offences were never reported to the police, who in any case had their hands tied? And what would it look like if we applied today's standards for sexual aggression? The cautious language of the reports conveys a sufficient impression of the vulnerability of Berliners to sexual aggression by the occupying powers eighteen months after the end of the war.

A DIFFERENT PERSPECTIVE

For a long time, perhaps even today, the stereotype of the barbarian Russian rapist has dominated the historical perspective. This distorted picture combines all of the historically bottled-up resentment and apprehensions of the German population regarding Bolshevism and the 'subhumans' from the East disparaged by the Nazis. The mass rapes during the flight and expulsion from the East and in Berlin confirmed the idea of the backwardness of the Russians that had been rife in Western Europe for almost two centuries. For the same length of time the Russians had been defending themselves against the notorious denigrating strategies of the West through deliberate shows of manliness and strength similar to those employed by Vladimir Putin today.[55]

Prejudices quickly come to the fore in discussion of the Red Army rapists. 'The Russians' had been ordered from on high to rape German women, Stalin had described three-day rape orgies as 'May festivities'; the Soviets were not punished for their deeds. The only truth in these statements is that Stalin is said to have made one trivializing remark: one needs to appreciate that 'a soldier who has gone through blood, fire and death will take his enjoyment from a woman'.[56]

The perpetrators of the time are reduced to two schematic types: the educated Tolstoy-quoting officer, who takes a defenceless German woman under his wing (and bedcover), and the drunken mobs of dirty illiterates from the hinterland, who attack German women of all ages. This scheme is indestructible, as the recent TV programme *Unsere Mütter, unsere Väter* once again demonstrated. There have been few attempts to date to see the matter from the Russian perspective, and I should therefore like to attempt to do precisely that.

The most obvious misconceptions about the rapes by the Red Army can be quickly cleared up. Raping enemy women was officially forbidden and punishable by death. Many perpetrators were executed without trial, shot summarily by their superiors.[57] If the perpetrator was brought to trial, the usual sentence was five years in a labour camp. The army command attempted to keep things under control as far as possible, not only because of the danger of indiscipline but also because the Soviet system was supposed to be superior and a model, and the

Red Army soldiers were meant to be liberators and not new tyrants. That is why soldiers were later quartered in barracks, access to outsiders barred, patrols carried out and curfews imposed. In Vienna all 'aimless wandering about at night' was prohibited. There was training in the correct way to deal with the population – unlike the US Army and the British, the Soviets were not forbidden to fraternize (a prohibition that the Americans also quickly relaxed). The existing rules and new measures did not appear sufficient, however, to put an end to the rapes. The factors fostering sexual aggression were evidently more persuasive than the deterrent or disciplinary measures.

I should like first to examine the possible personal motives of the men before looking at the more general structural reasons. What was going on in the minds of the men who were tempted to carry out acts of sexual aggression against women? When the Red Army reached German territory, they had already been through terrible experiences. In contrast to their hope that the simple Germans would turn away from their capitalist regime and cross over to their 'brothers' in the East, the Red Army soldiers first witnessed the Wehrmacht penetrating over 1,000 kilometres into the Soviet Union, occupying 1.5 million square kilometres of Soviet territory and defiling the 'mothers' and 'brides' of Russia, as the gender mythology of the time would have it. By the end of 1941 alone, the losses for the Soviet population had already reached 3.14 million dead, missing or captured.[58] It was not until December 1941 that the Wehrmacht was held up at the gates of Moscow. The tide turned after the victory of the Red Army at Stalingrad. With their growing superiority in men and materiel, they managed to liberate vast swathes of land. By the end of 1944, Soviet troops had lifted the blockade of Leningrad, and most of the Baltic, Byelorussia, Ukraine and the Crimea had been liberated. Confidence mounted, but the toll in loss of life did as well, with around 80 per cent of the members of the Red Army being killed or wounded in battle during the last weeks. More and more people from remote regions of Siberia and Central Asia were enlisted to fill the ranks. The cohesion of the units was weakened by the constant fluctuations.

Finally, at the beginning of 1945, two major offensive operations heralded the end of the Great Patriotic War. Large battalions reached East Prussia, Wartheland, Silesia and the Oder. Now around 3.5

million Soviet soldiers from the 1st, 2nd and 3rd Byelorussian Fronts, the 1st Ukrainian Front and parts of the Baltic, and the 4th Ukrainian Front combined with Polish units in January to form a 900-kilometre front from Memel to the Carpathian mountains. They hoped that, despite the heavy losses, the Vistula-Oder and East Prussian offensives would bring about the final and total victory over Hitler's Germany.

For the Red Army soldiers who now entered German territory in large numbers for the first time, it was not just any enemy territory but, as Elke Scherstjanoi writes, 'the soil of the main enemy, the places where they trained and where there most important reserves and homes were to be found'. Further operations in eastern Pomerania and the advance on Berlin from the Oder were the fulfilment of a statement made by Stalin a year earlier: 'Follow the tracks of the wounded German beast and deal it the death blow in its own lair.'[59]

The transformation of the sensitive officer

Vladimir Gelfand, a 21-year-old lieutenant in the 1052nd Artillery Regiment, a good-looking Jew from Ukraine with a high school diploma, literary pretensions, a Party member and admirer of the American president, Franklin D. Roosevelt, kept a diary throughout his entire war service and his time in the occupying army in Germany. His mental transformation, inurement and brutalization in the last months of the war are reconstructed here as a typical example of what was almost certainly a more general process.

On 14 January 1945, his unit was to the south of Warsaw. He and his soldiers were worn out from the fighting, but as Gelfand was an officer, he tried not to let it show:

> All around you artillery shells are booming, whistling, howling and roaring, and you sit there, between life and death, and can only wait for fate, which has already played its part several times in your life, to decide. . . . We are in sight of the enemy, and its furious assaults are aimed at our position and fill our hearts with desperate fear. The soldiers curse – they are in terrible shape. But I keep quiet and don't show my fear, because an officer has to have nerves of steel.[60]

Three weeks later, Gelfand's unit was 70 kilometres from Berlin. The fighting was still causing huge losses, and half of his men had been caught 'in the jaws of death'; 'It's an indescribable nightmare and nothing else.'[61] A week later, in Frankfurt an der Oder – Gelfand was being eaten up by lice, and it was raining incessantly. Two of his men had mutilated themselves in order to be sent home, and were shot for it. He had problems with his superior, was mobbed and denied military honours. But he would still have nothing to do with the crimes committed by his army against German civilians. He noted that the enemy women had disappeared 'since we pierced one with a lance and brought her back naked to the German positions'.[62]

The sight of German girls and Soviet prostitutes aroused him but he still didn't want to buy sex or obtain it by force. When Gelfand reached Berlin with the Red Army, he was overwhelmed by the prosperity and culture of his enemy. He thought that now it would all be Soviet, and he rejoiced at the great victory. He was convinced of the superiority of the Red Army, not only because of the way the war had turned out. When he stood near Colonel Antonov during a parade, he was deeply moved.

The first days in Berlin were the most memorable experiences in his life. He learned to ride a bicycle and met a wonderful girl, who urged him to protect her after having been raped for a whole night in front of her parents. She apparently said to him: 'You can sleep with me. You can do anything you want with me, but just you. I'm willing to fuck with you, to do anything you want, but just save me from these men with this sh…!' Gelfand was tempted, but he decided, according to his diary, to do his soldierly duty.[63]

But soon he started to get bored in Berlin. He started thinking more and more about the German women. His attitude was more than ambivalent: they attracted him but repelled him ideologically at the same time: 'The girls here are either dainty but cool, or passionate but moody. Others are ugly or have no figure. Russian girls are proud and very sensitive to all the refinements of conversation.'[64] The idealization of the virtuous Soviet woman at home and the demonization of the immoral Western woman was a traditional theme in the Communist ideology. The distinctions even included outward appearance: the made-up German woman with her fur coat and the unspoiled woman at home with her peasant's blouse. The Soviet image of German women was of a tantalizing but debauched creature, and German sexual morality, no doubt as a result of ideological indoctrination, was perceived as a pornographic cesspool.

Gelfand cultivated an ambivalent picture of women, not unusual for the time, as saints and whores. In the Soviet Union of Stalin's time, the relationship between the sexes was somewhat prim. Manliness was demonstrated ideally by fighting the enemy and in an ideological devotion to duty. Sexual passion was seen as a bourgeois vice. Lenin took a dim view of lust and advocated monogamy, claiming that healthy exercise and long sessions with piles of books were preferable to sexual activities.[65] After long hours at the workbench, a good Communist would rather attend a meeting or read *Pravda* than go to a woman. After 'bourgeois morality' had been abolished after the Revolution, divorce, abortion and family law relaxed, and after the disastrous famines of the 1920s and 1930s, the Soviets had once again established stricter rules of morality and tightened the laws. At the same time, fantasies about the opposite sex fluctuated wildly between romantic ecstasy and downright aversion, as Gelfand noted in his diary.

In spite of his reservations, Gelfand slept with a German, apparently consensually. It was evidently his first time, and he was bitterly disappointed at the discrepancy between the fantasies he had read about and the reality. Irritated by his day-to-day life as a soldier, he increasingly abandoned his romantic hopes of a proper love life. When he was stationed outside Berlin as an occupying soldier, he sought increasing contact with women, German and Russian, and contracted gonorrhoea. He became less and less selective – and considerate. One acquaintance, whom he simply refers to as 'the woman', was an anti-Semite. The bed scene with her had at the least some indications of force: 'She was not a one-night stand ... I continued to persuade her and started using my hands.'[66] His sensitivity gave way to the pragmatism of the gradual brutalization, isolation, disillusionment and ultimately uncouthness of the occupier. In the end he was only a man, who could not bear the 'imprisonment of the soul, the loneliness'. This is how he justified his indiscriminate sexual contacts, trivializing and ignoring the resistance shown by some of the women, including a 16-year-old girl. He contracted a venereal disease again, endured painful turpentine injections and catheterization, but this didn't deter him from his next sexual conquest.

Altogether, Gelfand's diary combines motives of revenge, resentment towards the Germans, frustration at his own situation in the military, loneliness and the conviction that as the conqueror he was entitled to treat women in a way that was at least very close to open violence and aggression.

Into the 'beast's lair'

The military letters of other young Russians and Ukrainians, Byelorussians and Balts, Kazakhs, Uzbeks and Caucasians, who were not officers like Gelfand, reflect the conflicting feelings that the soldiers wrestled with during the war and occupation period.[67] The first striking thing is the use of language. In their letters, the Red Army soldiers repeatedly refer to Stalin's description of the German Reich as the 'lair of the fascist predator'. The enemy is designated again and again as a 'bandit' or 'accursed German' or 'hateful German creature', blamed not only for atrocities committed against its own people but also for the fact that the soldiers have had to fight for three and a half years far away from their homes.

The letters by the Soviet soldiers are full of ill-concealed desire for revenge, which also has as much to do with the addressees – family and relatives – as it does with the letter-writers themselves. On 3 January 1945, Vladimir Ivanovic wrote:

Father, I am fighting on the soil of the enemy, the enemy who brought such misery and misfortune to you, my dear family, who caused the death of my brother and your son, who tore us apart. You lost your house and all your possessions acquired over the years. You have shed tears about everything the enemy did to our house, to our Vogorod. So now I am repaying it. In the enemy's country every one of our soldiers is master and everyone exacts revenge as he can. And there is no mercy in any house. Not for furniture, for watches, for mirrors. Their houses were nicely furnished. They left things behind. Everything is smashed to fragments. May their wives, mothers and the rest shed tears for everything that you have shed them for.[68]

The desire for revenge was directed at the entire German people, not just representatives of the Nazi state. Michail Aronovic, born 1915, wrote on 23 January 1945: 'They are all guilty and they are all condemned to death and that is why they are all trying to postpone the date of their execution. All the worse for their state and their generation.'[69]

A frequent cause of rage was the material wealth of the Germans. For years the Soviets had been preached to that their own system was fairer and superior, and that the German bourgeoisie and capitalists squeezed their own people dry and lived in the lap of luxury themselves. Now the Red Army soldiers were discovering that apparently most Germans lived well, not just the upper classes. Even after six years of war, they still had full pantries and lived in inconceivable comfort. The German Nazis had got rich, so it was said, from their forays through Eastern Europe. And so the soldiers were naturally entitled to everything they found in the German houses. The German standard of living was depicted as paradise. Pavel Vasilevic, born 1924, wrote on 25 January 1945 in a similar tone to his parents:

> As far as the trophies are concerned, I don't know how to describe them to you. Basically, the vodka is flowing in streams, there is all the food you could wish for, not to mention the magnificent palaces, where the walls shine like marble, where the silk curtains are seamed with gold, and you sink into feather beds like the sea when you lay down to sleep. I am sitting in the estate of a rich German; everywhere there are divans, armchairs, silk, the floors gleaming like mirrors. Imagine, soldiers who have never seen the like now feel like lords. This is not surprising, because they have had a hard journey and through their honest work have earned the right to take possession of these treasures. Now we are recovering from the terrible and difficult days of the past.[70]

The more the soldiers witnessed the atrocities committed by the Germans and the more they saw the wealth for themselves, the greater were the hate and frustration boiling up in them. Vasiliy Ivanovic, a captain, wrote on 27 January 1945:

> We are hitting them with all our might, dear Sura, to get our own back on the Huns and Fritzes, and their despicable women and their brood

of vipers are running in all directions. I don't think they will get very far. We will seek them out to the ends of the world, as comrade Stalin said, and we will exact our judgement over these dregs of humanity.[71]

The German fear of the Red Army appeared to increase the soldiers' rage even further. Major Anna Vladimirovna wrote contemptuously at the end of January 1945 about what wretches the Germans were: 'They all run and throw everything away. Like common vermin. They are afraid of their come-uppance. And you sense the power, the Russian pride and feel like singing.'[72] Again and again, the correspondents wrote that they felt no sympathy for the German women. Michail Borisovic, a fitter from Kiev, wrote: 'The men were the direct perpetrators of these crimes, and the women helped them, if not physically then morally, and the children were getting ready to commit the same crimes as their fathers, regarding themselves from birth as "superior to everyone".'[73]

Hate propaganda

The letters express not only personal feelings but also often official positions, which the soldiers were fed right until the closing phase of the war through training and propaganda. How else were the soldiers, who came from far away, to know that German women were rotten and worthless? Like the US Army, as we shall see later, they came equipped with an image of European – and particularly German – women as frivolous, lascivious and devoid of any moral values. Alexey S., a war correspondent, who was killed near Berlin, wrote home in February 1945: 'Germany makes a bad impression. It's not a country but a huge cattle yard. The mating and artificial insemination of women is systematic. The people are rotten to the core. The newspapers and particularly the magazines are full of pictures of naked men and women in all possible poses and positions. This is the most widespread literature.'[74]

The evidently exaggerated view of Germany among these soldiers raises the question of the extent to which military propaganda contributed to the attacks on German civilians, and women in particular. So there is no misunderstanding, Soviet war propaganda had sufficient information about atrocities to work with: the conditions when concentration camps like Majdanek or Treblinka were liberated do not need exaggeration. Every Red Army soldier knew of mass executions of his own people, the starving comrades who had been taken prisoner, the reports about Soviet slave labourers and Jewish concentration camp inmates. The men and women needed no training to know the terrible havoc that the German Wehrmacht and SS had wreaked.

Nevertheless, it is clear that Soviet war propaganda influenced the attitude of the Red Army to German soldiers and civilians. Soviet intellectuals had an important function in this regard. There is a famous poem by Konstantin Simonov from 1942 in which he calls on Soviet soldiers to show no mercy with the German enemy: 'Kill him! If your home means anything to you, know that if you don't kill him, no one will, so kill at least one! And kill more quickly! As often as you see one, kill him!'[75] Soviet propaganda portrayed the Germans as thieves, murderers, rapists, bloodsuckers and people with the morality of animals.

One of the propagandists working for the Soviets became particularly well known in Germany. Ilya Grigorievich Ehrenburg, born in 1891 in Kiev, had lived as a Bohemian in Berlin and Paris during the 1920s and fought with the anti-fascists in Spain in the 1930s. From 1940 he worked as a war reporter in Moscow. He was by no means Stalin's only propagandist, but he was the most well known. The *Deutsche Soldatenzeitung* described him as a 'blood-drenched monster in human guise' and attributed words to him that he had never published, in particular the invocation to rape German women. The originator of this invocation cannot be determined as it was contained in an anonymous flyer distributed towards the end of the war.

The lines published under Ehrenburg's name are by no means as unequivocal as Western propaganda claims. One of his most popular pamphlets was entitled 'About Hate' and contains the following: 'For us, the German soldier with a weapon in his hand is not a person but a fascist. We hate him . . . If the German soldier releases his weapon and allows himself to be captured, we will not touch a hair on his head – he will live.'

Elsewhere, Ehrenburg writes about the approach by the Soviet Army to German perpetrators: 'The men of the Red Army have not sought and will not seek revenge. They want to kill the child murderers, not their children.' And 'The Soviet soldier will not molest a German woman. The Soviet soldier will not abuse a German woman, nor will he have any intimate relationship with her. He is superior to her. He despises her for being the wife of a slaughterer and for having scheming friends. The Soviet soldier will pass by German women in silence.' And once again unambiguously: 'We are not after Gretchen, but the Fritzes who have given our women diseases, and we can say forthrightly that these Germans can expect no mercy. As for German women, they only disgust us. We despise German women for what they are – mothers, wives and sisters of executioners.'[76]

The reputation of the combatants should not suffer

There was plenty of hate propaganda by the Soviets, but no open invocation to rape German women – rather the opposite, with attempts to limit it. In February 1945, with an eye to the post-war European order, Stalin attempted to counter the hate speech by pointing to the difference between the Nazi regime and the population: 'Hitlers come and go, but the German people and the German state remain.'

The military leadership in particular had quickly realized that the vengeful mood of the soldiers had got out of control, endangering the progress of the Soviet Army. On 6 February 1945, Lieutenant-General Okorov, head of the Political Department of the 2nd Byelorussian Front, convened a meeting of the members of the Agitation and Propaganda Section. He warned them that the drinking, looting, arson and rape by the soldiers would damage the 'reputation of the Red Army as combatants'. It would be dangerous if they were now to become undisciplined and were merely to seek instant gratification: 'First they rape a German woman and then a Pole. The officer orders them to stop, and a soldier pulls out his gun and shoots the officer. Can a soldier like that fight selflessly? No.' All of the clobber, tulle and silk carried by the soldiers slowed the advance, and it is no coincidence that the Germans left all the breweries and distilleries undamaged but rather a tactic, speculated Okorov: 'They know that a drunken combatant can't fight.' He therefore demanded: 'Of course our people feel a huge need for revenge, and it is these feelings that have carried our combatants into the lair of the fascist beast and pushed them on to Germany. But revenge is not the same as boozing and burning.' It was time to explain to the troops 'that you will not be speeding up the defeat of Germany by beating to death some old German woman in the hinterland'.[77]

From February 1945, more and more directives were issued by the Soviet high command urging the troops to treat the Germans better. At stake was the reputation of the Red Army combatants as liberators and avengers, which should not be discredited through drunkenness, vandalism and intimate relations with Polish and German women.[78] In April, the commanders of the 1st and 2nd Byelorussian and the 1st Ukrainian Front were instructed about the need for a humane attitude to the German people and prisoners of war. A severe attitude invoked fear and just made the Germans more fanatical in their defence. The civilian population feared revenge and were organizing themselves into bands: 'This is not in our best interests. A more humane relationship with the Germans will make it easier for us to wage war on their territory and probably weaken the tenacity of the German defence.'[79] Two days later, the next directive was issued, forbidding looting and eviction without providing alternative housing.

Responsibility for the attacks was often shifted to other units. It was said that the infantry and advance units in particular gave free rein to their feelings. Further work was needed there, wrote the architect Boris Sergeevic in April 1945 to an acquaintance, so that people would understand that they were not fighting with women and for material objects but with 'Hitler's people'. He admitted, however: 'It is difficult to achieve in everyday life and we therefore often find ourselves following in the messy footsteps of our advance units.'[80]

By the end of April, the Soviets had advanced as far as Berlin. The initial impression of the Berliners was positive. Most of the population were loyal and interested in good relations with the occupiers. Many, particularly Communists, attempted to welcome the soldiers and officers and offered their services. 'The Berliners are strongly impressed by the contrast between what German propaganda said about the Red Army and its equipment and the reality', wrote the head of the 7th Section of the Political Administration of the 1st Byelorussian Front on 29 April 1945: 'The people are hoping for the establishment of military command posts so that a certain amount of order can be obtained and that an end can be put to the isolated incidents that still occur.'[81]

Apart from that, the number of rapes and other immoral behaviour had decreased considerably in recent times, he claimed.

A letter of the following day shows how misguided this optimism was in reality. On 30 April 1945, a representative of the People's Commissariat for Foreign Affairs of the USSR wrote to the Deputy People's Commissar for Foreign Affairs: 'In spite of the order by the war council to change the attitude to the German people, there are still many cases of rape. . . . The measures taken to date have not been sufficiently energetic.' He cites the example of a group of rapists who killed a Soviet interpreter and a sergeant from the Soviet command headquarters because they had attempted to prevent the crimes. The commanding officer himself was beaten up.[82]

The long-held opinion in Germany that Soviet war propaganda was responsible for the violence against civilians, and women in particular, and that the military leadership had encouraged it needs to be revised. The fact nevertheless remains that the acts of violence could not be prevented. The chronicle of events from the Soviet reconquest to the advance on Berlin and the occupation of the German capital provides a framework for a large number of terrible cases of sexual aggression. On account of their significance at the time, their exploitation for propaganda purposes and later instrumentalization in the Cold War, and not least the one-sided focus by scholars on the crimes committed by the Red Army, the often brutal acts by the Soviet soldiers have remained as the abiding image in the collective memory. A closer look at the actors, their war experience, their expectations and their indoctrination reveals the fateful way in which the warring parties and civilian population interacted and how their actions, prejudices and expectations were almost inevitably mutually reinforcing. The descriptions of the hunting down by Soviet combatants of German victims are like a preordained choreography, in which both sides knew their roles and played them out as if remotely controlled.

Immediate grounds

The explanations for the mass rape will be looked at in greater detail later on. For the time being, we can say that, from the individual soldier's point of view, there were immediate grounds for justifying such behaviour. One such ground was the motive of revenge for crimes committed by the German Wehrmacht and the entire Nazi system; revenge for the invasion of their homeland and the attacks on their families; revenge for their own dead soldiers, for shot partisans, murdered prisoners of war and slave labourers; revenge for the other victims like Jews and other persecuted groups whom the Red Army soldiers encountered as they liberated the camps; revenge for the pain and horror experienced by the soldiers themselves, particularly in the last weeks of senseless resistance by the Germans; and of course revenge for rapes by German soldiers.[83]

These grounds were used and reinforced by ideological propaganda to foment class hatred and rage at the humiliation of the Russian people by the Germans. Catherine Merridale, an expert in the history of the Red Army, saw in the Soviet soldiers a long bottled-up pain, 'not only in the war but through decades of humiliation, of disempowerment and fear'. The victory over Germany had given them the opportunity 'consciously or not . . . [to vent] anger that had built up through decades of state oppression and endemic violence in the Soviet Union'.[84] This motive applies particularly to those Red Army soldiers whose lives had been affected by Stalin's starvation policy, gulags and the Great Purge, and finally by the hardships of war.

Apart from the experience of German occupation and looting, frustration at the soldiers' own position in society and the army could be an explanation for the violence. We shall see that this also applied to the colonial soldiers in the French Army, who committed massive acts of rape in the south and south-west of Germany, and to the underprivileged African American soldiers in the US Army, who also risked their lives for a country that segregated them. And it also applies to other underprivileged groups in these armies.

A further motive for the violence at the end of the war was the resentment felt at the relative prosperity of the Germans. Many Soviet soldiers came from underdeveloped regions and could only dream of the running water, bicycles, watches and well-stocked cellars the enemy possessed. The wealth they encountered in the conquered land was a serious affront and was used for propaganda purposes to explain the looting of their own country by the Germans.

Hate, revenge and resentment were already generally accepted at the time as the reason for sexual aggression.[85] Internal military structures are also cited as explanations for the perpetrators' behaviour: the constant fluctuations in troop units, changing billets, house searches and requisitions, access to large quantities of alcohol and lack of discipline. All of these are good explanations, but in my opinion they do not shed sufficient light on the phenomenon of mass rape at the end of the war.

We cannot explain satisfactorily why all of these motives led specifically to sexual aggression without taking into account historical gender roles. Both the Red Army and the US Army also raped the women of their own 'brothers' and Allies – Poles and French women – as they advanced on German territory. And it wasn't only the wives, mothers and daughters of Nazis but also those persecuted by the Nazi regime. The acts were therefore based on a combination of ethnic and national revenge and power motives and gender-political factors, which we shall consider later after looking at the acts of rape committed by the Americans.

3

SOUTH GERMANY – WHO WILL PROTECT US FROM THE AMERICANS?

They softly entered the court and raped me and all the women. Even the old directress, who I can still hear screaming: 'Let me go, I'm an old woman.'

In a village near Pirmasens[1]

There are various reasons why the incidence of rape in the West was uncommon. One reason is that there was apparently a sufficient number of German women who were so attracted to the occupying soldiers that there was no need for force.

Günter Sagan in his book about the end of the war in 1945[2]

NO ONE'S TIME

At the end of the war, Moosburg an der Isar, 45 kilometres north-east of Munich and not far from the present-day airport in Erdinger Moos, was a small town with 10,000 inhabitants, dominated by two church towers of the same height. On the outskirts of the town was a large prisoner-of-war camp with as many as 200,000 inmates of all nationalities. In early March 1945, several thousand British and American officers were transferred there from a camp in Upper Silesia. It is said that the officers had to walk 70 kilometres and carried the weakened German guards accompanying them on their backs.

Six days before the end of the war, mayor Hermann Müller, who had been in office since 1933, decided to surrender the town without resistance. On 29 April 1945, American negotiators came to discuss the handover. At first everything ran smoothly. The commandant and mayor quickly agreed on the terms of surrender. The next day, however, armed Waffen-SS members began to dig in. An American officer said in rage: 'So that's what the word of honour of a German officer means.' American tanks rolled slowly towards the town.

The battle for Moosburg began at 10.15 a.m. The SS had to cede to the superior power and withdrew behind a bridge over the river Amper. The inhabitants took shelter in their cellars. Shells exploded. One of the church towers also came under attack. Fires broke out. There was fighting in front of the church. The first GIs appeared in the parish house. The square in front of the minster was full of tanks. The fighting continued in the distance. The SS had retreated over the Isar and blown up the bridge. Some of the German soldiers were hiding in houses. It was reported later that two teenage Hitler Youth members had shot at American tanks with revolvers.[3]

Was it this senseless but stubborn fighting by the Germans that galled the American military so much, or was it the 40,000 prisoners of war, including many of their fellow countrymen? At all events, the Americans began to loot the town with particular ruthlessness. If doors weren't opened quickly enough, they were blown open. Then the houses were pillaged from the cellar to the attic, not just for food but everything that would fit into the sheets, transformed into sacks for the purpose. Objects changed hands by the cartload: cartons of eggs, cheese wheels from the dairy, beds, mattresses, quilts, preserving jars, cookware and much more. The American soldiers strained as they dragged their heavy loads, dead poultry hanging from their belts.[4] In one cellar they discovered 80,000 litres of wine. They carried it off in bathtubs, washtubs, milk cans and buckets. The looting went on for eight days. But that was not all.

On Monday, the first day after the town had been taken, Moosburg's parish priest Alois Schiml received first word of rapes. If there were men in the houses the GIs entered, they were forced out at gun- or knife-point. One or two accomplices would stand guard. Several girls jumped out of first-floor windows and lay injured on the ground; others sought refuge in the parish house, where a room had been transformed into a shelter.

The military authorities ordered a list to be posted on the door of every building with the names and ages of all occupants. 'The effect of this order is not difficult to imagine. Seventeen girls and women, abused once or several times by negroes, were admitted to the hospital; other women and girls attended doctors' surgeries. Black Americans also raped a woman in the neighbouring village of Volkmannsdorf', wrote the priest.

He was particularly shocked by the fate of one serving maid. She was raped by a white GI wearing a steel helmet. She already had a history of depression, and the following day she became paranoid, particularly whenever she saw a steel helmet. She was given asylum at the parish house. After her mood appeared to have improved, she expressed the wish to return home. A few days later she tried to jump out of a second-floor window. She was admitted to the 'insane cell', as it was called, in the hospital. After around two weeks, she was allowed to leave this cell, but her fellow patients kept an eye on her. One afternoon, she saw three American soldiers with steel helmets entering the hospital. In her panic she ran up to the third floor, jumped out of the window and hit her head on the cobblestones, where she lay unconscious and covered in blood. An American doctor examined her and found that she had a skull fracture from the back of her head to her forehead, but she appeared not to have any internal injuries. On 1 August 1945, Schiml reported: 'She is still alive, is on the road to recovery and feels normal.'[5]

Well equipped, disciplined, smart

The last phase of the war began for the inhabitants of west and south Germany in October 1944, when the Allied troops crossed the Reich border for the first time near Aachen, occupied the territory on the left bank of the Rhine and pressed onwards to the Bavarian Palatinate. By late March 1945, the end of the war was also in sight for Bavaria. The Rhine had been crossed, the first territories in Bavaria taken, the Palatinate and Lower Franconia, all occupied in just a few weeks. In some places, particularly in the Bavarian Oberland, the French arrived first, followed by the Americans. After the German soldiers had shed their uniforms and hidden their weapons, and the last local party officials had abandoned their fight for every church tower and disappeared, it was often hours or days until the new military powers arrived. This period was known as 'no one's time', filled with fear and anxiety. The population formed reception committees, planned the official handover, sewed white flags and attempted to appear as ideologically inconspicuous as possible.

The Americans took over power in Munich on 30 April, occupying all of the towns and villages in Upper Bavaria on the days before and afterwards. The occupation was usually peaceful, and the population breathed a huge sigh of relief. 'It was as if we were celebrating a victory, so great was the joy at having been liberated from the jaws of a terrible monster that had almost swallowed us up', wrote the priest Kaspar Waldherr in Jetzendorf in the district of Pfaffenhofen/Ilm, describing the mood on the evening of 28 April, when the guns were finally silent. He expressed the widely held conviction that the Americans would be on the whole 'well behaved, considerate and helpful' and that the population was therefore very lucky not to have fallen into the hands of the Russians.[6] His colleague Johann Huber from Rieden gave voice to his preference even more clearly: 'The sooner they come the better. Just as long as it's not Ivan who comes. Anything is better than the Russians.'[7]

The GIs were welcomed not only because America was seen far more positively within the German population than the Communist Soviet Union. The first impressions also made the American soldiers appear more sympathetic. The priest Alfons Veit from Steinkirchen an der Ilm was impressed by the manly martial air of the American troops:

The American military police vehicles paraded in a smart and orderly fashion past the mayor. . . . And then a fighting unit appeared, filing through the village and back again; small tanks, a couple of large armoured vehicles and other vehicles, well equipped, disciplined and smart, equidistant, armed and ready for action, everyone in vehicles. The Americans arrived equipped in a way that had never before been seen. The entire army motorized! No one had told us that. What a sight! On the day before on the same street the remnants of the German army, undisciplined, with requisitioned horse-drawn agricultural vehicles . . . poor driven German soldiers . . . what an unequal competition.[8]

But the first impression quickly evaporated. Everywhere in Upper Bavaria, the arrival of the Americans was accompanied by looting, destruction, violence and rape. The soldiers of the richest nation in the world went from village to village and house to house, initially looking for enemy soldiers and weapons, taking watches and bicycles, radios, cameras, binoculars, jewellery, silver tableware, pocket knives and lighters as souvenirs, stocking up on spirits, food (especially eggs) and even live animals. Then the rape started, often in groups, once or several times in succession.

The American military tribunals, where a few of the crimes were later tried, discerned a clear pattern. Two soldiers would enter a house on the outskirts of a village at night. One of them would be armed with a pistol, and together they would go up to the first floor, where the women were sleeping. The armed soldier would take a woman downstairs and lock the front door. The women would then be raped one after another. The soldiers would leave the house, telling their comrades on the way where they could find women.[9]

Sometimes the GIs were taken to their victims by liberated slave labourers – a particularly perfidious form of revenge on the former German slave holders. Under the occupying forces, it was now the Germans who became defenceless victims without rights. In places like the tranquil Hörgertshausen in the district of Freising, there were cases of sexual slavery, in which the GIs requisitioned rooms for ten to fifteen females, who were constantly rotated.[10]

One feature that struck the army superiors was that the GIs raped

German women not only more often but also more brutally than they had, earlier, the women of their Allies in Britain and France. The German women were more frequently injured, beaten unconscious with fists or weapons, abused more frequently in the presence of their husbands or relatives, and more frequently penetrated orally or anally, according to the Military Prosecutor General.[11]

According to military statistics, around half of the rapists in the first months after the war were charged and brought to trial for assaults involving teenagers.[12] A quarter of the victims were unmarried, a quarter married, and 4 per cent widowed. The marital status of the remaining 45 per cent is not known.[13] The youngest reported victim was seven years old and was infected with gonorrhoea; the oldest, sixty-nine. The class distribution was even – middle-class women were just as likely to suffer as peasants. The Alpine herdswomen and dairymaids were particularly vulnerable to attacks by soldiers.

MODERATE INDIGNATION

The reports from the Upper Bavarian archbishopric Munich-Freising give a useful insight into the events at the end of the war and their immediate effect. Every ministry in the bishopric was to report to Cardinal Michael Faulhaber by 1 August 1945 on the events in the respective parishes in the last days of the war and the first days of occupation. The aim of these reports was primarily to list the material and immaterial losses by the church. Even at the time, however, the 540 reports were soon recognized as historical documents. The authors were aware that German society was at a crossroads, and they therefore attempted to record events, often in the form of chronicles and not without making their own political views known.

Although these observations cover only the first three months after the arrival of the Americans in Munich and Upper Bavaria, and although the ministers were almost certainly not informed of all the cases of rape (but probably in the first instance those affecting Catholics), the number of attacks listed is staggering. The archbishopric covered approximately the same area as the government district of Upper Bavaria. Over 2 million people, 90 per cent Catholic, lived in a thinly populated area of 12,000 square kilometres. Twenty-one communities reported 'several' rapes, without indicating precisely how many, and there was explicit mention of 131 cases (with names and often addresses). If we assume an average of three cases in the twenty-one communities that did not provide precise figures, the total number of rapes in the first three months of occupation, initially by the French and then by the Americans, runs to just under 200.

This number is only an approximation. It can be inferred from the reports that, in the eyes of the authors, the sexual aggressions in the communities were by no means the worst crimes. They wrote in greater detail and often with greater indignation about the looting by the soldiers, former prisoners of war, slave labourers and concentration camp inmates and the indigenous population. In view of the many detailed reports of property crimes and the often laconic list of sexual offences, it would appear on occasion that the churchmen were more interested in the intactness of their church spires and holy wine than that of the female members of their congregations. At all events, Georg Wall from Ebersberg did not sound too perturbed when he wrote on 21 July 1945: 'The arrival of the Americans was without incident; no shots were fired. There were a few reports of women and girls being raped.'[14] The use of words like 'a few' or 'isolated' in this and other reports would appear to indicate that in the eyes of the churchmen the female victims did not count for much.

Consensual sexual contact between German women and the occupiers seems to have given rise to greater indignation among clerics than violent aggression. For some it was already enough that women waved to the occupiers and rejoiced. 'Women in particular forgot themselves, threw themselves into the arms of the Americans and showered them with flowers', complained Joseph Mock from the Church of the Holy Cross in the Giesing district of Munich.[15] In fact, the same could be said of the attitude of women to Adolf Hitler, but we know today that in neither case was the euphoria confined to women.

The cleric Stephan from Oberhummel parish was particularly unpitying. He wrote that there had unfortunately been serious looting and rape. The 'greatest nuisance', however, came from the former concentration camp inmates, who 'ate themselves sick' from the good food offered to them. He also complained about the brothel established by the American soldiers opposite his parish house, where German women and girls (mostly speaking the Berlin dialect) were available, being paid with valuables, particularly 'beds and clothes looted from us. Evacuated women made themselves available in the most shameless manner day and night, especially to the passing negroes, in return for coffee, chocolate, etc., women whose husbands were in captivity or had recently been killed or here. The latest craze: dancing with negroes! It will be very difficult for the inhabitants to show compassion!'[16]

The average age of the priests was fifty-three years; they were mostly from modest backgrounds, and had been ordained on average twenty-seven years earlier. They were therefore experienced pastors who had known their congregations for many years: traditional and religiously conservative rural communities. The clerics played a key role in these rural environments, being involved in the rituals of birth, marriage, sickness and death; they were important points of reference and authority and for that reason were often involved in the decisions of villages to surrender or not, in some cases taking the initiative and coming out to meet the tanks themselves.

Before we reject the churchmen's reports as being overly biased, however, we should bear in mind that their judgements were by no means untypical for the time. We shall see that the tone adopted by the Upper Bavarian clergy was to predominate for a long time after the war. They thought no differently, if a little less flexibly, from the rest of the population about the events, which they believed they could divide neatly into consensual intercourse and non-consensual rape. The majority of reporters felt capable of making moral judgements about the women and assessing the attacks accordingly. A typical statement of this type: 'Three cases of aggression against girls and women are unfortunately to be reported. In two cases the women were quite obviously at fault themselves, but in one case the victim was a very virtuous girl from a good peasant family.'[17]

Refugees were basically deemed immoral ('the Banat Swabian girls are said to be particularly passionate dancers'),[18] as were evacuees, town women and women who, as camp followers, did not conform to the usual picture of moral rectitude. The rape of such women was evidently regarded as a minor sin and in some cases not even worth recording. Some reporters even turned the incidents round and accused the women of leading the men astray. Forty women and their illegitimate children were housed in Griesstätt in the deanery of Wasserburg, a fate of countless women who were labelled 'asocial' or 'degenerate'. The minister Jakob Christaller wrote that 'their impertinent and forward nature presented a great moral danger for the American soldiers'.[19]

Other groups of victims also shared this bad reputation in the churchmen's eyes. There is no doubt that the petty theft committed by released camp inmates, evacuees and refugees without means was a problem (apart from the property crimes by fellow Germans). It is difficult for us to understand today, however, how little compassion most priests and pastors had for Jews and other victims of persecution and enslavement. Their fate evidently aroused no sympathy but only annoyance and anger when they didn't behave as they should. Even after the end of the war, those groups who had been marginalized from the Nazi society were still seen as outside the moral mainstream and therefore unworthy of sympathy.[20]

Blame and women without conscience

As mentioned, I believe that there was a much larger number of acts of sexual aggression in the archbishopric Munich-Freising than the number reported, not least because it is evident, reading between the lines, that the Catholic ministers trivialized the occurrences or even blamed the women for them. They evidently felt capable of distinguishing between 'moral' and 'immoral' – in other words, between consensual and non-consensual sex. Thus the parish minister Josef Forster from Eichenried does not find it objectionable that women in his congregation landed in prison before the end of the war because they had relations with French prisoners of war. He found it much worse that now that war was over women 'made themselves available to Americans' without consequences.[21]

It would be anachronistic to apply present-day standards of what constitutes sexual aggression to the situation at the time. It is nevertheless legitimate to ask what the priest from Schellenberg near Salzburg meant with a sentence like: 'Serious molesting of women took place in only two or three families.'[22] An involuntarily comical but significant lapse was committed by Josef Gruber from Taufkirchen an der Vils when he wrote: 'Civilians were not injured or killed. In the first days of May, however, there were serious breaches of morality mainly by negro soldiers through the rape of several (eight serious cases) of girls and women.'[23] Rape in those days was not considered an injury. The point is that that the main problem in Taufkirchen – in the eyes of the churchmen – was the breach of morality.

It is thus highly likely that there were more rapes in the archbishopric of Munich-Friesing; many sexual aggressions were probably not regarded or perceived as such. Exaggerations must also be taken into account, depending on the political viewpoint of the reporter. Were 200 women in Bad Reichenhall really 'defiled' by 'Gaullists, Turks and foreign workers', as parish priest Matthias Kuhn from St Nikolaus parish reported on 25 July 1945? Some of the victims killed themselves, and one of the women was even granted a church burial. In this case, 'defilement' excused suicide, which was prohibited by the church.[24] Even if 200 rapes in Bad Reichenhall appears a little exaggerated, it was not completely invented, however, because Kuhn's colleague Eugen Abele from St Zeno also reported three days of looting and 'horrendous excesses; they also did terrible things of a moral nature to women and girls; for example, coloured Moroccans, who forced their way in at gunpoint at night'.[25] The recurrent reports of marauding Frenchmen in Upper Bavaria, which was occupied by the Americans, can be explained by the fact that for a short time the French army were the occupants, before being replaced by the Americans.

For some pastors, a narrow view of morality clouded the distinction between good and evil. What is behind the following report, for example? Ludwig Axenböck from Schönau parish wrote on 21 July 1945: 'An evacuated woman from Munich consorted with the Americans, caroused with them, was dumped from a car in the forest near Mailling, run over, fracturing her pelvis in five places, obliging her to spend around ten weeks in Aibling hospital.'[26] Is it possible that the occupiers just ran her over and nothing else?

Jakob Engl from Obertaufkirchen also has a strange understanding of right and wrong: 'Women and girls were also raped. Unfortunately, the girls themselves were to blame in some cases. They went out unnecessarily onto the streets, smiled at the blacks and begged for chocolate until the calamity occurred.'[27] A like-minded minister, Matthias Kern from St Wolfgang parish in Dorfen, wrote:

There were terrible and shocking occurrences in the first two weeks, when vehicles with black and white soldiers from Dorfen appeared almost every night, forced their way into houses under the pretext of looking for soldiers and attacked girls and women. Rape occurred unfortunately in perhaps five to ten cases. A few women without conscience, particularly from Munich, might have been to blame for showing a friendly attitude to the arriving Americans.[28]

Pastor Anton Kreutmeier from Moosach bei Ebersberg also wrote: 'There was talk about rapes, although in some cases the victims themselves were not completely without blame. One Yank is said to have apologized officially to a girl, saying that he was inebriated and had never done such a thing before.'[29]

'The search for girls is intensifying'

In spite of reservations about the utility of these reports as a source – reservations that also apply to the documentation on flight and expulsion – it would appear overall, to judge by the situation in the archbishopric Munich-Freising, that there was extensive mass rape throughout Upper Bavaria, mainly by US soldiers and occasionally by the French – for example, in Lochhausen, Obertaufkirchen, Feldmoching, Schellenberg bei Salzburg, Neumarkt, Oberau, Eberseberg, Grafing, Holzkirchen, Freising, Gammelsdorf, Palling, Miesbach (including children), Moosach, Kirchdorf bei Haag, Wolfratshausen, Otterfing, Traunstein and in Munich in the parishes of St Emmeram, St Achaz and Namen Jesu. In many communities the ministers write in general of the 'hunt for women and girls', as in Allach. Rapes leading to death occurred in the parish of Mariahilf in Munich, where a young woman from Welfenstrasse was molested and then shot by American soldiers.[30] In Unterstein bei Berchtesgaden, an 11-year-old girl was shot in the foot while running away and a woman injured herself jumping from a balcony; in Tittmoning, a woman died of a heart attack because her two daughters were being threatened by GIs; and in Schönberg, a young woman died from a botched abortion.[31]

Some of the parish reports were very vivid. In the idyllic village of Oberwarngau in the district of Miesbach, two sisters were mowing on the morning of 20 June 1945 when a GI emerged from the trees, shot one young woman and choked the other, dragged her into the shrubbery and abused her. Because he had no cartridges left, he tried to kill her by hitting her with a rock, but she managed to escape to the next village. The priest informed the American military police who 'after brief questioning brought the woman, who had a head injury, to Tegernsee hospital, where she was discharged after six weeks'.[32]

In Lenggries, soldiers broke a window frame in a farmhouse with their rifle butts, forced their way into the bedroom of a couple, threatened the husband at gunpoint and raped the wife, who was four months pregnant. A similar case occurred at the end of July in a mountain hut near Lenggries, although on this occasion the herdswomen were able to fend off the attack.[33]

Many similar reports from Upper Bavaria change our picture of the mass rapes after the war. The victims were not only homeless women in flight or vulnerable bombed-out women in Berlin. In Upper Bavaria, for example, victims also included people living in relative safety in the supposed sanctity of their own homes, surrounded by their own people, and possibly hitherto largely unaffected by the war. Isolated houses were frequently targeted by soldiers. The occupants were often woken from sleep and abused within their own four walls.

Eight cases of rape were reported in Oberbergkirchen. In most cases the perpetrators forced their way into the houses at night and threatened the occupants at gunpoint. Panic spread, priests instructed daughters to sleep with their parents and several families to group together. The protests by the population finally reached the military authorities. The company had to fall in before the victim. The woman would walk up and down the rows, recognize her assailant but refrain from naming him for fear of reprisals. The pastor at least managed to arrange for the women and girls who had been attacked to be examined for venereal diseases by the American military doctor. 'Worse damage was avoided in one case in this way', he wrote to his cardinal.[34]

Pastor Johann Schausbreitner from Stefanskirchen, one of the early churches to be founded in Bavaria near Mühldorf, which had a labour camp nearby as well as a satellite camp of Dachau concentration camp, kept a precise record of the rapes: two 18-year-olds, a 25-year-old farmer's daughter and a 69-year-old unmarried peasant. Several other women managed to escape.[35] This village today has just 500 souls, which means that even traditional and well-established communities were affected, and that the victims of violence could not escape the ensuing public disgrace.

These cases of sexual aggression towards German women, mostly by Americans, are richly documented in the files of the Bavarian police collected by the Ministry of the Interior. The scenarios are not dissimilar to the reports of rape by the Red Army in the East and in Berlin: the looting, the gang rapes, the brutality. The difference is that they are not the chronicle of a disaster that had been foreseen in advance. The population were completely unprepared for the aggression. The GIs appear to have been more bitter than the Red Army in the East at the deviousness and senseless resistance of the Germans fighting down to the last metre of territory. The local conditions, particularly in rural areas, where soldiers could break into houses at night with no danger to themselves, looting and raping the women, will have made it easier for them to commit these offences.

The frequent mention of the skin colour of the perpetrators in the source material, by contrast, is more a question of the prejudice at the time against other 'races'. In his study of American military court files, the criminologist Robert Lilly notes that African American soldiers did not commit more rapes but that they were punished more frequently and more harshly by the military tribunals. He surmises that acts by black soldiers appear more frequently in the sources because of the attitude of the reporters, who had difficulty in imagining that a white woman would have consensual sex with dark-skinned men.[36] Added to this were prejudices regarding the sexual and intellectual character of the black man, not only among white Americans but also within the German population.

Josef Koblechner from St Jakob parish in Wasserburg noted:

In the chapter 'Americans and women', the population was in for a great surprise. Before their arrival, many German women and girls were anxious about the American negroes. This anxiety was soon overcome. There were a few incidences of rape in the very first days, and in any case there is no convincing evidence that they were completely against the will of the women. In general, however, the negroes, when sober, proved to be harmless, good-willed, helpful and cheerful. They often played and joked like children. These observations were a veritable lesson for the German people as demonstration of the mendacious exaggeration of the Nazi race ideology.[37]

A 'FEELING OF GREAT INSECURITY AMONG OUR SOLDIERS'

With the increasing reports of rapes during the first weeks of the American advance, some people claimed that it was a planned tactic by the Germans. In June 1945, the military police commandant, Infantry Lieutenant-General Edwin Lee Clarke, said, in response to the rumours, that 'German women are creating a feeling of great insecurity among our soldiers by untrue charges of rape and that these tactics may be part of a German plan.'[38]

Clarke went about investigating the incidents. He questioned witnesses, read reports and concluded there had been one or two cases of seduction but without any sabotage motive by the enemy. In most other cases, the victims had resisted as proof of rape. Some women had jumped out of windows and risked breaking a leg. Others had been badly beaten by their assailants. Two cases of younger victims, involving a 13-year-old and an 18-year-old girl, both virgins before the assault by 'negro troops' and both from well-off families, were clear, as was a case in Thuringia, in which the victim had been eight months pregnant. He concluded: 'It is my opinion that the allegation of the creation of a feeling of 'great insecurity' among our soldiers by untrue charges of rape is FALSE. I am further of the opinion that these so-called tactics are not a plan of sabotage by the Germans, and that there has been no evidence to support this latter allegation in any of the areas occupied by the Corps.'[39]

All of the cases had taken place in the houses of the victims at a time when the GIs were forbidden from fraternizing, and contact by members of the military with the German civilian population was strictly controlled.

Most of the rapes had occurred, according to Clarke, during the rapid advance. This pattern had already been observed following the landing in France. As soon as the troops stopped, the rapes would decrease, he hoped. Nor did he find any confirmation of the rumour that women had been falsely accusing soldiers of rape in order to obtain a legal abortion.

Gang rape in Frankfurt am Main

One of the cases examined by Clarke was a cause of particular concern for the military authorities in June 1945. Walter M. C., a private in the 204th Field Artillery battalion, had been charged with fraternization.[40] He was accused with four other soldiers of having stood by as two German women had been forced into a house at gunpoint and raped by three fellow soldiers. This incident was discussed in military circles and even reached the ears of General Dwight D. Eisenhower, commander-in-chief of the Allied forces in Europe. C. attacked his commanding officer, Brigadier General Slack from the XXth Regiment, who, he claimed, not only referred to the three rapists several times as 'dirty bastards' but also threatened to ensure personally that they would hang and be buried within thirty days. C.'s defence strategy consisted merely of claiming that the alleged rape was in truth a cunning ruse by German women to weaken the American army.

The defendant's diversionary attack resulted in a review of the hitherto reported and investigated cases of rape in Germany. In April 1945 alone, thirty-seven soldiers, two-thirds of them white, had been convicted of rape. A further sixteen cases were being heard, and only five had been dismissed for lack of evidence.

From the list of convictions presented to the senior military police authorities for investigation of the accusations, another case in Frankfurt stands out, ending in several severe injuries. On 13 April 1945, Private Samuel J. B. from the 526th Infantry Battalion was sentenced to death by hanging. He was accused of having violated the ban on fraternization, assault with intent to kill of Margot B., Luise B., Alwin F. and Emilia S., and rape of Miss R. All these offences were committed on the same day. It sounded like a would-be killing spree.

At midday on 27 March, a man appeared at the house of the 31-year-old Margot B. It was Samuel J. B., who ordered her to come out because she spoke English. She took a small dictionary with her. The court record states: 'I couldn't understand exactly what he was saying except for the word "basement". He was pointing his gun at me, and I was afraid he would shoot me.' They went up a few steps, where her mother was waiting for her. When the soldier saw her, he shot. The mother was hit in the arm and knee. Margot B. ran to her. The soldier followed with his rifle raised. He ordered her to leave the house with him. At this moment, 15-year-old Alwin F. arrived, a delicate boy for his age. He tried to understand what the soldier wanted but understood only the word 'wall'. When Alwin took a step towards the soldier, the latter shot and hit Alwin in the stomach. In court, where she identified Samuel J. B., Margot B. later testified that the soldier had not appeared normal, waving his rifle in all directions and screaming 'kill you'. She watched Alwin collapse and tried to run away. The accused then shot at her and hit her in the upper arm and chest.

On the same afternoon, Maria R. was walking down the street and saw a GI marching three Germans with raised arms in front of him. He ordered her to join them. She later identified the man as Samuel J. B. They stopped in front of a store. The men were allowed to proceed, but Maria R. was ordered to enter the store. In the passage was a second soldier, Frank B. The first soldier, Samuel J. B., ordered her into a side room and told his comrade to keep watch. He told Maria R. to take her clothes off, which she refused to do. 'Then he pointed his rifle at me, but I swept it aside. He showed me a box and said that if he opened it I would be dead immediately.' He ordered her repeatedly to take her clothes off, then he hit her with the rifle butt. 'I was a bit dizzy and fell against a table.' He turned round and took his pants off. Then she had to lie on the ground.

In the cross-examination Maria R. was asked if she had resisted or at least called for help. 'I said to myself that it would be of no use. No one would come to my aid.' The storekeeper, who was in the next room, was detained by the other soldier. Frank B. opened the door repeatedly and attempted to enter, but the rapist sent him out. Then the other soldier took over. Maria R.'s resistance became weaker and she felt her strength leaving her. 'Perhaps I could have resisted physically a bit more, but I was exhausted.' After ten or fifteen minutes, it was over. Then the first soldier came back and raped her again. According to her it must have lasted half an hour. Then new Americans came into the room, who had been summoned by a German civilian. Among the

Americans was Lieutenant-General Blakefield. When he saw what had happened, he ordered Samuel J. B. to get up and arrested him.

Blakefield later testified in court that the victim was extremely agitated, even hysterical. She was crying and laughing alternately. Her posture was clearly defensive. The examination by the military doctor revealed that she had light contusions and grazing behind her ear, which could have been caused by a weapon, and bruises on her back and thigh. The storekeeper testified that he had seen the rapes through a crack in the door and obtained help. He particularly recalled the tattoo of a woman on the back of the accused.

His story was obviously different. He claimed to have spoken to Miss R. on the street and asked: 'How about a fuck?' She took him to the store, undressed and lay on the table. 'I stood up and said that it wouldn't work well on the table and that she should lie on the floor. When I was finished, Frank B. came in and asked: 'Could I get a piece of ass?' and I said to him: 'Ask her yourself.' The young woman did not resist or call for help, he continued, nor had he used force.

The court believed the witness. She had put up sufficient resistance and been forced at gunpoint, and it was to be assumed that the accused would have used the weapon, given that he had shot three civilians the same day. He was sentenced to life imprisonment with hard labour and a dishonourable discharge from the army.

As this case illustrates, the defence council resorted to a tried and tested strategy that is still used today. The lawyers attempted to call the woman's reputation into question. As Lilly describes on the basis of his random sample, this tactic was also used by the perpetrators. They objectivized their minor-age victims as 'chicks', 'a lay' or 'a lying bitch' who is 'good for pricking'. They trivialized their deeds as a process that transformed a girl into a woman, for which they should in fact be grateful. Another defence strategy in court was to ask the victims whether they had been members of the NSDAP or another Nazi organization. Even the fact that their husband or father had fought in the Wehrmacht was used by the defence as a mitigating argument. When in one case the victim stated that she had been a virgin, the defence asked whether she had ever been to a Nazi youth camp, stating that it was common knowledge that the Führer sought new blood and that her claimed intactness was less than credible for that reason. The accused in this case were nevertheless sentenced to life imprisonment.[41]

Physical resistance by the woman was the main criterion for establishing whether the sexual contact had indeed been rape or whether the victim merely claimed it. This was often a stumbling block for the German women. The questionable argumentation was further complicated by the impression by American military tribunals that German women did not defend themselves as vigorously as British or French women – not to mention American women – would do. This observation is made both in the court files discussed by me and in the cases Lilly studies. If it is true, the question arises as to why German women resisted less. There are two possible reasons from the victims' point of view. First, the women expected to be raped by the foreign soldiers because Nazi propaganda had prepared them for it; and second, they were no doubt disarmed by the fact that they would be killed if they refused.

One victim from Berlin, asked by the social scientist Erika M. Hoerning, explained her own behaviour retrospectively as follows: 'As I said, there were eight Russians . . . very brutal, and I must tell you that I didn't scream or do anything else. I whimpered because everybody talked about raping and then being shot in the neck, and I was terribly afraid of that.'[42] Lilly believes that this might even have brought about an escalation in the sexual assaults. Some soldiers, he surmises, might have interpreted the lack of physical resistance as consent, not least because they were also unable to communicate verbally and were not in fact allowed to do so, because the ban on fraternization included even speaking with the civilian population. Moreover, they often took a no as a bashful yes.[43]

I believe that this argument is viable only to a limited extent. There were no doubt plenty of verbal and non-verbal opportunities for misunderstanding between the soldiers and their victims. Non-consent is expressed not only through vehement resistance and verbal means. The sources speak again and again of victims who cried, pleaded, begged, attempted to flee and resist physically, and of soldiers who held down their victims by force and threatened them with weapons. It is difficult to interpret these situations as consensual sexual contact. The slogan 'copulation without conversation is not fraternization' cannot be used to justify the assaults at the time.

The mitigation strategy used by the occupiers was nevertheless effective. Lilly believes that incidents in Britain or France that would have been prosecuted as rape might have been interpreted differently in Germany. He mentions a case in Aldekerk in the Lower Rhine region in which two GIs alternately raped a 19-year-old girl twice in her house. The victim cried and was in pain. After the act the soldiers drank wine with her and her mother and then the girl was once again abused. One of the GIs took a ring from his finger, gave it to the victim and said: 'You me Frau.'

A military doctor confirmed afterwards that the victim had been a virgin. The soldiers had not hit her or pointed a weapon at her, and the rifles had been just within reach next to the bed. One of the soldiers said afterwards that he had given her the gold ring in the belief that she had earned it as recompense for the sex. The military court nevertheless sentenced both soldiers to life imprisonment with hard labour for the rape. The appeal court reversed the judgement, however, finding the accused guilty only of fraternization and promiscuous behaviour with an unmarried woman, transforming the sentence into a year's hard labour and discharge from the army. They reasoned that the victim had not resisted physically or complained, and the weak signals of resistance like shaking her head and crying were completely normal behaviour for women in her position. This judgement reflects the widespread belief at the time that women wanted to be conquered and that a healthy degree of feigned resistance was part of the morally approved image of female sexuality.

After studying court files for the period March to September 1945, Lilly comes to the conclusion that the military courts increasingly trivialized rape. In the descriptions, earlier epithets like 'brutish' or 'bestial' were rarely used. He claims that the changed language was indicative of an increasingly blasé attitude by those involved. The anal and vaginal rape of the 60-year-old Anna K., for example, is described laconically as: 'He satisfied his lust.' Other cases speak merely of 'satisfying sexual needs' or say that the perpetrator intimidated his victim in order to initiate sexual intercourse.[44]

The sentences for rape also changed. In Britain and France, where there had already been problems with rape by GIs, rapists – particularly blacks – were more frequently sentenced to death, with the possibility in some cases of mutation to life imprisonment. In Germany, however, perpetrators could expect lighter sentences. Lilly surmises that this had to do both with appearances and with internal considerations. The army did not wish to demoralize its soldiers in the face of the enemy, and in any case the women of the vanquished enemy were worth less than the women of the Allies or those who had suffered under German occupation.

DISCUSSION

We should avoid compartmentalizing these events as incidents in a higher-level battle of the sexes. Sexual assault is not a male privilege, and the experience of being sexually assaulted is not a female privilege. Present-day feminist theory no longer uses this binary code as a pattern for identifying perpetrators and victims, but takes account of the interaction of social, ethnic, religious, age and other categories in the individual. Sexuality is understood as situational or enacted: in other words, acquired and visualized only through interaction with another – not least through rape. Regardless of whether the sexual assault is between men, between women, or between a woman and a man, it is ultimately a question of the exercise of power in a patriarchal setting that makes the victim into a 'woman' – in other words, disempowered.

Systematic rape in war and crisis regions has once again recently come shockingly to the fore. The terrorist organization Islamic State in Iraq, Syria and Libya, the radical Islamic sect Boko Haram in Nigeria – is rape part of the arsenal of all wars? My historical study of the rapes at the end of the Second World War is designed to counter such generalizations. On the contrary, I seek to identify the factors that led to these crimes in a particular historical constellation.

Ideas of masculinity and femininity

To understand the gender culture that was partly responsible for the mass rape, we need to go back further in time, to the bourgeois era when the male–female 'emotional culture' changed from a sensitive and friendly relationship to a polar confrontation. On the one side was the soft, emotional woman in need of protection; on the other side the aggressive and rational man. This confrontation of the sexes during the nineteenth century fostered in men 'aggressive and competitive affects in the market society', competition, rivalry, warlike hardness.[45] The female subject by comparison was reconstructed as being emotional, empathic and tending to sentimentality. The consumer society of the early twentieth century reinforced the sexualization of women, while men adopted a power-oriented, uncompromisingly heterosexual gender role that left little scope for mutual attraction and empathy for others. It was in this charged male–female atmosphere that the concept of a 'war of the sexes' emerged in the early twentieth century. It became fashionable to speak of the supposed irreconcilability of the sexes.[46]

The battle of the sexes was not a German or European phenomenon but one involving the entire modern world: press, academics, political parties, doctors and psychiatrists explained that men and women were not meant for one another and that the relationship between the sexes was a battleground, in contrast to the utopian bourgeois idea of the previous century of complementarity: the man operated in public, the woman in the home, both working towards a peaceful family life based on love, respect and tolerance. Meanwhile, the biologism and Darwinism of the late nineteenth century produced a conflictual model based on feelings and sexuality. Experts now claimed that women could not separate sex and love, while men used sex above all to pass on their genes. The quality of the desire was also completely different: men wanted hard sex, women cuddly sex. A real man needed to dominate, possibly with a hint of violence, and a real woman would yield to this need in the interests of natural selection of the stronger.

Ideas like this meant that even before the First World War prostitution and trafficking in girls increased greatly. The number of prostitutes in the German Empire rose, for example, from 100,000 to 330,000. The trend was even more marked in times of war, when the military set up brothels and controlled prostitution to give soldiers access to sex. This did not stop many soldiers from believing that they had a right to sexual war booty. The penis as weapon, the sex act as surrogate for fighting, the diametrically opposed nature of the passive woman and the aggressive man – all this produced an explosive mix in the relations between the sexes. Where simple organizational categories were questioned, there was a need for hard contrasts so that women would feel feminine and men masculine.

The women's emancipation movement, the increasingly open homosexual milieu, psychoanalysis, the first sex-change operations all shook the traditional ideas of masculinity, not only in the Western world, but also in the East, where Communism advocated equality of the sexes. In the Soviet Union, the ideologically ordained but only fragmentarily implemented gender equality was not particularly welcomed by men. Women should have children and work, and the link between production and reproduction was therefore a central focus of gender politics. Despite this, women were usually stuck in the lower-paid and less prominent areas of politics and industry.[47]

In the early twentieth century, therefore, the dominant male model came increasingly under pressure. The male image was of workers and fighters, but machines made physical strength less important, as work could now be carried out by less skilled immigrants and women. At the same time, from the First World War onwards, the fighting affected civilian life more and more and thus impacted not only on men. As the sociologist Andreas Reckwitz puts it, the male position was 'doubly destabilized: at home and at the front, which affected very many more civilians than previous wars'. It was now no longer the 'privilege' of men to fight, to prove themselves in war and, if need be, to die heroically for the fatherland. This could explain why the post-war periods after 1918 and 1945 saw a radically new gender order.[48]

Masculinity also suffered in the USA in the 1930s. The economic crisis caused mass unemployment and wage cuts, making millions of family providers reliant on welfare. The fear of a soft and 'feminized' nation was greater for some people than the threat of war with Germany. It gave rise to a movement aimed explicitly at strengthening men, shoring up the health and strength of the nation through physical fitness and male vitality. The outbreak of war was an ideal moment for combining male and soldierly images. The 'real man' could prove himself in a particularly hard situation full of deprivation, physical stress and boundless violence.[49]

British soldiers also had to deal with contradictory male virtues in the war: on the one hand an honourable and emotionally controlled or 'tempered' bourgeois masculinity as a contrast to the hyper-masculine Nazi maleness, and, on the other hand, a heroic, steady and soldierly masculinity to defend the attacked 'female' nation.[50]

The idea of soldierly comradeship as an exclusively male domain that didn't require women, who stood for home, family and security, played an important role in the punishment of aggressive sexual practices.[51] A comrade was someone with whom one could do things together. Getting up to tricks meant, above all, non-marital sex with women:

> Adultery with comrades was what made a soldier's life interesting . . . Boozing and going on the rampage gave the male society the feeling of being able to flaunt the formal rules of military order and even more so the morality of bourgeois life. Demonstrating disdain for women, talking of sexual matters in a crude and unmannerly way, talking smut were all signs of real maleness.[52]

It was not primarily sexual needs but rather the need to fit into the soldierly community and to prove oneself among comrades that counted.

This is the background to the frequent commission in groups of rape and other crimes in the Red Army and in the US, British and French armies. It was not just a matter of punishing the enemy but of interaction with comrades. 'The victims themselves scarcely seemed to feature in their minds as people. . . . The passion in question was largely their love for each other, and also their grief – undrownable despite oceans of wine and schnapps – for all the people and the chances they had lost', as Catherine Merridale describes it.[53] The desire for comradeship and the fear of being seen as a coward were both reinforced by the group rapes. Merridale tells of a Red Army soldier who was invited to select a German girl from among a group of terrified captives. His first fear was that his own men might think him cowardly or even impotent if he refused.[54] The same phenomenon can be observed today in male initiation rites in student fraternities or gang rapes by criminal bands.

Gaby Zipfel points to a further motive for the soldierly violence against women and civilians. The soldiers hid their vulnerability in war by directing their power to harm against female or feminized people. They compensated for their own fear and weakness through male aggressiveness. The victim did not have to be a woman. The mass rapes in Nanking in 1937 during the Second Sino-Japanese War also included the anal rape of men and forcing men to sexually abuse one another. In the Bosnia war in the early 1990s, Serbian soldiers also forced men to have intercourse with one another.[55]

The dramatization of sexuality and gender roles in wartime, the male experience of downgrading in their countries of origin, the subconscious insecurity with regards to identity in view of the growing women's labour force created a climate of anti-female aggression in both the West and the East. This made women into particular targets for male frustration in the last phase of the war and the post-war period. The most extreme expression was rape, but there were also other forms of reaction to masculine insecurity, such as the shaming rituals through the public shaving of the heads of supposed collaborators in France and Germany. Compulsory examinations of female 'sources of infection' can also be seen in this light, not to mention the merciless discipline in homes for 'destitute' girls and, not least, the constant suspicion that rape victims had in fact consented to the approaches by the occupiers and had even sought financial recompense for their immoral behaviour.[56]

It is repeatedly pointed out that the victims of the misdeeds committed by the Allies and German soldiers in the Second World War were the vanquished population and that they were part of the sexual conquest of a country. War-related rape is categorized within the semantic field of violent attack on the rights, property and collective honour of others.[57] However plausible this might sound, in my opinion this highly abstract explanation does not help us to understand what happened. The concept of symbolic collective rape, like the earlier idea of a natural male sex drive, runs the risk rather of normalizing sexual violence in war and presenting it as an unavoidable evil.

It would be more useful in my opinion to consider that it was rather the specific experience in dealing with the sexes and the established behaviour patterns in the different armies that led to the eruption of sexual violence at the end of the war. Rapes had occurred as the armies advanced on Germany – the communal acts had already been 'tried out' by the Americans in Britain and France and the Soviets in the East.

Alongside the acute war-related opportunities for the mass rape of German women, the interaction of ethnic, sexist and specific social factors might be a further reason why the fate of German women has never been recognized or sympathized with. They have never been delineated as a victim group, as they were not raped solely as Germans or as women. As we shall see, this had ambivalent consequences in the attempts to come to terms with what had occurred. Treating the terrible events as the violent fate of a nation helped in particular in discussion of German flight and expulsion, but it also meant that for a long time the fate of the individual women was ignored and has still not been recognized today. It was a woman's fate, leading in a post-war society interested in re-establishing male dominance to a devaluation of a group of victims who were 'female' and hence inferior.

A 'SEXUAL CONQUEST OF EUROPE'?

The decision for the second time in a generation to send soldiers across the Atlantic to fight at the side of the Allies against Germany was initially anything but popular with the US population. It was not until the Japanese attack on Pearl Harbor in December 1941 that the mood changed. After the initial goal of liberating the countries occupied by the Germans, of disarming the enemy and bringing the main persons responsible to justice, the aim was to restore security and order and to re-educate the Germans to build a democracy. The long-term objective of the United States to consolidate the American influence in Europe and to keep the Soviets in check was ultimately to require presence of US troops abroad for many years.

The prospect of permanent stationing in Europe under living conditions much worse than those at home was not popular with the soldiers. Noble political motives on their own were often not sufficient to motivate the ordinary troops. In her book *What Soldiers Do*, about the sexual conquests by GIs in France at the end of the Second World War, Mary Louise Roberts points to another motivation used by the US Army to lure soldiers – the reward for the efforts and hardships of war could also be of a sexual nature in the form of European women.

Roberts shows that the US Army, in its attempts to inspire the young men to fight, quite deliberately disseminated an image of French and European women as sexually hungry and open-minded. In the military newspapers and propaganda leaflets, the prospect of a long and hard struggle to liberate Europe from the German aggressor was blatantly made more palatable through the prospect of gratitude by the women.[58] Countless cartoons and photographs showed American heroes being embraced and kissed by the women in the liberated countries. Roberts claims that the 'conquest' of women fulfilled a dual purpose: on the one hand, as a trophy for the American soldiers themselves; and, on the other hand, as a strategy in the power struggle for domination in the country. Consensual and non-consensual sex by foreigners with their wives and daughters clearly demonstrated to the men of Europe how insignificant their position had become in the world.[59]

Thus, the raping by American soldiers did not begin after they had crossed the Rhine but right after the landing in Normandy, where there was fighting, looting and destruction by US troops. French women suffered on account of their reputation among the American men as being particularly easy prey. The prolonged US propaganda to encourage and sexualize the American soldiers had its consequences: 'The myth of the manly GI turned out to be *too* successful. Sexual fantasies about France did indeed motivate the GI to get off the boat and fight. But such fantasies also unleashed a veritable tsunami of male lust.'[60]

The conquest and liberation of Europe was made to look like a romantic affair – expressed by laughing women in the arms of American soldiers – but in reality the French were obliged to complain continuously to the military authorities that the soldiers sought sex in public in broad daylight, peacefully sometimes but also by force. Parks, ruined buildings, cemeteries, railway tracks all appeared ideal for this purpose.

In spite of the numerous complaints, the American army command did nothing to discipline its troops. Instead, it justified the behaviour of the soldiers by pointing to the military – in other words, male – inability of France to resist Nazi Germany, and decided high-handedly that social ills like the open and secret prostitution, particularly of young girls from rural areas, and the growing rate of infection with venereal diseases were a French problem – as long as the American public, particularly women, remained untouched by it.

When the complaints of rape by the French increased and came to the attention of the American media, however, the army leadership resorted to pointing the finger at African American soldiers, whom they prosecuted and punished with particular severity. In October 1944, 152 American soldiers, including 139 blacks, were convicted of rape in France. Within a single year, forty-five black soldiers were executed there for rape. This was fine with the French, who were also particularly interested in the prosecution of dark-skinned perpetrators.

Roberts believes that the disproportionately large number of black GIs involved, according to official figures on rape in France in the summer of 1944, was due not only to the French women's fear of 'the black man' but also to a structural factor: most of the complaints were about rape by members of the supply units, in which there was a higher proportion of blacks than in the fighting units. They were less mobile than the other units and it was thus easier to prosecute someone for an offence. At the time, however, people naturally sought a different explanation for the disproportionately large number of African American suspects: as mentioned earlier, black men were thought to have more powerful urges and weaker control. Some 77 per cent of all rapes for which convictions were obtained in France involved African Americans; later, in Germany, the proportion was to dwindle to less than a third.[61]

Roberts' study clearly shows that the behaviour of the American soldiers in France was already similar to what was to come later in Germany, albeit not with the same brutality. The tacit acceptance of sexual promiscuity, also as a hoped-for antidote to the homoerotic climate in the army (forced sexual restraint was seen as a cause of homosexuality), ultimately counted for more than the question of whether the sexual objects belonged to a friendly or enemy nation. Contemporary witnesses already noted the violent and intensive nature of the 'fraternization' of GIs in Europe. The obvious comparison between the conquest of sexual partners and the conquest of the enemy, whose human dignity and equality were denied, was also made at the time.[62] As Karen Hagemann puts it, erotic fraternization became a 'myth rather than a stab in the back'. The fact that their honour had been wounded because they were unable to fulfil their male duty and protect 'their' women was used by German men to exonerate and dissociate themselves from any feelings of guilt and to direct their aggression instead against the 'Yank lovers'.[63]

Rape sweetened with a bar of chocolate

The American writer and journalist Meyer Levin, who worked as a war correspondent during the Second World War, admitted that, after what he had seen in Theresienstadt concentration camp, he felt a need in himself for revenge in the form of rape:

> In war there is a reversal of the general code of the community of men. It is right to kill, and with this sanction comes a compulsion to reverse all other civilized injunctions: to steal, lie, blaspheme, and rape. ... Thus theft is transformed into loot, rape in Germany was accomplished through the medium of a bar of chocolate and was known as fraternization.[64]

In other words, the eyewitness was saying that, for the Americans, fraternization could be a euphemism for rape. This self-critical appraisal is striking and reveals how deceptive it is to regard the pictures of American soldiers in their tanks being enthusiastically welcomed as the reflection of a harmonious reality. Behind these images was far more than just the well-earned rest and relaxation of battle-tested soldiers.

It is quite possible that the sexual violence by the Americans was also the result of prejudices and mutual misunderstanding. Petra Goedde believes that contact between black Americans and German women escalated rapidly because of mutual prejudices – German women regarded black men as being driven by lust and reacted strongly when African Americans made advances, while the Americans acted under the false assumption that German women had fewer problems with ethnic barriers when it came to sex than white American women. The GIs had heard that European women in general were less sexually inhibited than the women back home. This alone provided enough material for misunderstandings. Moreover, the difference between a 'respectable' woman and a prostitute was not always evident to GIs, while German women failed to realize that certain behaviour on their part signalled consent to the GIs.[65]

Undoubtedly, there were also many consensual relationships between German women and American occupying forces. Of the 70,000 or so mothers of occupation children, only around 5 per cent claimed that they had become pregnant through the use of force. German women were fascinated by the relative prosperity of the American soldiers and in the destruction of post-war Germany dreamed of starting afresh in the New World. They saw the good physical shape and optimism of the GIs in contrast to their own often burnt-out and disabled men, marked by the fighting and captivity. But above all it was extreme hardship that prompted women (just as much then as today in countries where sex tourism is rife) to become involved with foreign soldiers. One example illustrates the poverty and hardship in the German population at the end of the war. In a weekly report of July 1945, the mayor of Bad Wiessee, today a prosperous town in Upper Bavaria, wrote to the district council in Miesbach: 'As indication of the continuing poor food and health situation of the population, not only general poor health but also fainting fits have been observed on occasion even with mild infectious diseases. Around one third of the population are visibly undernourished, and children have even been seen rummaging in dustbins for American food.'[66]

For that reason, the GIs and German women had certain mutual interests. For black soldiers in particular, who were not allowed to marry white women in the USA at that time and suffered from many other forms of discrimination and segregation, the prospect of a relationship with a white woman might well have been just as tempting as the prospect of a better life and even emigration for a German woman. The moral judgement, still to be found in present-day historiography, that German women were particularly uninhibited, sexually starved and morally destitute continues to be coloured by the negative interpretation of the events at the time.

UNBROKEN ASSERTION OF POWER BY THE OCCUPIERS

The American occupation zone consisting of parts of south and central Germany, Bremen and Bremerhaven had an area of 116,000 square kilometres, approximately the same as the Soviet zone. The American military command in Frankfurt was responsible for 16.7 million Germans. The basic attitude of the Germans to the Americans was ambivalent. The victorious power was idealized as a stronghold of freedom and equality and as a protector but at the same time demonized for its lack of culture, materialism and aggressive hegemonial policies.[67] The GIs were seen as prosperous, relaxed and friendly towards children (the latter also applying to the Red Army), but also as boorish philistines, libidinous, childish and uncultured.[68] As was the case in Berlin, the sexual and other violent aggressions by the Americans did not cease with the end of the war but continued to perturb the population for years, doing little to improve the ambivalent relationship of the Germans to the 'occupiers'.

In the district of Traunstein alone, several incidents were reported in the course of a few weeks in May 1946, a year after the end of the war. When these incidents also included murder, the population rose up in anger and demanded the 'removal' if possible of all 'foreigners' to improve legal security in the region.[69] In a wealthy district on the outskirts of Munich, a saleswoman in a health food store was raped in June 1946 by two American soldiers. She was out walking when a light American military truck stopped 20 metres away. One soldier with a cocked rifle ordered her to come with him into the trees.

> I said in English: "No, I won't come with you, I'm a respectable girl." Then he pointed the rifle at me and said forcefully: "You will come with me." I stuffed my knitting in my handbag and tried to run away. He grabbed me by the arm, pointed his weapon at me and pulled me into the undergrowth ... After the intercourse he was friendly and instructed me not to speak of the incident to anyone, not even his comrade.

But that wasn't the end of it. The other soldier threatened to shoot her if she didn't also go into the trees with him. After the woman had undergone this rape, the first American asked her if she would meet him again at the same place the next morning, to which she agreed. 'They gave me two cigarettes and a piece of chocolate and drove off in the direction of Gräfeling.' The women went straightaway to a doctor, who confirmed a genital injury, and then to the police.[70]

This case shows how self-assured but also how ignorant the Americans were in their behaviour. They had no scruples about attacking in broad daylight in the belief that they could buy themselves out of trouble with a hand-out, and even repeat the act. They had nothing to fear from the German authorities, and while they respected their own administration it did not stop them from acting in concert.

In Hochbrück bei Oberschleissheim, the 32-year-old Käthe C. was also attacked from an army vehicle in June 1946. She resisted vigorously and was beaten and clubbed for her pains. Here again a comrade kept watch during the rape. Afterwards, the assailant told her to be quiet and say nothing to his superiors. When further soldiers approached in another vehicle, they helped her and took her to the military police. Another report from the same region speaks of a hotel in which four American soldiers requisitioned a room and repeatedly brought women there.[71]

Until the entry into force of the Paris Treaties in 1955, the German police and jurisdiction were powerless in the face of these attacks. Neither the Americans nor the Allied soldiers in the other occupied zones could be charged by them or in the occupiers' courts. It was only after 1955 that German jurisdiction was extended to all non-criminal proceedings against natural persons from the Allied armies, albeit with very limited means, as we shall see later in the paternity claims against members of the occupying forces.

A further source of irritation was the fact that, even after the official end of the occupation status, the American armed forces refused repeatedly to cooperate with the German police. Evidence was not recognized, perpetrators were protected, and victims criminalized and intimidated. They were sometimes sought out at home by American investigators and interrogated with a lie detector without being given the opportunity to call a lawyer. If proceedings were instigated, they were in accordance with American procedural law, which also included cross-examination, a procedure unknown in Germany.

The German Child Protection League wrote to the Federal Ministry of Justice on this account in August 1956. The 15-year-old schoolgirl Erika L. had broken down in Würzburg after being cross-examined. The American doctors stated the next day that she was capable of testifying again, but she broke down once more as soon as the questioning started and had to be admitted to hospital. She had been raped by eight American soldiers. During the cross-examination, which lasted several hours, no account was taken of her youth or sense of shame and embarrassment. The Child Protection League described this procedure as a 'second rape' and appealed to the politicians to offer better protection, at least to minors, before American courts. But the Minister of Justice was hesitant in answering. He said that the prosecution of members of the American armed forces was the responsibility of the army, and the accused had the right to test the witness' credibility by cross-examination. In this case at least, the third questioning session took place in the girl's home, sparing her the need to confront her attackers again.[72] We should not forget that the tactic of accusing rape victims was not just a speciality of American military justice but still remains a popular defence strategy for casting doubt on the victim's credibility.

The Bavarian press also repeatedly complained about the mild sentences handed down to American soldiers convicted of rape. The acquittals in the trial for rape of the 12-year-old I. S. in 1959 gave rise to furious protests.[73] Worried members of parliament and church leaders asked the Ministry of Foreign Affairs if it would not be possible by diplomatic means to ensure that German women and girls were left alone. Violence increased every time a new unit was stationed. In 1963, in the town of Gelnhausen in Hesse, where units of the 3rd US Tank Division were stationed, for example, there was such a rise in property theft, vandalism and violence, even eighteen years after the end of the war, that the population began to wonder who would protect them from the Americans. After the rape of a 37-year-old woman by a US soldier, the town council protested to the garrison headquarters, while five citizens took the law into their own hands and beat up a black soldier. *Der Spiegel* carried a detailed report saying that the lack of security on the streets had also destroyed public confidence in the American sense of justice. On two occasions, civilians had followed soldiers who had been caught in the act to their barracks, only to see them ushered to the safety of the extraterritorial site by the sentries. Between 8 August and 25 September alone, twenty-one offences had been perpetrated by members of the army. A police officer who asked to see the papers of a GI who was in the process of stealing a floodlight from a building site suffered a broken finger. Although the local commander, Colonel James Terry, promised an improvement, it was to no avail. After a pile-up of German vehicles caused by American smoke grenades, a GI forced his way at night into a couple's bedroom and only ran off when they cried loudly for help.

'The people of Gelnhausen quickly realized that there was no point in reporting incidents of this nature. A young post office worker who had been beaten up by US soldiers and had identified the perpetrators in the barracks was later badly beaten up again by the same soldiers.' The population also resented the fact that convicted delinquents were not imprisoned but 'rehabilitated' in the barracks. Often they received only a reprimand and a dressing-down from their commanding officer. A drunken captain who caused a traffic accident killing two and injuring several others got off with a warning and a 400-mark fine. The inhabitants of Gelnhausen reacted to their legal powerlessness in their own way. A father whose daughter had narrowly escaped being raped bought a handgun. The rapist of the 37-year-old woman was never caught.[74]

It was not unusual for women to be attacked in the open, sometimes even when accompanied by a man. On 4 December 1951, the 26-year-old clerk K. S. was walking home with his wife in Bad Kissingen. Shortly before they reached their home, they were stopped by two drunken US soldiers. One grabbed the woman by the shoulders and tried to drag her off. Her husband intervened and demanded that the soldiers leave his wife alone. She managed to get away but the other soldier punched and injured the man. He was able to escape and call the military police, who arrived while the two were still on the rampage. The MP merely told them half-heartedly to go home and then drove off again.

In Würzburg in April 1952, two women, also with a man, were importuned by American soldiers. The German man stood in front of the women to protect them. One of the soldiers punched him and the other threw a rock at his head, causing a suspected skull fracture.[75] Bad Kissingen town council complained in winter 1951, in a letter to the Lower Franconia regional authority, that a striking number of incidents of this nature took place especially around Christmas time.[76] The inhabitants of Bamberg were also concerned at this time by the numerous incidents involving GIs. Apart from rapes, there was also vandalism, shooting, fights, theft and even murder, frequently under the influence of alcohol. When complaints from the communities where the US troops were stationed began to increase, the Bavarian president Hans Erhard finally wrote to the US Landeskommissar Oron

J. Hale in January 1952, saying that, although he had no right to criti-
cize the behaviour of the occupying army, he believed that there was
an urgent need to teach particularly the lower-level commanders the
'poor service that this behaviour rendered to the joint interests of the
West and the prestige of the greatest democracy in the world'.[77]

The appeal was well intentioned but had little effect. In the last
three months of 1952 alone, the Bavarian Ministry of the Interior
received reports of 227 serious incidents involving American soldiers,
including 18 attempted or successful rapes.[78] A year later, in the last
three months of 1953, there were 260 reported breaches of security by
US soldiers, even more than in the previous year. 'The population is
particularly concerned about the many attempted or successful sexual
offences committed by US soldiers', wrote the Bavarian Ministry of the
Interior.[79] The area close to military training grounds was considered
particularly dangerous. Most of the recorded attacks were group rapes.

These examples from Bavaria were repeated in other regions under
American occupation. Years after the end of the war, the sexual suppression of Germany, a reaction to the suffering of war and the incredible
hardship that the Germans had inflicted on their enemies, had apparently turned into a gesture of power through sexual acts.

PARALLELS AND DIFFERENCES

Although it will not have made much difference to the victims which
uniform the soldier who raped them was wearing, I believe it would be
useful to compare the Soviet and American offences, not least as the
aftermath and collective memory are so different. As we have seen,
the acts themselves were similar. After months and years of fighting,
the soldiers of both major victorious powers had already committed
rapes on their allies in the East and in Britain and France, respectively.
Following their encounter with the horrendous crimes committed
by the German Wehrmacht and the liberation of concentration and
extermination camps with their piles of corpses, the sexual violence nevertheless increased exponentially. It was directed at a population that,
through fear and also for reasons of ideology and self-righteousness,
had put up unexpectedly fierce resistance. The relative prosperity of the
enemy provoked rage and envy not only among the Soviets. The GIs in

Upper Bavaria also looted, stole watches, bicycles and other valuables. Moreover, both of the armies had been encouraged through propaganda, and through rumours of the allegedly immoral life of German women, to believe that every soldier was entitled to a female trophy.

On the other hand, we see the fear of 'Asiatic beasts', but also of African American troops; the belief that they were particularly uninhibited and uncivilized; the vague expectation of retaliation for the misdeeds of earlier years. The threat of weapons and the legal insecurity probably also made the victims appear more passive, a conviction that was reinforced by the general preconception by the Allies of the defeated German people as cowardly and wishing to curry favour, and of a nation that was notoriously willing to accept and obey orders.

After the first phase of conquest, the documented American rapes often appear to be mere demonstrations of power. They took place in broad daylight, in groups, without the slightest fear of the German authorities and only mild apprehensions about their own. The population realized this but had no choice but to resolutely call for a bit more discipline. Some group rapes appeared to have had a systematic character, for example when Soviets and Americans set up temporary premises in which they were able to abuse women for days on end.

It is also interesting to note that the divergent strategies by the two major powers for dealing with the Germans appear to have made no difference to the rape problem. The Americans initially called for a strict ban on fraternization, while the Soviets only gradually screened their troops from the civilian population. As we shall see with the French, who billeted their soldiers in civilian homes so that they lived in close contact with the conquered people in south-west Germany, none of these approaches brought about any improvement in terms of sexual assaults. Apart from the various structural and situative factors fostering a culture of rape among the soldiers, it was above all the image of women – and German women in particular – and the gender roles of the time that brought about the sexual violence that marked the conquest of Germany by all of the occupying forces.

4

PREGNANT, SICK, OSTRACIZED –
APPROACHES TO THE VICTIMS

Mummy, if only we could be together. I am so afraid because I haven't had my period. It will soon be ten weeks. I hope that the Good Lord hasn't done this to me.

Gabi Köpp, fifteen years old, alone in flight[1]

I don't want charity. I want my rights like any other mother. I don't see why I should have to suffer the consequences of the lost war for the rest of my life.[2]

Margaret S. in a letter to the Federal Ministry of Social Affairs

I do not belong to the large number of mothers with illegitimate children but to the special group of war victims, and I believe that the government should not deny me this moral recognition.

M. K. from Bremen in her petition to the Federal Ministry of the Interior on 12 June 1951[3]

VICTIMS TWICE OVER

In September 1961, the 35-year-old housewife U. G. appeared before Opladen local court. She was informed of her right to refuse to testify but said that she was willing to do so. She related that in the late afternoon of 8 May 1945, she had been walking from Weede to Steinweg in the district of Segeberg when, at around 7 p.m., she saw a British motorcycle driver leaning against a tree. His hand was on the pistol in his lap. He addressed the two women and asked in broken German how old they were. At the time U. G. was eighteen and her friend just sixteen. The soldier told the friend that she was too young for him and she was able to get away. 'I wasn't able to escape', continued U. G.; 'He grabbed hold of me so that I couldn't free myself. He was like an animal, you could say, and threw me onto the ground, tearing my blouse in the process.'

When U. G. later spoke to her friend, the latter said that she had wanted to fetch help but couldn't find anyone. U. G. related the incident to her mother, who told her she should wait first for her next period. But it didn't come. A pregnancy test was carried out by the health department in Bad Segeberg. Her mother wanted her to have an abortion, but they were told at the department that abortions were strictly forbidden. On 30 January 1946, U. G. gave birth to the child of the British rapist. Now, fifteen years later, she swore that her testimony was true. She hoped to receive a hardship allowance for her daughter.

One of the aspects of the mass rapes after the war that still remains to be discussed is the fact that in many cases the suffering of the women did not end with the rape. Many victims had to endure humiliation for years afterwards. Especially for those who became pregnant as a result of the rape there was very little chance of starting over again after the war. They were despised by society and had to fear that their husbands would leave them, or discovered that, encumbered with an 'occupation child', they had little chance of finding a partner who would marry them. And they had to bear the financial costs of the outcome of the rape.

Unwanted pregnancies were just one of the consequences of sexual violence at the end of the war. Those women who had 'only' become infected with a venereal disease and had to deal 'only' with

the psychological consequences or were marginalized in society were
to discover painfully how German society dealt with victims for whom
they had no sympathy.

For U. G., the story continued. Two months after her court hearing,
a municipal councillor at the Amt für Verteidigungslasten [department
for losses incurred by foreign defence troops] in Düsseldorf stated that
she had provided no proof of rape and requested that the friend who
had run away be questioned under oath. The witness was heard on 21
December 1961. She added that they had both started to cry when the
soldier spoke to them and she had told him that she was very young and
had a sick mother at home. The soldier then grabbed her friend by the
arm. She could not say whether her friend had resisted. Her testimony
satisfied the judge, however, and on 14 March 1962 U. G. received
a decision in her favour, granting her a hardship allowance for her
daughter of DM 65 per month backdated to 1 October 1958, minus 50
per cent to take account of state welfare payments. The total amounted
to DM 1,300. The child was now sixteen years old and was to receive a
hardship allowance of DM 42 per month until she completed her voca-
tional training in 1965.[4] It had taken twenty years for compensation, at
least of a financial nature, to be obtained for the rape.

The social climate at the time and the institutions dealing with the
women in many cases provided no help for the victims, but rather wors-
ened their situation. Insensitive gynaecologists and unpitying jurists
decided on abortion requests and compensation claims; authoritarian
welfare workers controlled their household and child allowances if the
women had had a child as a result of the rape; and brutish policemen
assisted the occupation forces' military police in fighting suspicious
'sources of infection' with venereal diseases – often with the same occupying power that had committed the rapes. And the reputation and
credibility of the women were always at stake. Post-war society was
more interested in struggling to restore the supposedly lost 'morality'
than in dealing with the consequences of acts of violence suffered by
the German population in the Nazi era and war.

FRATERNIZATION

Few people are aware today of the mass rapes committed by GIs and soldiers of the French Army. Unlike the acts by the Red Army soldiers, these crimes have not entered the collective German memory. Even in small communities, they have been forgotten or suppressed. The images of fraternization are much more vivid: women and girls who landed the nearest muscle-bound GI allegedly for a cigarette or a pair of nylon stockings or simply because they found the well-nourished American soldiers more attractive than the emaciated German men. It was said that Americans took six years to defeat the German soldiers but it took only one day and a bar of chocolate to get a German woman.[5]

It is difficult today to understand the indignation at women who had relations with occupying soldiers. At the time, however, both the occupying powers and the Germans had different reasons for wanting to prevent contact between the military and civilians. For the Germans, there were questions of loyalty to the nation and the soldiers who had been killed or taken prisoner in the field, while the Americans, British, French and Soviets feared that informal contact with the enemy population could weaken and endanger their own troops. Moreover, the Allies wanted the Germans to feel in no uncertain terms that they had lost the war and that they could not expect any sympathy or clemency.

It was for that reason that, as early as 12 September 1944, General Eisenhower forbade private contact with Germans: 'Every friendly German civilian is a soldier of hate in disguise . . . A smile is the weapon they use to disarm you. Do not fraternize.'[6] This attitude was reinforced by the ban on fraternization in early 1945, designed to prevent any unnecessary personal contact. After Germany's surrender, however, the ban on contact proved to be neither enforceable nor desirable, because the occupying powers were reliant on the help of the Germans in administering the occupied territories, and were also intent on re-education and democratization. By October 1945, the American ban on fraternization had been officially lifted.

At the same time, the term 'fraternization' acquired a second unofficial meaning – namely, consensual (hetero-)sexual contact between German women and Western soldiers and other members of the armed forces.[7] Even if 'fraternization' is generally associated with American soldiers, the British had similar ideas about the nature and intentions of German women and warned their soldiers accordingly. In a 1944 manual, the British soldiers were warned that 'under the shock of defeat, standards of personal honour, already undermined by the Nazis, will sink still lower. Numbers of German women will be willing if they can get the chance to make themselves cheap for what they can get out of you.' Marriage was forbidden by the British as a precautionary measure, since the German girls would become British if they married British men and exploit all the advantages of this nationality. They would not be doing it out of affection: 'When once they had their marriage lines, he would have served his purpose.' They were also warned that the Germans might use attractive women as spies: 'Don't be too ready to listen to stories told by attractive women. They may be acting under orders.'[8]

For rape victims – in particular, of Western Allies – this judgement had fatal consequences. Women had great difficulty in shaking off the suspicion of fraternization, even when they had been victims of sexual violence. One of the main problems was that rape in general – and not just at the time – was often seen as a misfortune brought upon the women by themselves, the result of the unstable female character. Rape by a Western soldier, rather than a Soviet, who in the Nazi ideology belonged to a lower species, doubled the lack of credibility.

There were concrete arguments that combined with social anxieties and the sense of shame to form a complex structure that militated against women. On the one hand, there was a real need for food, cigarettes and other commodities available in large quantities to the US soldiers. There was also a fear of the sexual and emotional attraction of the 'victors', which was also experienced as an insult to German men. This fear nourished the collective fear of an 'emasculated' German nation. Rejection and resentment of foreigners and other ethnic groups fuelled this mixture of emotions and needs.

The German population generally regarded those who fraternized as prostitutes. Women did not sell themselves because they needed to or because they were uprooted, but because they didn't want to work. As such, they were an insult to all of the men who had sacrificed themselves in the fight for the German fatherland; they had their fun while the former soldiers suffered; they damaged the 'health of the nation' and burdened the public sector by spreading venereal diseases; and they endangered the moral discipline of the young. Above all, however, they threatened the bourgeois family model with its established gender roles; they were the only ones to blame if Germany lost its dignity after the war. Their extramarital relations with soldiers of the occupying powers undermined morality and decency; through their consumption of American men and products they contributed to the 'Americanization' of Germany, to sexual libertinage, materialism, and 'miscegenation' in the event of contact with black soldiers. The only good thing to say in this moral discourse was that the 'Yank lovers' at least protected respectable women from the sexual advances of members of the occupying powers.[9]

Some observers even connected the supposed moral decline in women with the Nazi past. After the Hitler regime had forced people into 'mental prostitution', it did not take much for them to take the step to physical prostitution.[10] This was a strategic argument that associated the supposedly immoral women with the Nazi ideology.[11] Sexual contact with foreign soldiers was interpreted as a continuation of the immoral period before 1945 and a betrayal of the German people.[12]

Careful study of the reports of fraternizing women reveals that one group of women in particular – lower class, non-local city dwellers – were accused and even publicly singled out by having their hair shorn and other shaming rituals. Their mere existence appeared to stand in the way of the desire for consolidation of sexual and family morality after the war. 'Unfortunately there were flirtations between Yanks and German girls and women. There were even friendships with blacks, fortunately only in the case of two or three dishonourable women (two from Silesia!)' wrote Albert Michel, minister from Alling in the district of Unterpfaffenhofen in the summer of 1945.[13] The pastor Joseph Hort from Gündlkofen bei Moosburg also didn't mince words in identifying those who perturbed the traditional public order: 'Sympathy for the evacuees is usually misplaced. They are lazy, thieving, argumentative, accusing farmers for the smallest thing, and need to be chased out of our Bavarian province as soon as possible.'[14]

GIs don't need to rape

The prejudicial moral condemnation, particularly of urban dwellers and strangers, combined at the end of the war with the humiliation of defeat for German man. The problem was not the killing in the country's recent past, in which the men had been deeply involved, but the moral disintegration of the present, which was projected onto the women. The persistence of this point of view can be seen in the professional reconstructions today that still fail to question the prejudices of the time. Otherwise serious histories of the occupation period deal with the subject of rape under the heading 'fraternization', boldly connecting two aspects that are in fact quite disparate – the voluntary, if sometimes needs-driven, relationships between GIs and German women, and the sexual aggression of the occupiers. This distorted representation culminates in an inflexible thesis that has kept us in ignorance, even today, of the rapes by the Western allies; according to this thesis, sexual aggression by the Americans was 'limited' because German women were very welcoming. In other words, the GIs didn't need to commit rape because the women wanted in any case to have sex with them.[15]

This thesis is based uncritically on discussion at the time of the relationship of German women to Western occupying forces. The truth in these claims made at the end of the war is not questioned, and the conclusion is simply drawn that 'cases of rape in the West were isolated and had various causes. One was that there was apparently a sufficient number of German women who were so attracted to the occupying soldiers from the outset that there was no need for the use of violence.'[16]

The GIs, writes the historian Klaus-Dietmar Henke, were in an unfortunate position, compared with their French and German comrades, because the US Army did not wish to provide military brothels for them. But the 'attraction' between American soldiers and German women was great and there was a mutual need for distraction, tenderness and sexual adventure. Curious about the smart and well-fed charmers from the fabulously rich and superior America, 'fraternization' by German women started on the day they arrived. The non-fraternization policy of the American Army, the prohibition of any private contact by soldiers with the enemy civilian population, could not compete with this force of attraction. In the eyes of this specialist on the history of the American occupation, there were therefore hardly any instances of rape. During 1945, he estimates, there were around 1,000 to 1,500 cases.[17]

The prejudice that still exists in historical research today is due to the intensive attack at the time on fraternization by German women. The contemporary sources, which are in reality highly questionable, are the chief witnesses in this incorrect assessment.

There are not only the memoirs of German men with battered egos, like the jurist Dietrich Güstrow, who was a public prosecutor in the Nazi era and a judge and mayor after the war. When the Americans arrived in his village in the Harz, he had to put up with having eight American soldiers living in his home, which was particularly hard for his fanatically nationalistic Prussian mother to swallow. The frustration was all the greater when their Russian servant, a slave labourer, suddenly confronted the Güstrow family. She flirted with the Americans and insisted on her right after liberation to decide for herself when she would work for the family. The rapid rise of the former slave labourer to become a self-assured member of the victors was a typically bitter experience for the Germans at the time, particularly the heads of the families, who were used to exercising unlimited power. Güstrow described the young American officer as an 'ill-behaved man' who refused to 'cooperate' with the Germans and brazenly insisted that the US soldiers were not 'visitors' but had come to Germany as conquerors.[18]

It is against this background of a disempowered German patriarchal system that no longer had control over its women and had to stand by as they fraternized with the new masters that the criticism of this all too willing fraternization is motivated: 'It was not long before we discovered that nothing is as erotic as power.'[19]

Another questionable source regarding the apparent immorality of German women is to be found in the reports of the time by American soldiers. Many GIs wrote home boastfully from Germany – like this one: 'The girls here are all well-rounded. Perhaps it's because I have been away so long, but they all look pretty to me. It's forbidden to fraternize, but I reckon they don't mind our eying them. Everywhere I've been they're all the same, a bunch of flirts.'[20]

These are the mirror image of the German documentation, expressions of triumph over a humiliated patriarchal society.[21] No one can deny that the American soldiers and German women were strongly attracted to one another and that the need for distraction, tenderness and sexual adventure was not one-sided. But those who look at the large number of rapes by American soldiers will seriously question whether that was all there was to the story of German–American sexual contacts.

The sexual order of the time, influenced by a bourgeois Christian sense of morality, the hierarchy of feelings, makes it practically impossible today to determine the real nature of the sexual relations. But to explain them merely as indication of a search for 'human warmth and entertainment' sounds like an extreme simplification.[22] We would not dream of making such a supposition in the similar case of the sex trade between tourists and locals in poor countries. I therefore agree with Jennifer V. Evans that the idea of fraternization by German women needs to be fundamentally revised. Only by looking more closely at ideas of gender and morality at the time (and to some extent today as well) can we shed light on the grey area between open violence, forced prostitution and consensual sexual contact – grey zones in the power hierarchy of Germans and Americans, women and men.[23]

Public morality above all

Another major obstacle to a reasonable approach to the rape victims was the attempt by post-war society to restore *Sittlichkeit* ('public morality').[24] After the years of Nazism and war, there was a movement in Germany to clean up the distorted value system by restoring sexual morality, of all things. It was thought that the battered society – as Germany saw itself – could recover only on the basis of a solid morality. There was therefore an all-party interest in the alleged threats to *Sittlichkeit*: pornography, prostitution, writing harmful to young people – but also materialism and sexual profligacy. To those fighting for decency, women who abandoned themselves voluntarily out of pure craving and hedonism were a perfect target.[25]

Post-war society operated on the tried and tested principle of seeking a scapegoat as a way of avoiding a personal admission of guilt.

Responsibility for the disaster of the Second World War and the Shoah was established by inverting the cause-and-effect relationship. If the Germans had recalled their traditional bourgeois values in time, if the Weimar society had not taken the first steps towards pluralism, if the churches and patriarchal family heads had been stronger, all this wouldn't have happened. In other words, everything that contributed to the disappearance of the good old days before 1933 was made responsible for the later moral and military defeat. In this way, "traditional values" were disconnected from Nazism, and the crimes of the Nazi regime ultimately interpreted as having to do with the relaxation of morals before 1933.[26]

This morality rhetoric had its price: politicians, administrative employees, welfare services and police, doctors, psychologists, social workers and criminologists, clerics – of course – all united to deny that the decline of morals was a *consequence* of the lost war and that immorality was a *consequence* of the distortion of values by the Nazis and of the economic impoverishment and occupation. This meant ultimately that the German women had not been raped at the end of the war and during the occupation because of the population's own immoral behaviour under the Nazis. Even worse, in the tradition of mistrust of the supposedly unstable female morality, the rapes were often seen as a further problem of questionable morality. Put succinctly, in this way women who were in reality victims because of the criminal acts of the Germans under the Nazis were seen as having to be cured of their immorality.

To restore the morale of the Germans after 1945, the morality brigade championed two causes: the fight for sexual decency and the rescue of the bourgeois family. A typical example of this was articulated by Peter Schmittingen, priest of the parish of Günzlhofen, in summer 1945:

> The foundations of the family had been extensively shaken. The absence of a strict paternal hand, the early and often long separation of husbands and wives, the annoying idleness and pleasure-seeking of young women . . . the fear for children, particular boys, who so many people believed would merely become cannon fodder, very often also the fear for children on account of future religious concerns, the heavy

work and associated emotional fatigue and turmoil, the absence of male friends and the fear of girls that they would never find a husband if they were too choosy and narrow-minded in terms of morality, and other things besides all resulted in a gradual decline in moral standards and a blurring of the lines between good and evil.[27]

The author of these lines thus interpreted the Nazi era as a time of moral decay in his own community and blamed the behaviour of women for it. Let it be clearly stated that women were of course also responsible for the Nazi crimes. But this is not what worried the priest; he was concerned, rather, at the weakening of the bourgeois patriarchal social order with its traditional gender roles through the supposedly immoral behaviour of women. After 1945, the finger was quickly pointed at groups of people thought to be particularly responsible for all that was wrong. In many cases it was the city dwellers, evacuees and strangers, who brought shame to the German people on account of their 'wantonness and dishonourable behaviour towards the Americans'. Another priest from the parish of Ising im Chiemgau put it more bluntly still: they 'hang around like lazy swine at the lake and stand greedily around the campfires in the hope of getting a piece of chocolate or the like to satisfy their craving. And they dream of perhaps finding someone who will take them away to a far-off land ... only forceful discipline can teach respect to these immature and wanton young women.'[28]

After the strangers and the supposedly criminal displaced persons liberated from the camps, the next scapegoats in the conservative post-war morality discussion were the young and women in general – first of all single women, unmarried mothers, 'infected' and 'neglected' women.[29] Women who had dealings with the former 'enemy' – they were called 'Veronikas' – were an ideal target for accusations. Originally, the term referred only to women who had become infected with a venereal disease as a result of sexual contact with the occupying soldiers, known as 'VD girls', standing for 'Veronika Dankeschön' and also the English abbreviation for venereal diseases. In the US Army, it soon became customary to use this designation for all German women who allegedly thanked their 'liberators' by presenting them with a venereal disease. Later, the term was used for all women who were not living in socially accepted circumstances.

In this climate, women who had been raped also quickly came under suspicion. Who knows whether they had been assaulted or whether they had voluntary had sex with the enemy? Was their venereal disease or pregnancy really the result of an act of violence? Did they have witnesses? Or some other proof? Had they gone immediately after the act to a doctor or the police to describe what had happened, or had they preferred not say anything? Wasn't the rape really a defence to cover up their own dissolute way of life?

It is no exaggeration to state that women who were raped in the late 1940s and early 1950s were symbolically assaulted a second time through the constant questioning of their integrity by neighbours, doctors, officials and other welfare authorities. The post-war discussion of morality exaggerated the problem of female morality to the same extent as it trivialized the actual crimes committed in the Nazi era. Women who were unmarried or not living in respectable circumstances but had venereal diseases and were uprooted, possibly pregnant, were unlikely to have their abuse recognized, because in the strict sense they had no honour that could have been violated. Fallen women, as they were called – in other words, unmarried pregnant girls and prostitutes – were seen as social cases that constituted a danger to the public.

Girls like Anna

The accusation of sexual degeneracy hung like the Sword of Damocles over every woman whose lifestyle was deemed 'asocial'. Many a young girl who had been sexually abused was labelled in this way. Anna K. was born in East Prussia in 1932. She was one of seven children, and their father worked as a warehouseman. She described her life until the age of twelve as 'normal'. She went to primary school and felt happy and well looked-after by her parents. The first bombs fell in early 1945, and refugees needed shelter. The family made space, and Anna shared a room with seven others.

One day she heard cries in the next room. She watched a woman giving birth without any assistance. Anna was twelve at the time. 'It was terrible to watch – and I couldn't do anything to help. I just stood there, I don't know how long. When help came, I just heard someone say it was too late. Mother and child were both dead. After I witnessed that, I was no longer a child anymore.'

But there was worse to come. On 27 April 1945, Anna and her family were woken by loud shouting and cries. They quickly got dressed and went to the door. The Soviet soldiers were there. Before she realized the danger, Anna was picked out of the group and dragged away by a Russian. She screamed. He pushed her down into a cellar, stuffed her mouth with a rag and called his comrades. 'Then they removed my underwear and had their way with me. It was terrible. I don't know how I got back to my parents.'

Anna K. wrote this report at the end of a stay in a home. The self-examination had been ordered by the management to find out whether their 'ward' had mended her ways. And yet they also illustrate the terrors that Anna had to endure, only to end up in a German institution. After the rape there was the escape. In Königsberg (Kaliningrad), she and other children were ordered to remove corpses from the houses and streets and take them to the woods for burial. Anna got typhoid fever. When she was discharged from hospital five months later, her mother was no longer living. With her father, she now had to look after her remaining siblings aged two, six, nine and eleven years. In early 1947, the dearth of food in the East was so great that the rest of her family starved to death: 'They died on 5, 25, 29, 30 and 31 January. It was the most terrible time for me because I had to bury my brothers and sisters and my father on my own.'

Left to her own devices, she joined a group of boys who went on forays to find food for themselves. She cut her hair short and wore a jacket so as not to look like a girl. She moved around, later seeking work as a household help, but kept on running away. In this way, she came to the attention of the authorities and ended up in a home. Her greatest wish, she wrote finally in her report, was to find work that she enjoyed, if possible with children. 'This is basically my life story. I was unfortunately unable to provide more details because my memory of the past is just so terrible to recall', she concluded.[30]

She was admitted to the reformatory with the official diagnosis of 'sexual degeneracy'. According to one statistic, this diagnosis applied to almost 80 per cent of the female inmates of the reform schools after the war, while boys were mostly admitted for theft. Since the Weimar era, this group had been increasingly the target of 'public health'. It was not a question of curing the 'wards' but of ridding the community of diseased elements – in other words, of preventing undesired reproduction, abortion and venereal disease. The situation of asocial juveniles became even worse during the Nazi era. They were classed as 'morally feeble-minded', and the eugenic principle meant that they were incarcerated in juvenile concentration camps, subject to forced abortion and sterilization, often without their knowledge and agreement.

After the war, the same people still held most of the responsible positions in the welfare and health sector. For homeless raped girls, the fact that there had been basically no change in attitudes to sexual vulnerability was fatal. Degeneracy was a 'deep-lying pathological character defect' characterized by an 'abnormal lack of restraint and inability to form attachments due to shallowness, either innate or acquired, and an inability to sustain emotions and willpower, leading to a loosening (or under-development) of the inner perception of moral values', was the description of the notorious child and juvenile psychiatrist Werner Villinger. He had been involved in euthanasia and forced sterilization during the Nazi era, and after denazification became dean and rector of the University of Marburg and president of the Society of German Neurologists and Psychiatrists.[31]

The 'treatment' in such cases of 'sexual degeneracy' was as might be expected. As it was believed that the girls did not have the mental capacity to 'sublimate' their excessive impulses, the only possible therapy was 'honest' work in the disciplined environment of a home. The girls concerned were generally older than the boys and were kept longer in care. Girls with frequently changing sexual partners were seen as the problem, rather than their sexual partners. It was sufficient for a girl to be seen in 'bad company', to be heavily made-up or provocatively dressed, to go dancing until late at night, to masturbate, to have sex as a minor, to have venereal disease or get pregnant – regardless of whether it was the result of rape, abuse or consensual sex – for her to be caught up in the clutches of the 'welfare' agencies.[32]

Becoming a 'vagrant' through the loss of one or both parents was enough for a child to be admitted. Of the 1.6 million children and juveniles who became orphans or semi-orphans as a result of the war, 80,000 to 100,000 were considered 'unattached, homeless, unemployed and without a profession' and thus automatically welfare cases.[33] No one knows how many of them were raped in the East or in post-war Germany. They were not discharged until they were considered re-socialized – in the case of women, in other words, when they had found a man and got married, because marriage and family were seen at the time as the only effective 'medicine' for women.

Post-war society thus submitted young women like Anna, who had been thrown off course in the war by devastating experiences and tragic losses, to a bombardment of misdirected moral discourse. Girls like Anna were regarded as extremely sexually vulnerable *because* they had been raped and orphaned and were homeless and unemployed.

A danger to 'public health'

Everywhere in the country police were rounding up young women. In a major raid in Erding near Munich in November 1946, the Munich criminal police arrested a number of juvenile girls and arraigned them before the military tribunal. Some of the girls were admitted to Algasing hospital, where venereal diseases were treated; others were released because there was no evidence that they had committed an offence. 'As no one bothered about the girls, they continued their sorrowful lifestyle', wrote the welfare department in the Bavarian Ministry of the Interior in November 1946.[34]

The practice of placing supposedly degenerate women and girls in homes was so widespread after the war that, on 31 November 1946, the Bavarian Minister of the Interior received a cry for help from the director of the Upper Bavaria regional authority: there were no places left in the institutions, and referral to reform school should be seen as a last resort. Account should be taken of the fact that a certain amount of degeneracy in the morally loose segments of the female population was an inevitable product of occupation in any country and could not therefore be eradicated in its entirety. To prevent the institutions from becoming even more overcrowded, a staggered approach should be adopted. Before admission, the juveniles should be given a warning, which could be entered on the person's identity card. Degenerates from other occupied zones might be sent back to their home towns.[35]

The Traunstein police reported on 27 October 1947 that R. P., a girl with highly infectious syphilis, had escaped from Traunstein hospital. When the police caught her, she stated that another patient had frightened her by claiming that she had to pay 4.20 marks a day for her hospitalization. As she had no money, she had climbed out of the window of the men's toilet at 6 a.m. and run into the forest, discarding her hospital clothes on the way. She had headed in the direction of Trostberg and got on a train at Nussdorf station. She was arrested when she returned to fetch clean clothing. R. P. was described as a 'danger to public health'. As Traunstein hospital could accept no responsibility for her and the police considered the girl to be 'highly impressionable', she was transferred to the hospital bay at Stadelheim prison in Munich.[36]

After the war the risk of infection with a venereal disease increased considerably in the population as a whole, not only because of the rapes. In 1946, 0.5 per cent of Germans were infected with gonorrhoea and 0.2 per cent with syphilis, double and triple the rates for 1934, respectively. High incidence was reported not only in cities like Bremen and Bremerhaven, which were hubs for American troops stationed in the country, but also in many other towns and even rural regions. In the rural district of Eichsfeld in Thuringia, an absurd rate of 44 per cent of juveniles and 70 per cent of adults was claimed. The church, schools and doctors called for counter-measures.[37] Weekly statistics were kept in Saxony on the spread of syphilis, gonorrhoea and soft chancre. At a conference to discuss combating infection, psychiatrists and neurologists in the Soviet-occupied zone spoke in November 1946 of a 'state of emergency'. Treatment centres had to be set up there that were also open at night. After 'numerous armies' had marched through Germany, venereal diseases were omnipresent not only in towns but also in the countryside. In Greifswald in the province of Mecklenburg, for example, over one third of the 3,246 infected persons were from rural areas.[38] It is no longer possible to determine today what percentage of those persons had been raped.

The metre-thick stacks of files with lists, tables and implementation regulations in the federal archive in Berlin-Lichterfelde on this topic alone are indication of the way in which, after the war, the German administration under Soviet occupation moved from fighting the military enemy in the field to combating venereal disease. The authorities appeared more concerned about public health than about the circumstances under which the diseases had been contracted. The reason for the increase in venereal diseases is evident. Whereas two-thirds of those infected after the First World War were men, after the Second World War two-thirds were women. The registers at the treatment centres for venereal diseases regularly listed 'Russ. soldier' as the source, indicating that the sexual contact was rarely voluntary.[39]

Despite this, women were the declared target of the counter-measures. They were regarded as 'sources of infection'. Raids were directed against them, aiming in the first instance at enforcing examinations, hospital admission, official registration and sometimes even travel bans. In Hesse in early 1947, over half of all female patients in hospitals had been compulsorily admitted, as compared with only 6 per cent of the men.[40] This was due to the fact that the German authorities had no influence over the Allied soldiers and that Soviet soldiers in particular were reluctant to go to the doctor for fear of disciplinary consequences. In addition, the (morally degenerate) German women were seen unilaterally as the spreaders of diseases. At a conference of the state and provincial health departments in March 1946 in Berlin, doctors pointed out that not prostitution but 'sexual intercourse with frequently changing partners on its own' was of epidemiological relevance. Not even 10 per cent of the female 'sources' had been identified.[41]

Among the American soldiers, the infection rates also rose to such an extent that it was feared at the end of 1946 that a third of the GIs could be infected with a venereal disease.[42] For that reason, the military administrations decided to fight at least this battle together with their former enemies. The Americans and the Soviets began to examine and treat not only their own soldiers but also the German women. Everyone who spread diseases was to be forcibly treated in hospital, registered and re-examined at regular intervals. Those who refused treatment were to be admitted to welfare homes. Fines and compulsory labour for a month were ordered. The lifestyle of cured women was to be regularly checked.[43] Patrols and inspectors visited bars, clubs, suspicious boarding houses and other relevant venues. Certain groups were examined as a preventive measure, including the nursing staff in paediatric hospitals, women suspected of prostitution and refugees.

The battle cries of the German doctors recalled the pathos of the Crusades:

Mindful of its moral mission, the entire medical profession should get to work. When we consider how much unhappiness we cause to our people every day we delay combating this scourge, when we bear in mind the damage that an unchecked source of infection can cause, when we realize how relentlessly these plagues sap the life and working energy of our people and threaten the very foundations of society, no doctor with a sense of responsibility can stand idly by. . . . The demographic consequences of a poorly treated venereal disease are drastic. . . . Added to this is the serious loss of workers during this reconstruction period.[44]

The 'fight against venereal diseases' was not just about the dangers of sexually transmitted diseases themselves but, above all, about the implied decline in morals and, in particular, the new grey zones between 'sexual intercourse with frequently changing partners' and 'covert prostitution'. The discussion focused not on the individual situation of women but on the 'purity' of the 'communal blood' of the entire people and the wish of the occupying forces for their soldiers to be protected from infection. The German authorities did not recoil from targeted denunciation. In summer 1948, for example, the *Landsberger Presse* called on neighbours to keep an eye out and to report any suspicious occurrences to the housing department. The names of women suspected of prostitution were also made public, not to mention the usual reprisals like residency prohibition in certain places, or admission to a workhouse or reform school. Two weeks later the town council had to recant, as the accusations proved to be exaggerated or untenable.[45]

Post-war society was reluctant to differentiate between consensual and non-consensual sexual contacts, between women who prostituted themselves out of need and victims of rape. In cases of doubt, it was the woman who was blamed. Even if women had no reason to believe that they could have been infected, they were sometimes forced to undergo a medical examination. They only had to be in the wrong place at the wrong time and to be caught by a patrol. In Landsberg am Lech between August 1948 and March 1949 alone, 128 women were picked up from the street and forcibly examined. Only half of them were infected. In Berlin on 23 November 1946, a special action to combat venereal diseases was instigated. Some 400 people were rounded up and taken to Friedrichshain hospital. Of them, 11 women and 4 men had gonorrhoea, and 4 women and 5 men syphilis.[46] In Bamberg in 1946, no fewer than 3,300 persons were admitted to a specially established temporary hospital for examination on suspicion of venereal disease. Half of the patients were diagnosed with a disease and treated free of charge. The experience of being arrested at random by uniformed men, placed in vehicles and finally forced to undergo a gynaecological examination must have been traumatic for many women, all the more so if they had been victims of an earlier sexual assault.

Sixteen-year-old Else B. was arrested by a German policeman in Bremen in 1946 and handed over to the American military police. She was suspected of being infected with a venereal disease. At the police station, military policemen attempted to rape the young woman, but she managed to fend them off. In their disappointment, the military police put her in a bunker, which served as a police lock-up. The inmates had nothing to eat, no fresh air, no possibility for washing. Else was menstruating. She had to wait three days before seeing a doctor. He established that she did not have a venereal disease and that she was a virgin.[47]

THE ABORTION PROBLEM

The fear of getting pregnant was a particular torment for many of the raped women. They frequently discovered they were pregnant quite late on, because the physical and mental strain caused irregularities in their menstrual cycles and even the complete absence of periods. When a woman was certain that she was pregnant as a result of having been raped, whether she wanted to or was able to have an abortion depended not only on her own attitude but also on external factors. It was easier to obtain an abortion in the Soviet occupied zone than in Catholic Upper Bavaria or Baden, where, in spite of sympathy in some isolated cases, doctors and hospitals often refused to treat women.[48] During flight, women looked in despair for possibilities of terminating pregnancies, as we know from Ruth Irmgard Frettlöh, whose mother ultimately gave birth to an unwanted child, who died after just four months.[49] Sources from Catholic Upper Bavaria describe failed self-induced – and sometimes fatal – abortions.

Abortion in Germany was regulated at the time by paragraph 218 of the Civil Code (BGB). It was basically illegal, subject to long terms of imprisonment and only allowed exceptionally under special circumstances. Under the Nazis, the ban was lifted in the case of 'undesirables'. During the war years, 'ethical abortion' was allowed in the occupied eastern regions in the case of rape by soldiers or civilians.[50] The fact that legal and illegal abortions after war-related rape were allowed has led the historian Atina Grossmann to conclude that the partial lifting of the ban on abortions at the end of the war was the result of the racist attitudes of the Germans. Grossmann, who only looked at the case of Berlin, writes that abortions were performed right up to the last month of pregnancy and that, with the approval of the church and the occupiers, women ended involuntary pregnancies 'on a fast assembly line'.[51] They didn't want to bring the inferior offspring of 'Mongols' or Slavs into the world.[52] Abortions were officially allowed and accepted by society out of a 'mixture of sympathy for the raped women, racism, hurt national pride and male solidarity'.[53] This assertion is backed by the extensive collection of affidavits at Berlin-Neukölln department of health from women seeking an abortion.

Grossmann takes a fundamentally critical attitude to the handling of German victims of war. This is possibly the reason that the historian is less than objective in this matter. There can be no question of 'assembly-line' abortions from an individual or an official point of view. The Neukölln records indicate that the authorities were in no way enthusiastic about relaxing the abortion law and, on the contrary, they often blocked abortions. And women did not seek an abortion frivolously or for racial reasons – they did so as a matter of survival and to save their relationships.[54]

After examining several hundred applications for abortion in the archive of the Neukölln health department, I found only one single case citing an ideological motive of this type. As the applications were formulated in cooperation with doctors and officials, an opportunistic attitude by the women might have been expected – in other words, if they had believed that their cause would have been helped by citing racial grounds, we would also find this reflected in the records. German society was not 'politically correct' and there would have been no reason to suppress racial feelings, as we shall see later. We can therefore assume that the applications in Neukölln reveal the true motives of the women concerned.

It is difficult to say why so many women attempted to abort on their own without medical assistance. It is estimated that 27,000 illegal abortions were carried out in 1946.[55] I am convinced that, even in these cases, the main reasons were the shame at the illegitimate child, the fear of social stigmatization, the economic consequences and, with married women, concern at the survival of their marriages.

Legal patchwork

The request for termination of pregnancy on account of a sexual crime was dealt with differently at the local level, not only in the West and the East or as a function of the occupying power but also within the different occupied zones. Doctors could terminate the undesired pregnancies but were obliged to observe strict criteria. In most cases, the justification for abortion was the fear of serious psychological consequences for the victims of these unwanted pregnancies.

For a short time, the town of Greifswald was particularly generous. The Lex Gryphiswaldnis of 29 May 1945 stated that every woman who so wished could have an abortion in the University Women's Hospital, although this was soon restricted to medical and ethical indications with approval of the official medical officer. In South Württemberg-Hohenzollern, a confidential decree was promulgated on 18 January 1946 demanding that the ban on abortion should be lifted only if rape had been proved beyond doubt and adverse psychological consequences were to be expected. In Baden in the French zone, the head of the German justice department sent a memorandum on 18 December 1945 to the senior public prosecutors stating that, apart from strictly interpreted medical indications, neither ethical, eugenic nor social indications could be used to justify abortion. A 'clemency rule' existed for cases of particular hardship, however. We shall see below how rarely clemency was shown on the matter of abortions. In Hanover, it was up to the doctor's discretion whether pregnancies as a result of rape were terminated, provided that the women had reported it to the medical officer. This decree was revoked by order of the military government on 14 August 1945, although a loophole remained in the form of a combined medical and ethical indication. In the Soviet occupied zone, a committee had first to verify the circumstances of the pregnancy. Courts and public prosecutors were instructed, however, until further notice, not to press charges for violations of paragraph 218.

An official argument for the partial lifting of paragraph 218 for rape victims was the fact that society could not demand of a woman that she brought a forced pregnancy to term because this would cause her to lose her personal freedom and condemn her to motherhood against her wishes.[56] For a long time, therefore, the woman's rights were given priority over those of the unborn child, a priority that was later to be confirmed in West German legal interpretations.

'For twelve years we hoped for an Allied victory'

On the basis of a directive of 2 August 1945, in Bavaria a commission consisting of three doctors, including a public servant, decided on abortion requests. Prior to this the American military government had been responsible for approving the waiving of paragraph 218 and had promptly forbidden abortions. Rape by a GI was not recognized as sufficient reason for the termination of pregnancy, which was also illegal in the USA at the time. As Silke Satjukow points out, it was not in the interests of the Americans to approve abortion officially because this would have been tantamount to recognition of the large number of assaults by their own soldiers.[57] When the German authorities were allowed to decide for themselves, they made abortion conditional on the approval of a medical commission, which, however, only recognized medical indications.

The callousness with which medical officers argued is demonstrated by the case of an interpreter for an American unit, who requested an abortion after having been raped. The medical officer refused, stating that the woman, who was married, had evidently not sufficiently resisted the assault. It was 'understandable' that she was now suffering from a reactive depression on account of the pregnancy: 'this is likely to be observed, however, in any happily married woman who has an affair in her husband's absence.'[58]

A similarly cynical argument can be found in Stuttgart. The American justice department there stated that an abortion was acceptable only if the mother's life was in danger. The term 'violence' was relative. Was it rape if a woman accepted a ride in a jeep from an unknown soldier on a deserted street or if she claimed to have been hit and bitten during intercourse?[59]

As the mother's health had to be endangered for an abortion to be approved, the applications often speak of severe depression. On 18 September 1946, for example, the husband of a forty-year-old woman from Munich who had been raped requests permission for the pregnancy to be terminated because his wife was becoming more and more depressed by the day, thus severely jeopardizing family life.[60]

But the women victims were not to have it so easy. The Medical Council of Bavaria claimed to the Bavarian Ministry of the Interior at this time that the psychiatric diagnosis in the applications designed to demonstrate serious psychological grounds for an abortion had not been made with sufficient care: 'A purely psychological indication for termination of a pregnancy cannot be accepted merely on the basis of a psychiatrist's opinion but only as a result of an existing psychopathology that justifies abortion.' In other words, the Medical Council of Bavaria recognized only the perverted eugenic abortion practised under the Nazis, while psychological stress as a result of an external event like rape with subsequent unwanted pregnancy was not regarded as a medical indication. The letter went on to state that, in general, applications for termination of pregnancy as a result of rape would not be accepted in future.[61]

The attitude was thus very narrow-minded, and applications could take months to process, while for the pregnant woman, naturally, time was running out. I. O. from Penzing bei Landsberg wrote a desperate letter to the Military Government on 1 October 1945:

On 10 May 1945 I was stopped by a soldier in American uniform and in spite of strong resistance was forced at gunpoint to submit to him. The soldier was drunk, and there was unfortunately no one nearby to help me. My family and I were always staunch opponents of the Nazi regime and suffered under Nazi rule for twelve whole years. . . . For twelve years we hoped for an Allied victory that would restore equal rights and liberate us from a terrible way of life that had become almost intolerable for peace-loving people. Trusting the discernment of the American military government, I request this approval, because the assault committed against me and its consequences once again threaten to destroy my life instead of allowing me finally to work quietly and peacefully thanks to the Allied victory for a better life than was possible under the Nazis.[62]

Women seeking an abortion in Bavaria met with a particularly uncompromising attitude. Religious doctors tended in general to refuse. For example, A. K., who had been raped by Czech soldiers in Sudetenland, was informed by the medical officer in Nördlingen that she should have the child and apply to a religious organization for the child to be taken into care.[63]

At the end of 1946, the heads of the state justice departments reviewed the problem at an interzonal conference. They decided that abortions would be allowed in future if the pregnancy could be proved to have resulted from rape and if the pregnant woman had reported the rape within a very short period (around one week).[64] As we have seen, it was almost impossible to make a report at this time, however, because the German police were not responsible for the investigation of such cases. Official sources also show that for women who could not meet all the requirements, the only possibility was to seek an abortion without official permission. At least one backstreet abortionist is mentioned in the records, a midwife in Feldkirchen near Munich, who is said to have carried out a large number of abortions.[65]

Grounds for abortion

Women in Berlin-Neukölln seeking an abortion were required to produce an affidavit confirming the violent origins of the pregnancy and a medical certificate on the length of pregnancy.[66] The archive contains over 300 affidavits. Not all of the women give a reason for not wanting the child. As mentioned earlier, however, there is only one case in which a woman, already in the seventh month of pregnancy, explicitly requested an abortion because she didn't want 'under any circumstances to bring a Russian child into the world'.

Most of the other women stated that they were engaged, married, widowed or already had children. They mentioned saving their marriage or hardship because, for example, their husband was a war invalid, or the need to work. They pointed out that they had been forced to have sex against their will and at gunpoint – the threat with a weapon was considered necessary at the time for the act to be recognized. One woman wrote:

> I have had two children. The older one is three and a half, the second died in hospital of measles and pneumonia at the age of eighteen months. In my current situation I cannot afford to have a third child. In addition, I am obliged every month to accept welfare payments. My husband was in the military for six years and has been missing for one year. I am therefore left totally to my own resources – and so one child is enough! I hope for your understanding. I. H., 27 September 1945.

Women often gave the name of a person who could confirm the assault. This was possible because the rapes often took place before witnesses. In the case of E. H., her landlords and her own four children were present. Many of the applicants had been raped several times, which naturally increased the chance of becoming pregnant – A. S. nine times, B. B. in Upper Silesia eighteen times. She had two children, lived with her mother and claimed that she had no more baby clothes. B. E. was raped in St Blasien in the Black Forest by a Moroccan. She was a Red Cross nurse and feared that if she had a child she would lose her job. Hildegard S. had been raped 'many times' as she fled from Silesia. Her husband had been killed in the war. She didn't even have a change of clothing for her eight-month-old child: 'Please understand my situation and allow me to terminate the pregnancy. I am speaking the full truth.'

C. V. stated that she had been married without children for twenty-two years. Her husband had just returned from captivity. E. H. had been for two months in the refugee camp in Fürstenwalde, where she had been raped and made pregnant. She was expecting her wounded fiancé to return any day: 'Given the misery I have had to suffer, I do not want under any circumstances to bring a child into the world.' G. W. also expressed her fears: 'I have been married since 23 August 1941 and have two children aged four and eighteen months. My marriage is at risk and I therefore request that the pregnancy be terminated.' G. D. also saw a threat to her marriage if she failed to obtain an abortion.

H. S. threatened to kill herself. She had been evacuated in 1944 from Westphalia to East Prussia and had had to flee in January 1945 with a four-month-old baby. The child had been run over by a tank. She had had to work for several months for the Soviets. Now she was six months pregnant and wished to return to her husband in Gelsenkirchen.

> I urgently request that the child be taken away from me. I am not in any state emotionally to give birth to a child conceived under such atrocious circumstances. I have gone on living only in the hope of the medical assistance I now request. In this condition I shall not under any circumstances give my husband the news of the death of my little boy. I implore you to help me and to admit me to an institute, as I have no food here and wish to return home as soon as possible. If I do not receive a positive response, I will no longer be able to remain living. I hope that you will appreciate my situation and remain, with gratitude, Mrs H. S., 14 September 1945.

Our examples, which could be continued at will, indicate that some women would have given birth if they had been able to count on support. Their requests and letters clearly disprove Atina Grossmann's racism thesis. In the Bavarian applications, there is not one single case connecting the request for an abortion with the skin colour of the father. We have already heard about cases of women who request compensation for children resulting from rape. Here, too, there are no arguments on the grounds of race.

This does not mean that racism did not play a role in society. As we shall see, the authorities were indeed influenced in their decisions whether to recognize rape or not by the ethnic origins of the soldier concerned. For the time being, however, it would appear that in many cases the reasons for wanting an abortion did not differ greatly from those involved in any case of unwanted pregnancy: economic consequences and fear of personal repercussions. The danger to an existing marriage was a promising reason at the time for applying for an abortion. Concern about the survival of the family was prominent, a factor that was also determinant in considering compensation for the children of rape. Siring by men stigmatized as being inferior was secondary to the question of morality and restoring family values after the war.

NO ONE'S CHILDREN

Pregnant raped women who did not want or were unable to obtain an abortion had two possibilities open to them: to keep the child or give it away. In 1956, there were officially just under 3,200 children resulting from rape in West Germany including West Berlin. It is not known how many were brought up by their mothers, but we do know that of all the occupation children, as they were called, 73 per cent remained with their mothers and only 7 per cent ended up in homes. The rest were brought up by maternal relatives, usually the grandparents, or by foster or adoptive families (which was not uncommon for illegitimate children after the war). These figures were officially collected and surprised the authorities themselves. This also disproves the thesis that rape victims seeking an abortion did so mainly for racial reasons.[67]

According to official statistics, in April 1953 there were 202 children who had been *proved* to have been conceived as a result of a rape by a member of the occupying forces. Almost all of them were being brought up by their mothers, some by their grandparents, and a few in adoptive families.[68] Mothers were reluctant to put their children in homes not just because of the costs, which they would have had to pay themselves until a financial arrangement had been agreed for them. As we shall see from eyewitness accounts, the women very often took the children to heart, in spite of the terrible circumstances in which they had been conceived, regarding them as their own flesh and blood and suppressing the way they were conceived. There were even some women who regarded the child as the only positive aspect of a horrendous time.

Even with half-caste children of African American or North African soldiers and members of the occupying authorities, the proportion of children in homes and with foster families was only slightly higher than with white children.[69] Contemporaries nevertheless noted that single women with coloured children had less chance of finding a husband. For that reason, thought was given to establishing special homes for 'mulatto children'. In summer 1953, a clergyman from Switzerland offered to accept a number of occupation children from West Germany into his community. He called his project Action for No One's Children.[70]

The children were designated 'occupation children' by the authorities despite the fact that around a third of them had been conceived during the last days of fighting before the official start of occupation. Their legal situation was precarious. They were German citizens. Only the French occupying forces granted the children of relationships with their soldiers the possibility of French nationality. For pronatalist reasons, the French even claimed such children, although they did not pursue the claim with any force. The other occupying forces did not make any attempt to claim custody for the fathers of these children, and in the case of rape such requests would probably in any case have been ignored.

Thus it was the German mothers and the German state who were responsible for the children. Until the Paris agreements entered into force in 1955, German courts had no jurisdiction over child maintenance claims for illegitimate occupation children in any of the three zones. Claims for maintenance could not be asserted in the occupation courts either. It was only after 1955 that German jurisdiction was extended in general to all non-criminal cases against natural persons. Even with children who were not conceived through rape, maintenance payments were made by the fathers in only 1.7 per cent of cases for white children and 2.1 per cent for black ones.[71] In 1956 in Munich, all of the fathers known to be alive were summonsed, but only 10 per cent of the soldiers and members of the occupying authorities responded to the friendly invitation and only 6 per cent ultimately acknowledged paternity, mostly men who had been in a long-term relationship with the German mother and even intended to marry.

The children basically had the same status as German illegitimate children, but they were worse off financially because they were not eligible for an orphan or war invalid allowance. Thus the legal right to being raised 'to bodily, spiritual and social fitness' was less secure than with illegitimate children with German fathers.

The complex legal status with regard to maintenance payments for the children resulting from rape was thus a further heavy burden for the abused women. Of course, the men committing the rape didn't leave an address, but it sometimes happened, especially when occupying troops were billeted in the houses of German civilians, that the women knew the name, rank and company of the perpetrator and child's father, or had at least sufficient fragmentary information to find out who had made them pregnant. This did not mean that they were able to obtain financial support from them. Even after 1955, there was still a yawning gap between the legal situation and the reality. The headquarters of the US Army in Heidelberg, which was meant to serve the summonses of the guardianship courts – the army refused to serve the soldiers directly – often failed to fulfil its duty and even advised the soldiers in writing that they were not obliged to pay child maintenance and that coercive measures by the German courts were not supported or followed up by the US headquarters.

In many cases the German courts were unable even to ascertain whether a summons or order to pay had been served at all. Or they received a curt reply that, in spite of the precise details of his identity, the accused soldier had not been found by the headquarters. Or the cases were terminated summarily because the soldier concerned had been posted. Once he had departed to the USA, for example, it was impossible to follow up maintenance claims. Legal assistance, even between states within the USA, was unusual. There was no compulsory registration or poor people's courts that might have paid for an insolvent father.

The US occupying forces tried all kinds of obfuscating ruses. In one case the headquarters in Heidelberg informed the local court in Munich that in its opinion the accused did not have to appear for the paternity hearing because he thought that the child's mother was a prostitute. When it was pointed out that prostitutes also had legal rights, the accused appeared but denied having had any intercourse and claimed that the mother had many sexual partners. A blood test was ordered, upon which the accused was posted back to the USA. The pretext that the women had slept with several men was a popular excuse. If necessary the GIs were even willing to produce witnesses. If an enforcement writ was issued, the bailiff was simply denied admission to the barracks. And if everything else failed, the soldier was hastily posted back to the USA.[72]

The USA was not the only country to refuse to pay for the consequences of the rapes committed by its soldiers. In a High Court decision of 24 July 1950, the British also confirmed that maintenance claims against the father of an illegitimate child born to a German mother in Germany could not be asserted in England. A maintenance decision by a German court was enforceable in England only if the accused had been in Germany at the time the proceedings were instituted or voluntarily recognized German jurisdiction. Members of the occupying forces were excluded in principle, even if they acknowledged paternity.

As stated, France promised to care for the children of French soldiers, but the mothers had to cede all rights to their children, and the promise that the child would be with its biological father was not kept. Instead, the French Red Cross put the children up for adoption. In 1955, maintenance claims against fathers were allowed, and German mothers could have a German custody decision checked by a civil court at the place of abode of the father, but this was usually a protracted and most often fruitless endeavour.[73]

Like the American and British, the Soviet military administration also refused to care for occupation children. It had enough of its own war orphans and did not want 'children of the enemy' in its own country. In any case, the acknowledgement of paternity and payment of maintenance did not exist in the Soviet Union. Although the Civil Code, according to which the father was liable for maintenance, applied to the Soviet occupied zone, the Soviet military administration attempted to obstruct the assertion of this right. Later regulations in connection with the troop stationing agreements and the sovereignty agreement after 1955 did not cover maintenance claims for children resulting from rape at the end of the war at all.[74]

'THE OTHER VICTIMS ARE ALSO TAKEN CARE OF'

Raped women who had a child did not at first receive any support from the German state either beyond the normal social security that depended on the mother's income. But was it fair that women victims of war-related rape should suffer not only mentally but also financially? Were the women not in this situation as proxy for the defeated nation? Was their sacrifice so much less significant than the sacrifices made by the soldiers and war invalids, the displaced persons and refugees? Were they not just as entitled to an allowance for their child as the fighting men? These questions were discussed for a decade after the war.

It is often claimed in the literature that after 1949 the question of the mass rape of German women was barely discussed – not at all in the Soviet occupied zone / East Germany, and less and less in West Germany as well.[75] The documentation on flight and expulsion by the Federal Ministry for Displaced Persons, Refugees and War Victims has already been mentioned as a refutation of this assertion. A much more important aspect of public discussion in the West of the rape of German women by Allied soldiers is the treatment by society of these questions and of its consequences, namely the children. Discussion was conducted not behind closed doors but also in parliament and the media. The question of justice for rape victims who had been made pregnant bothered post-war society increasingly, not because the public had particular sympathy for them but because it touched on the important topic of bourgeois family morality. The husband of one of the victims made this clear in an appeal to the federal authority responsible: 'If they are not to question the principle of justice, mothers who are left to their own devices and have borne the sacrifice without being able to get rid of the burden like others should not be deprived of a modicum of gratitude and assistance. The victims and casualties of the fighting in the East are also taken care of by the government.'[76]

Basically it is a question of the acknowledgement by society of the decision against abortion and in favour of the child conceived as a result of the war and through violence. Against this, however, was the fear that the state could be burdened financially by more and more groups of victims of the war. It couldn't or didn't want to pay even more reparations. For that reason, it was decided early on that rape victims were not in the same category as invalid soldiers and were not therefore entitled to a pension or compensation for pain and suffering, even if the act had been committed during the fighting or as a result of the war. For war victims to receive financial recognition there needed to be physical or mental injury, and rape was not considered as such.

Motherhood of an illegitimate child or the obligation to look after the child could not be regarded as personal injury. This option was not open to the women victims. But there was still some doubt as to whether the discussion would end there.

Concern for the bourgeois family

A particular hardship for rape victims was that there were children resulting from rapes whose mothers were legally married but whose husbands were missing or in captivity. Although these children were legitimate under the law, they were not entitled to an orphan allowance, with the result that public welfare was available to the mothers only in the case of demonstrated hardship. Legitimate children received both war pensions and invalid pensions because of the legal relationship with the deceased father. This also meant that a returning soldier whose wife had been raped had to provide for the child that was not his own as long as his income was above the level making him eligible for welfare.

This injustice towards German men ultimately stimulated discussion after 1950 of possible compensation for rape children. Added to this was the growing pressure from the victims and the war victim organizations. The associations lobbying for those who had suffered from the war emphasized in particular the military and patriotic sacrifice by raped women as a way of pushing their claims. They were, of course, most interested in cases from the former German east. Thus, the Sudetendeutsche Landsmannschaft, Reichsbund der Kriegs- und Zivilbeschädigten, Sozialrentner und Hinterbliebenen, und Verband der Kriegsbeschädigten (VdK) appealed to representatives of the state to do something about rape victims with children. Many of these women had been army, staff, intelligence, navy, anti-aircraft, air raid protection and SS auxiliaries and Red Cross nurses who had found themselves in Soviet captivity, where they had been raped and made pregnant. These cases, they argued, were clearly a result of the war and eligible for compensation in the form of pensions or therapeutic care. Otherwise they were reliant on welfare, as they were frequently unemployed. If they worked, however, the support was withdrawn. This treatment was unfair and unworthy of a 'civilized state'. Also, claimed the VdK, there was the danger that maternal feelings would suffer.

Ways should therefore be sought to compensate for this hardship: 'We owe this to the unfortunate German women and girls who have living proof every day of the time of their most profound humiliation as women.'[77]

Very few politicians and administrators shared this view initially. It was not denied that many children had been conceived as a result of rape and could therefore be considered by extension as victims of war or its consequences, but the assumption that the state should be responsible for these 'unasked-for' children was incorrect, argued the opponents. The mother was still connected biologically to the unwanted child and was therefore responsible for its upbringing and welfare.

Not 'just any unmarried mother'

Once it had been unleashed, the discussion would not be reined in. Individual women and husbands who felt they had been betrayed personally approached authorities and politicians to assert their financial claims and also to restore their honour. In June 1951, M. K. from Bremen submitted a disciplinary complaint against the Federal Minister for Displaced Persons, Refugees and War Victims as he had not replied to several applications by her. She came from East Prussia and had attempted in vain to escape in January 1945 with her parents and siblings. Her mother had died in February 1945 and her father had starved to death two years later. In September 1945 she had been raped by a Russian soldier in Sellwethen in East Prussia (now Yegoryevskoye) in the presence of her sisters. She had been twenty-two at the time and 'intact'. On 19 April 1946 her son Hans-Dieter was born. Now, after having been accepted in West Germany as a late returnee, she was treated like 'just any unmarried mother'. She couldn't understand that the state helped those who had lost a family member as a result of the war but not those who had gained one for the same reason. She felt herself to be just as much a victim of the war as those who had suffered physical injury or material loss. It was particularly important for her not to be lumped together with women who in her eyes had merely 'fraternized'.

The women and girls who threw themselves into the arms of the advancing troops in return for chocolate or cigarettes and ended up with a child as a result were treated no differently than I am. This is a debasement of my status that I oppose. I am not just one of the large number of unmarried mothers but in a special category of war victims and demand that the state does not deny me this moral recognition.[78]

The combination of the fate of displaced persons and ethical principles produced a rhetoric in which flight and expulsion from the former German east were used as a decisive argument to distinguish the women concerned from those who had allegedly 'thrown themselves into the arms' of the Western Allies. This is possibly the only legitimate explanation for the self-assurance of the raped mothers. E. B. from Middle Franconia wrote in April 1951 to Elly Heuss-Knapp, wife of the President at the time, that she had been driven out of Upper Silesia 'like an animal'; 'We were at the mercy of these brutes, whose outrages did not stop at old women and children.' Her daughter Ingrid, whom no one was looking after, was the result of rape. She received a war widow's pension of 27 marks and could not earn anything to supplement it as she was severely physically handicapped as a result of what she had endured. She received 18 marks per month for her daughter. She didn't know how she could feed and clothe the children.[79]

The subject was also debated in parliament. The SPD member for Bielefeld and 'mother of the constitution' Frieda Nadig spoke up in particular for the rape victims and asked whether the children could be granted assistance.[80] The problem of foisting the matter on the welfare authorities ignored the human tragedy suffered by these women, since the decision by a raped woman nevertheless to bear the child was a sign of a deep-seated morality. But the Federal Ministry of the Interior considered the existing welfare arrangement sufficient, prompting the Bielefeld *Freie Presse* to comment that this was a miserable answer.

The case of pregnancy following rape by an American soldier also came before the parliamentary Petition Committee. P. S. from Heroldsberg near Nuremberg stated on 22 November 1955 that her daughter B. S. had been raped in Nuremberg on 4 August 1946 at the age of nineteen by the American soldier A. W. H. She had given birth to a daughter. The application for compensation of 45,000 marks submitted to Claims Office Team 7728 on 31 January 1950 had been refused for substantive reasons. The father of the victim, as the child's

guardian, then wrote to the Federal President and various federal min-
istries requesting maintenance for his ward and compensation for his
daughter. He was informed that compensation was possible only if the
child's mother had been physically injured or her health impaired. The
Law on Compensation for Occupation Damage did not allow for compensation for the costs incurred by the mother for maintenance and
education of the child resulting from rape, since the law only provided
for reimbursement of the costs incurred through an increase in the victim's needs, for example as a result of health treatment. The child itself
could not demand any compensation either because there was no case
of damage to be compensated, since the child had not been physically
injured or its health impaired by the rape. The damage incurred by the
child because the biological father did not pay maintenance was not
occupation damage.[81]

But the resistance from within the administration began to crumble
as it came under increasing pressure from another debate, namely the
restoration of family values. The mood ultimately swung in favour of
compensation for forced motherhood. In North Rhine-Westphalia the
regional welfare associations decided to offer special welfare payments
to raped women and girls, available even if the legitimacy of the child
was not disputed by the husband of the raped woman but his income
and assets made it unreasonable for him to have to support the child
alone. In this way, it was argued, 'the child could remain in some cases
in the family without the legitimacy being disputed by the husband
and the child having to be put in a home'.[82] In a memorandum to the
regional authorities, the Federal Ministry of the Interior also now considered it desirable to help families generously in cases where the wives
or mothers could credibly demonstrate that they had been the innocent
victims of rape. This was the responsibility of the welfare authorities at
the regional level.

In my opinion, this change of attitude by the federal decision-
makers did not come about because of the justified concerns at the legal
situation of children resulting from rape. The rape victims and their
emotional state was not the focus either. The politicians and officials
were most concerned about protecting the family, which in the 1950s
was of great significance in the discussion in West Germany about the
restoration of moral values. The decisive argument was that husbands

should not be expected to finance children of rape that were not their own, since otherwise the family could well break down, leading to even more single women and illegitimate children as a result.

The Protestant church used similar arguments in favour of compensation for raped mothers. The Landesverband der Inneren Mission der evangelisch-lutherischen Kirche in Bavaria supported its plea for maintenance with a particularly vivid example:

> Margarete F., a married woman, gave birth on 27 February 1946 to a half-caste child resulting from a rape by a negro. Both the mother and her parents had been extremely taxed by the situation and had difficulty coming to terms with it. The child was put in a home immediately after the birth and through our mediation came into a foster home in Winkelhaid bei Altdorf.

The raped woman nevertheless had to pay 30 marks a month for the child's maintenance. Her husband divorced her when he returned from the war and paid no maintenance, either for the wife or for his own legitimate child. Mrs F. now wanted to remarry, but the new husband refused to pay maintenance for this 'nigger child'. The mother had therefore stopped the payments, with the result that the local welfare authority was billing the father of the child's mother. The grandfather was a pensioner with a gastric disorder. His wife, who was also sick, still worked so as to improve the family's income situation.[83] According to the churchman, this represented a moral and human hardship that the state should put an end to. The bone of contention was thus the question of the continued existence of the family and not the woman's experience of violence.

There still remained the conflict between the desire to protect the family and the fear of endangerment to the family from women lacking bourgeois morals. The suspicion that the single mothers had 'fraternized' and then claimed to have been raped so as to make unjustified demands would continue to stick. Those dealing directly with the victims were very hesitant. On being asked by the Bavarian Ministry of the Interior, the Working Committee of the Bavarian State Welfare Associations, for example, considered that in the event of rape 'special welfare arrangements for women and their children in general were not applicable' because it was impossible to produce evidence to the contrary, opening the door to misuse (of state subsidies). The state was only willing to act in the place of the defaulting payer of maintenance in the interests of protecting and encouraging the family if the woman's 'moral character' was unimpeachable.

The dispute between the various actors regarding compensation payments to rape victims who had been made pregnant, which went on until the mid-1950s, can ultimately be reduced to this social contradiction: on the one hand a gender model that suggests that even raped women basically had lax sexual morals and were thus responsible themselves for their fate; on the other hand, the need to name the suffering caused by the enemy and in this way possibly to make good Germany's own guilt, but also above all to strengthen the 'healthy' family.

No repayment for the suffering of the victims but compensation for the children

As late as June 1956, Federal Minister of the Interior Gerhard Schröder from the conservative CDU party rejected compensation for women who had been made pregnant through rape by members of foreign armies. On 17 December of that year, a ruling was finally arrived at. On the basis of the Law on Compensation for Occupation Damage, under certain circumstances compensation could be provided from federal funds for maintenance for children resulting from rape by members of the occupying forces. The extent was determined as a function of the amount the father should have paid according to the law.

The ruling was continuously fine-tuned for a long time. By limiting it to occupation children in the narrow sense, i.e. children conceived against their mothers' will on the territory of the future West Germany between 1 August 1945 and 5 May 1955, it soon became obvious that a large number of mothers would get nothing – namely all those who had been raped while fleeing during the last weeks of the war. The Berlin Senator for Finance immediately complained in March 1957 that all of the known 200 'Russian children' living in (West) Berlin would receive no compensation under these circumstances.[84] The ruling was re-examined.

The number of eligible women gradually increased. Applications for compensation could now be made by mothers who had been raped before the official start of occupation; mothers who had been raped in the former colonial territories in the East; mothers who had been deported and forced to work in the East and had been raped and made pregnant there; mothers who had been raped by members of the occupying forces who weren't soldiers but civilians or their dependents; refugees who had been expelled and fled and who did not acquire German citizenship until the 1950s. The general criterion was that the rape and pregnancy were due to the war and post-war situation. The duration of the monthly allowance, initially limited to the end of the child's sixteenth year, was later extended to the end of its education or the age of twenty-four. The Amt für Verteidigungslasten [department for losses incurred by foreign defence troops] was responsible for approving applications.

There was no discussion of real compensation for suffering due to the rape. It was finally admitted in a letter in August 1956, from the Federal Ministry of the Interior to the Federal Ministry of Finance, that even if rape did not cause any external injury, it caused emotional damage 'as the side effects of an act of violence [could] lead to extremely severe emotional shock',[85] and compensation for suffering might therefore be considered. It could never be put into practice, however, because the number of potentially entitled women was too great. The Federal Minister of Finance knew very well why he opposed payments to rape victims: it was to be feared that an extension of the acts eligible for compensation would prejudice other cases; put another way, there might be other victim groups who hoped for compensation for their wartime trauma.

For that reason, at the end of December 1956, it was decided that only the above-mentioned compensation would be paid to mothers of rape children on the basis of the compensation paid for occupation damage. The Ministry of the Interior and the Ministry of Finance agreed that the compensation should have two purposes: '50 per cent for the child's maintenance and 50 per cent to compensate for immaterial damage to the child's mother'.[86] After a lot of hesitation, the matter was finally settled – at least in theory.

FIRST THE FRENCH, THEN THE PUBLIC AUTHORITIES

Doubts as to the credibility of the rape victims were still almost impossible to remove. There was great concern that some women would come up with the idea 'for the child's mother to claim and testify to rape without the necessary conditions having been met so as to obtain money for the child'.[87] In other words, it was seriously believed that masses of women would falsely claim to have been raped merely to obtain a small monthly allowance.

As late as 1960, the Federal Ministry of Finance considered how it might assess a claimant's application. It was not enough for a rape to have been 'plausible', as this would only demonstrate the 'probability of the claimed facts but would not represent proof'. An affidavit was not therefore sufficient to determine that a rape had actually taken place. An authority should not be satisfied with a mere probability and should not under any circumstances make its decision on 'instinctive deliberations or general suspicions', but should establish certainty according to generally applicable empirical rules for determining the truth. Although final proof could not usually be provided, the child had to have been the product of rape 'with a probability bordering on certainty'.[88] But when is a claimed rape really a rape with a probability bordering on certainty?

The rules of procedure stated that a mother could apply for compensation only if she could describe the course and circumstances of the rape in minute detail. Short answers in a questionnaire and affidavits were not sufficient. An offence was deemed to have been committed only if the perpetrators proceeded using either physical force against the child's mother to 'break her resistance' or an unequivocal and serious psychological threat. Proving this in the case of war-related rape was a nerve-racking affair for the women, since the jurists made everything dependent on the mother's credibility.

Women were assumed to be credible if they could describe the incident coherently and without contradictions:

In addition, her general personality was decisive, as demonstrated by her general appearance and the way she described the incident. It is also normally useful if not vital for the authorities to obtain assistance in their decision on the personality of the child's mother on the basis of the assessment by trustworthy persons who have known her for a long time and can reliably judge her character.

A further guide in determining whether rape had taken place was the reaction by the woman concerned. Only those who immediately informed a relative or close friend and consulted a doctor 'if only to prevent the risk of infection' were considered credible. In addition, the place where the rape allegedly took place, the circumstances and whether the child's mother associated with members of the occupying forces needed to be taken into account.[89] In a nutshell, when in doubt, decide against the applicant.

A study of the application processes reveals depressing details of humiliating and routine suspicion. In the state archive in Freiburg, there are over 200 applications for compensation for the maintenance of children resulting from rape. Most of the fathers were French soldiers.[90] The documents also provide an insight into the extent of the rape problem under French occupation. In 1955, there were officially 471 occupation children resulting from rape in the whole of Baden-Württemberg. According to my formula, this would be equivalent to 47,100 rapes, which inevitably, because of the great mobility at the end of the war, will not all have occurred in the south-west.[91]

The German people had a historical prejudice in particular against Moroccan, Algerian, Tunisian and Senegalese colonial soldiers dating back to the French occupation of the Rhineland after the First World War, a period known in the collective memory as the 'Black Shame'. The horror stories about 'Moroccan' rapists were just as embedded as the prejudices against the raping 'Mongols'. The encounters between the population of south-west Germany and the French soldiers apparently followed the same preordained choreography as in the East, Berlin and Upper Bavaria.

In the border areas in particular, however, there was also a lot of sympathy and a sense of kinship with their close neighbours, and the abhorrence at the deeds was just as great as with the Berlin Communists in respect of the Red Army, or among those who had initially welcomed the Americans so warmly regarding the actions of the GIs. A woman from Freiburg wrote indignantly to the French military government

that she had always respected the French hitherto: 'Then you came
. . . and what now? Your black soldiers have raped whole villages of
women. Your officers have done nothing about it and have themselves
given orders or taken part in these atrocities.'[92]

Rapes are known to have taken place in Stuttgart, Freudenstadt and
Konstanz.[93] Particularly in places where the army had encountered
strong resistance, there were 'free nights' in which the soldiers could
make use of the German enemy in every respect for up to forty-eight
hours.[94] The French historian Marc Hillel reckons that there were 385
rapes in Konstanz, 600 in Bruchsal and 500 in Freudenstadt. As in the
archbishopric of Munich-Freising, Catholic clergymen in the bishopric of Freiburg documented hundreds of cases. In many villages, there
were dozens of sexual assaults.[95] Responding to the violent excesses,
the French authorities stated that they were doing exactly the same
as the Wehrmacht and SS had done in occupied France. Attempts
were nevertheless made to restore discipline. Brothels were established,
and the army leadership made the occasional example and executed a
convicted rapist. In 1946 a French parliamentary inquiry committee
came to the conclusion that 'regrettable aberrations' had taken place
during the invasion.[96] Many of the offences did not take place directly
after the fighting, however, but later during the occupation.

After the decree regarding compensation payments for children
resulting from rape, applications were received from women from the
smallest villages and hamlets who had been made pregnant against their
will by an occupation soldier. It might be due to a special south-west
German piety that the victims' stories were investigated and handled
with harsh and meticulous care and stringency. Approval was extremely
rare.

It did not suffice for the women to describe the circumstances of
the rape and even provide the name of the perpetrator. The officials collected further, supposedly more objective testimony, so as to
obtain a faithful picture of the incident and, above all, of the claimant's character. The character references from social welfare workers
and statements by neighbours, doctors and relatives were ultimately
determinant – in other words, it was bourgeois respectability and the
women's family background that were pivotal. The criteria for assessing the incidents were at all events irrelevant: the women's lifestyle,

their housekeeping and child care – in short, their morality and sense of family, rather than the injustice they had suffered, were what counted.

It cannot be repeated often enough that the assessments by welfare workers, experts, witnesses, decision-makers in the offices and courts, and the descriptions by the victims themselves are all sources requiring a certain critical historical discernment. All of these actors were following their own agendas and made use of rhetorical argumentation. We cannot say today who was telling the truth; all we know is the motives. What we can infer with certainty from these sources is the degrading and routine suspicion to which the women were exposed. It gives us an insight into the mean-spirited worldview of the welfare workers, psychiatrists and officials in the 1950s.

As an unmarried mother, F. F.[97] from Altenheim in the district of Kehl, who was even able to name the perpetrator, one Ali B. from Tunisia, was regularly visited by welfare workers. Their impression helped with the decision as to whether she was eligible for compensation on account of war-related rape and pregnancy:

> There are no complaints about the raising of the child, who is being brought up as well as possible in the home of F. The mother is currently unemployed and thus at home, which does not prevent her from continuing to see coloured members of the occupation force and openly admitting that she obtains things from them that she needs to subsist. The house is nevertheless clean and tidy. . . . The child is well developed for her age. Because it is a coloured occupation child, it is often the cause of conflict in the family. The stepfather is also not a good father in this regard . . . refusing to contribute to the child's upbringing.

The welfare worker added that the child was developing well, was big, strong and hard-working, but only an average pupil, ready to get up to all kinds of tricks, helping with the housework and in the neighbourhood. In spite of the poor circumstances, she could remain without problem in her present environment.

There was nevertheless the impression

> that a rape had not taken place. Frau F. also had her first child without being married, so that it can be assumed that the child G. was conceived

with the claimant's consent, all the more so given the report by the state health department in Kehl: "Although morality and decency are not important focuses in the home of F., there is nothing to be said about the child's upbringing."[98]

It was not a question of the child's welfare, however, but of the morality of the child's mother. The fact of having another illegitimate child was sufficient for the authorities to question the claimed rape.

The children should not learn the circumstances of their conception

Rape was not sufficiently demonstrated either in the case of H.-M. T. from Villingen. There were no records available from the hospital to prove that an examination had taken place after the act. The victim had not released her doctor from the obligation to confidentiality, and another witness was too old to remember. The alleged perpetrator, Aziz T., adjutant in the French Army, also refused to acknowledge paternity. The victim herself had put her story on record with the South Baden Regional Authority, stating that it was impossible for her to provide any proof. She didn't initially tell anyone about the rape. When she discovered she was pregnant, she even claimed that it had occurred of her own volition: 'I continue to do so today because I wish at all costs to prevent my daughter from learning the way she was conceived. The girl already has it hard enough coming to terms with her "differentness", and it requires a lot of strength but also a lot of love to understand and come to terms with it.'[99] The rape victim had thus kept silent out of consideration for her daughter and was now suffering the consequences. In judging the case, the child's welfare was the least important argument.

The grounds for the decisions clearly illustrate the importance for the authorities of the personal appearance, the 'good impression', of the claimants. A. A. from Nenzingen/Stockach is a case in point. She was awarded 60 marks a month until her daughter turned sixteen. The claimant was able to produce not only a witness to the rape by a 'coloured' Frenchman in a pigsty in May 1945 but also confirmation from two doctors that she had applied for an abortion, which would have been approved except for health considerations. When the girl was five, the mother married and the daughter was legitimized. The authorities were satisfied in this case that rape had occurred. Apart from the facts themselves, the 'resocialization' through marriage and the protection of the new family could well have been decisive.

I. Z. was also believed. According to a record, her claim was credible because she had spoken hesitantly and only after a number of questions. The details were visibly embarrassing for her, and the social worker did not have the impression 'that she was reciting a prepared speech. Moreover, her general demeanour was that of a modest, simple but self-assured woman without sufficient imagination or acting capabilities to have thought up the salient points of the story herself. It can be assumed that she really was the victim of rape.'[100]

'Rape is much less damaging to a reputation than consensual intercourse'

A particular feature of the French occupation was that the soldiers were billeted in private houses. (The Americans preferred to requisition quarters for themselves alone.) The proximity of the civilian population and the stationed soldiers not only increased the danger for the locals but also made it more difficult for the victims to have their stories of violence believed. This was the case with I. Z., a dietary assistant from Baden-Baden, whose appeal against the rejection of her application was turned down in February 1962 by the South Baden Regional Authority. Her husband, a doctor, had been killed in the war. In autumn 1945 she lived as a 27-year-old with her parents, where Dédé was also billeted. The soldier lived in quarters separated from the family by a glass door. After a few months, he forced his way one night into Z.'s bedroom and raped her at gunpoint. He left shortly afterwards. He said simply: 'C'est la guerre!'

I. Z. didn't call for help or inform the authorities afterwards. She gave birth to the resultant child far from her home so as to avoid the shame of being seen pregnant and unmarried by friends and neighbours. She regarded the rape as a 'disgrace' that would remain with her forever and that could never be made good, as a stain on the reputation of her highly esteemed and respected family: 'Any criminal can return to a normal life and regain respect after serving his sentence. I will never be able to restore our family's good reputation.'

Her father managed to discover where Dédé was living. I. Z. travelled to France to remind the father of her daughter about his maintenance obligation. She learned from Dédé's mother that he was married and had two children but would be willing to take in his youngest daughter: 'My poor daughter was devastated at the thought of having to go to France and live in primitive French circumstances, much, much different from ours.' A planned marriage with a German fell through, as the fiancé was unable to get over the rape: 'I keep on asking what I did to deserve this. I was not able to go back to work . . . Perhaps I could have remarried . . . And what if something happens to me? An orphanage would be the only solution.' Her daughter was a 'delightful child', well brought-up and with a loving and honest character. She was attending secondary school.

But none of this had any effect. The jurists refused to accept her argument that she had wanted to protect her reputation and that of her family and had not therefore informed the authorities about the rape. They believed the opposite, considering it 'proper and natural' to inform the authorities after a rape, since 'being a victim of involuntary intercourse was much less damaging to a reputation than consensual intercourse outside of marriage'.[101]

The belief that rape was less damaging to a reputation than consensual sex with a member of the occupying forces is revealing. Even in the late 1950s, there appear to have been conflicting views of morality. On the one hand, society was keen to defend the family and sexual morals, making it more acceptable to be raped by a soldier than to sleep with him voluntarily. On the other hand, rape victims considered the moral pressure that would burden them and their children if the circumstances of the conception were known to be unbearably shameful, because they knew that their credibility would be questioned. An insoluble dilemma.

I. Z. described the unreasonableness of the authorities as 'unworldly'. Not only was no action taken against the assaults by the occupying powers in autumn 1945; not only had she been unable at the time to 'cope emotionally' with the stress of making a report – in her eyes, it would have been an 'affront to good taste' to peddle such an embarrassing incident. In addition, the adoption agreement and guardianship files would be accessible to the child when she came of age 'and for

that reason alone the rape should not be on file, because it could pro-
voke feelings of inferiority in the child and cause an emotional shock'.
But the authorities were unmoved: 'application admissible but not
granted'.[102]

The application of A. M., by contrast, was approved. She had been
repeatedly raped over a long period by a Russian soldier in West
Prussia. It was possible that the East German victim of a Red Army
soldier could expect more sympathy in Freiburg than an ordinary
unmarried local woman raped by a Frenchman.[103] This hypothesis is
supported by the following case history. J. R. stated that she had been
raped for the first time at 9.30 p.m. on 9 June 1945 by the French adjutant Louis M. She was working at the time in the French officers' mess.
The assault was repeated three times in June 1945. For the authorities,
this meant that 'at least the subsequent incidents cannot be regarded
as rape. Because of the short period in which the incidents took place
(one month) it cannot be determined on which occasion the child was
conceived.' But the claimant insisted that all of the intercourse with the
Frenchman had been involuntary: 'I didn't know how to get away from
him. I was told that they would force me to come back and work in the
mess if I left. . . . I never said anything about this intercourse, because it
was never recognized at the time.'

She was still refused recognition. On the contrary, she was now
accused of adultery. There were 'substantial grounds for suspicion': the
repetition three times of the intercourse with the Frenchman and the
refusal to make serious efforts to escape from the situation by leaving
the job were indicative of the 'silence of a guilty conscience' on the part
of the accused. J. R. was not ultimately convicted of adultery, because
the judges could not rule out intimidation on account of the 'unnerving
impressions of war and collapse'.[104] In retrospect, of course, we cannot
say who was right: the claimant, who had the accusation of 'fraternization' hanging over her like the Sword of Damocles, or the authorities
with their scepticism. But formulations like 'the silence of a guilty conscience' and the preconceptions as to how a woman should react after
being raped reveal the inquisitorial morality of the authorities.

Sexually inexperienced girls suffered particularly in this regard. P. R.
from Offenburg was a kindergarten teacher in Ettenheim and slept in
a room with four of the children she was looking after, aged between

one and eight years. The door had to remain unlocked because of the children, which offered an opportunity for the three Frenchmen billeted in the house. She was so shocked that she didn't tell anyone about the rape, even her employers. It was only eight days afterwards that she went to the doctor, who told her she should return in a month's time. When she did so, the doctor informed her that abortions were forbidden. She consulted the priest in Ettenheim 'but he couldn't help me either'. She gave birth to a son at the end of October 1946. In her application for maintenance in January 1958, she wrote: 'I affirm by affidavit that I had never had sexual intercourse before. For that reason it was terrible for me and [I] couldn't tell anyone. Today I know that this was false modesty.' This claim was also turned down.[105]

Voluntary association with a black man is beyond imagination

Apart from the depressing stories of the women, the records of the South Baden Regional Authority and the Freiburg Tax Office show that German society in the 1950s was not yet ready to abandon its prejudices and strict moral criteria. There was no willingness to try to understand the situation of the women and children concerned; nor was there much tolerance for other ethnic groups.

Because T. S. already had an illegitimate child, it was not initially believed that she had been raped. In November 1962 the Tax Office revised this opinion – the child was black. The argument that she already had an illegitimate child was valid only 'if it had been a white member of the occupation forces of the time . . . For a woman who already had a child, voluntary intimate association with a man would probably not have bothered her. It is this thought in particular that persuaded us that the claimant's statement was true.'[106]

Several other cases confirm that decisions as to whether a raped woman should receive compensation for her child or not were openly based on racist criteria. Prejudice against black soldiers was not just a south-west German speciality. Representatives of the Nuremberg Tax Office wrote to the Federal Minister of Finance in August 1959 about a local incident in which R. M. from Allersberg had been raped in November 1945 by a black US soldier. She came from a respectable family, her father and brother working for the post office, and she had not gone immediately to a doctor or the police out of shame and consideration for the 'rural circumstances'. The authorities were nevertheless willing to believe the victim because 'it is unlikely that the claimant would have given herself voluntarily to the negro. This assumption is suggested above all by her reputation and that of her family.'[107]

'I LOVE THIS CHILD AS MUCH AS THE OTHERS'

The effect of the rape on the relationship between the women and children can also be touched on here. There are frequent references in the applications for support to the fact that the mother loved the rape children just as much as the legitimate ones. These are, of course, also targeted statements, as the women hoping for compensation had also to demonstrate their maternal instincts. For example, H. R. wrote in January 1959 to the Federal Minister for Family Affairs that she had fled Pomerania in 1945 with four children aged three to ten years. The fifth child was the result of a rape, and as a war widow she requested the same treatment for it as the legitimate children: 'I ask you, Minister, are these children outcasts to be treated like cattle? I love this child as much as the others, because I also carried this child beneath my heart.'[108] I. D. from Coburg also wrote that she cared for her child, who resulted from rape, with all her heart: 'I love my child, even if it was conceived in an act of brutal and crude violence and I didn't even see the father with my own eyes, because I was forced to the floor as I resisted and blacked him out so as to be able to submit more easily to his unlawful demands.'[109]

In the following case, a child resulting from rape was even described as replacing the woman's legitimate children, who had died. H. S. had been raped during her three-year Russian captivity in East Prussia. Her legitimate children, aged six and ten years, died within a week of one another. Her parents also starved to death. The son from the rape, wrote H. S., was her all and everything: 'I am so sick that I can no longer have children. The child had no milk or sugar until 1948. He was completely undernourished. He was nine months in hospital in plaster with severe scoliosis. My husband wrote that I should go to him, but without the child. As a mother I couldn't do that. He had the boy declared illegitimate and doesn't provide for him.'[110]

We also hear from fathers, however, who accepted the rape child as their own. A mother wrote to the Federal President Theodor Heuss that she found it particularly praiseworthy that her husband, a displaced person, behaved properly in every respect towards the child and did not treat him differently from his own children: 'In the end, this child – even if it was conceived in violence – is also a living being having the right through being born to an existence and thus demands, and should indeed demand, my tireless maternal duty.'[111]

Occasionally, of course, there are glimpses of less noble maternal instincts. Some women clearly hoped that the French occupation authorities would take the child. As has been mentioned, France was the only victorious nation after the war willing for demographic reasons to accept occupation children and bring them up as French citizens. France's interest in the children was well known, and there were even rumours that poor mothers had their children taken away from them, even if they were unwilling for this to happen. Calls by the French administration for such children to be reported heightened the fear of child abduction.[112]

Pressure does seem to have been exerted on some occasions. M. T. from Krauchenwies near Sigmaringen wrote in her petition to Federal President Heuss that, when her son was six months old, two men from Tübingen asked whether she wanted to give him away to be brought up in a French family. 'What kind of mother would give away her child? In any case, Germany needs them as well', she wrote indignantly.[113]

M. L. from Bad Krozingen fought a long and difficult battle with the authorities. After her failed request for an abortion, she did not want 'under any circumstances' to keep the child resulting from rape by a French officer. She had been a Red Cross nurse in Russia during the war, held an executive position and, according to the authorities, enjoyed great respect in her surroundings. All that the 37-year-old knew of the father was that he was Algerian and had been posted on the day after the rape.

The State Health Department in Freiburg confirmed to M. L. in October 1947 that it was possible for the child to be adopted in France. M. L. replied that she didn't want to keep the child another minute, as she still loved her husband, who had been killed in the war, too much to bring up other children. She had already sacrificed her health as a

Red Cross nurse and now she was expected to keep a child that had been forced upon her.

> Out of the question. I can't find any love for it. And I don't think it's right that these men should get away with it so easily, simply by returning to France, while the others have to see how they can manage ... I certainly haven't deserved to have my life turn out this way, at my age and certainly not on account of such a vile scoundrel.

She repeated defiantly: 'I don't have any time for the child and won't bother trying to look after it.'

On 12 January 1948, the district juvenile department in Mühlheim took over guardianship of the child. Only two weeks later, the mother declared that she wanted to bring up the child after all. 'Mother and grandmother get so much pleasure out of him and are devoted to him', it said in the records of the district welfare office. In 1955, M. L. married a businessman from Ettenheim and moved with the child to him. A year later the new husband adopted the boy.[114]

The case histories offer shocking testimony to the difficult lives of the rape children. Mothers had children taken away from them, although they were clearly well looked after, simply because they looked 'negroid'. One boy was put in the children's home in Konstanz and then in Villingen, where he was to be handed over to the occupying forces. The welfare worker wrote on 24 March 1950: 'From what I have learned to date about the child's mother and her parents, they are quite unwilling to accept the child in their own household. L. S. shows no maternal feelings or love for the child.' On 2 May 1950, the mother was deprived of custody. The child was put up for adoption in 1951, but his foster parents could not decide whether to adopt him. L. S. married a watchmaker in January 1953. She died two years later of a heart attack. It was only after her death that the husband found out about the child's existence. Although the consistently negative attitude of the child's mother and her parents to the illegitimate child was unpardonable, it was understandable given the fact that she had been raped as a young girl and 'didn't want to be constantly reminded through the child of this terrible experience'.[115]

The to and fro between custody and giving away children resulting from rape was no rarity. Depending on their situation, some of the raped women gave the child to their own parents, particularly when they were unmarried and had to work; others put the children in homes because they wanted to start a new family. Putting a child in a home seems to have been used as a threat, should the children create difficulties. E. X. from Achern was raped by two drunken French soldiers on her ten-minute walk to work. When the daughter F. was six years old, she went to live with the grandparents because the new husband didn't want to have the girl with him. She was told that if she made difficulties she would be put in a home. The welfare worker noted that the girl had promised to behave and had not caused any problems to date. She helped the grandmother at home and there were no complaints from school 'although the teacher is not particularly happy about her being there'. After eight years of school, she was nevertheless put in a home 'where she is being taught all the tasks required of her'. She clearly needed a strict education with good guidance and instruction.[116]

In this way, the suffering of the rape victims was carried over to the next generation. It started with the rape itself, continued with the refusal of a request for abortion, making the victim dependent on welfare, and ended in many cases with expert opinions and lawyers, who appeared in principle to consider the victims insincere. For better or worse, the raped women and their children were often at the mercy for decades of the arbitrary behaviour of authorities – first foreign soldiers, then German officials.

It is evident that the attitude to date to the mentality of mothers made pregnant through rape has been too one-dimensional. It is not true that the main grounds for wishing for an abortion were racial. The relationship to the children resulting from rape was also ambivalent, with sentiments ranging from complete rejection to love, seen as a consolation at a time of great hardship. The child's skin colour was not necessarily a concern. By contrast, the encounters of the women with German authorities was repeatedly coloured by manifest racism and narrow-minded morality.

5

THE LONG SHADOW

And then he asked me: 'Which one did it?'

I looked at them, all seven or eight, and thought: 'Now's your chance to get your own back – for all the pain, for the mortal fear, for these humiliations and the stigma.' That was my first thought. My second thought was: 'Eva, pull yourself together. They are also human. They are the Russians you have been waiting for.' I looked from one to the other, recognized them all, including the small fat one who had been particularly mean. I looked them all in the eyes, and in their eyes I saw only one thing: fear. I said to myself: 'It's not worth it for even a single life to be lost on your account and on account of the disgrace they've brought upon you.'

Eva Ebner in her recollection of the line-up of the Red Army soldiers[1]

According to her neighbours she still called out for help at night.

Psychiatric report on a patient raped by Frenchmen[2]

THE EFFECTS OF THE EXPERIENCE OF VIOLENCE

What was life like afterwards for the rape victims? Were they marked forever, or were they capable of leading a fulfilling life in spite of what they had experienced? The effects of sexual violence depended on a number of factors, personal and external: on the resources for facing up to it, on the individual living situation, but also on the collective interpretation and – not least – the acknowledgement of the victims by society.

We hear repeatedly of women who didn't have the strength to continue living. There are rumours of dozens or even hundreds of women in some parts of Berlin, in places in the East, but also in Upper Bavarian villages, who committed suicide after what had been done to them. Particularly young girls, religious and elderly women and those who could not identify with others who had suffered the same fate had difficulty coming to terms with the experience of violence and the humiliating consequences. The literary critic Marcel Reich-Ranicki once commented on the question of whether the journalist Ilya Ehrenburg had really urged Red Army soldiers to systematically rape German women by saying that an invocation to rape was not as bad as an invocation to kill (of which there were plenty of examples from Ehrenburg's pen).[3] Given the many suicides as a result and the severe psychological consequences, this comment is equivocal to say the least.[4]

The psychiatrist Albin Segmüller wrote a doctoral thesis right after the war on 'reactive suicides and attempted suicides in the post-war period'. The cases he described demonstrate the suffering of the women after the event. A twenty-year-old attempted to kill herself with twenty Bromural tranquillizers for fear of an examination in an American military hospital. A forty-year-old took tablets and cut her wrists because she feared, after her husband had been killed in the war, that she had been infected with gonorrhoea by an American soldier. Another patient committed suicide because of an 'unwanted pregnancy by a negro'. Among the female victims, Segmüller identified the typical refugee fate as a reason for suicide: homeless, having lost all of their family, unemployed, raped and infected with a venereal disease or pregnant. And then the humiliation of an embarrassing medical examination by order of the occupying powers, in which the victim would be required to describe what had happened.[5]

We know of victims with lifelong physical and psychological traumas. Today we would call this post-traumatic stress disorder. Psychiatrists and psychologists now distinguish between objective and subjective trauma factors – for example, how anxious someone is in general versus the objective extent of the threat. For that reason, it is not possible to generalize the effects. The few researchers who have studied the psychological stress caused by the war-related rape of German women (unfortunately only the victims of Red Army soldiers) reckon that around half of the victims suffered post-traumatic stress disorder. This high figure is explained by the fact that the victims were also subject to other war-related trauma, such as bombing and other forms of military action, expulsion from their homes and the loss of family, friends and relatives: 'The multiple and sequential traumatization resulting from war experiences in general increased the likelihood of a post-traumatic disorder. The considerable demands of everyday post-war life, the reconstruction of their own and their families' existence were an additional burden.'[6]

Among the acute signs of post-traumatic stress are depression, disturbed social behaviour such as outbursts of anger, anxiety and nervousness, guilt feelings, emotional numbness, amnesia, sleep disorders and nightmares, and psychosomatic problems. The symptoms can occur years after the event, for example following a build-up of negative experiences or when current events, such as news reports of mass rape in present-day conflicts, awaken memories of the past. Elderly persons are apparently particularly at risk of developing or redeveloping post-traumatic stress syndrome, as mental and psychological resistance becomes weaker with age, coupled with the unbalancing effects of incisive changes in life and approaching death.

The psychologists Svenja Eichhorn and Philipp Kuwert identified after-effects even at an average age of eighty years in a random sample of twenty-seven women who had been raped by Soviet soldiers. They included lifelong impairment of sex life, relational difficulties with family members and a generally reduced enjoyment of life. The researchers also studied the coping strategies of the victims. Over a third had attempted to suppress the experience, while around a fifth had actively attempted to come to terms with it.[7]

After the war, however, there were few possibilities for the victims to come to terms with their fate in this way – not because the topic was suddenly taboo, but because people simply didn't talk about their mental problems in those days. It was not part of the German social culture, and the social climate did not encourage it. People were brought up to 'deal with life'; they were 'hardened' as children and learned to avoid giving an impression of excessive sensitivity to pain and emotionality.[8] The inability to speak about experiences, feelings, physical and emotional suffering was 'the real cultural phenomenon of the post-war years'.[9] The consequences of the war were internalized, something to be dealt with by the victims, who barely had a language to do so.

Suffering without words

Many women never spoke about their rape. As we have seen in some of the applications for compensation, young women who had never had sex before did not even inform their parents of their misfortune. Later, they often had to explain why they had not spoken immediately about it.

If the women became pregnant and couldn't or didn't want to terminate the pregnancy, they could no longer keep quiet about it. There were cases in which the rape victims invented a consensual sex encounter. Although society thought it more 'honourable' to have been raped than to have had voluntary sex with an occupation soldier, the women themselves apparently sometimes felt differently. The rape was so shameful that they preferred not to bring it up. The victims wanted to protect their families and in some cases, as we have seen from the Freiburg records, went as far as giving birth somewhere else. These were probably not isolated incidents, because illegitimate pregnancies before the Second World War were often kept secret in this way.

If the rape produced a child, the mothers, as we have seen, often kept quiet for another reason: they wanted to spare their child the knowledge of the way it had been conceived. They did not wish to impose on the next generation the suffering the victims often experienced for the rest of their lives, and the rejection by society. It was already bad enough to be stigmatized as a 'Russian brat' or 'negro child'. It is questionable whether this policy of silence was successful.

Today there are organizations that help these children to find their fathers.[10]

Apart from fear of social opprobrium and family 'disgrace', many women also kept silent because the war-related rape was often interpreted as fraternization. The reversal of the burden of proof – it was the victim rather than the assailant who had to prove her innocence – was onerous, as the accusation of having had sexual contact with the occupation soldiers was difficult to shake off. We also know that some rape victims were urged by their families to keep quiet about their fate.

The case of Gabi Köpp, who, as described earlier, was raped several times as a fifteen-year-old as she fled from Posen (Poznán) to Hamburg, is particularly revealing. Her mother could not and would not help her to come to terms with these traumatic experiences, telling her daughter that if she had anything to say she should write it down. Gabi Köpp tells what it was like not to be able to talk. At some point she abruptly discontinued her diary because she could no longer stand the recurrent nightmares caused by the intensive recollection of the terrible experiences. She had to begin by trying to forget about the things she was not allowed to speak of.

Köpp wrote later about her initial attempt to face up to her situation: 'In retrospect I can see today that my stamina lasted instinctively just long enough for me to get over the worst part of my flight by writing it all down.'[11] The fact that this diary existed at all was a bone of contention in the family: 'As if I had done something wrong, the story told in these densely written pages was declared taboo.' She kept the document in a safe. It was not until early 2005, on the sixtieth anniversary of the liberation of Auschwitz, that she opened this Pandora's Box and began to transcribe the notebook onto a computer. The renewed confrontation with what she had experienced in flight was possible only after years of psychoanalysis.

No diagnostic category

Before we accuse families and post-war society too hastily of being generally unfeeling, we should recall that the idea that rape could cause severe psychological trauma was not yet accepted. The concept of post-traumatic stress did not become an official diagnostic category in psychiatry until 1980. Until then it was not believed that the psyche could be pathologically affected by a bad experience. Not least because post-war society did not want to award pensions for war-related mental suffering, in Germany the 'neuroses' of returnees were also attributed to the personality of the individual and not to the experiences themselves.[12] It was assumed that someone suffering from the effects of a trauma must have had an existing mental illness.[13] As we have seen, this also applied to war-related rape victims. Because they had no physical damage, they had no hope of a war disability pension or compensation for pain and suffering, unless they had a history of mental illness.

An expert opinion from the psychiatry department in Reichenau in 1957 illustrates the uncertainty regarding the problem of rape victims. G. F.[14] from Breisgau/Hochschwarzwald district, who worked as a laundress in a station hotel in Immendingen, was brutally raped four times by French soldiers on 8 December 1950. Her head was banged against the floor of the vehicle, a French ambulance, until she lost consciousness, her mouth was held closed, she was strangled, beaten and finally after half an hour thrown out onto the street. By chance, a doctor came by and notified the (German) police to make a report. At the time, G. F. was fifty-two years old.

She was admitted to the psychiatric ward, not because she was diagnosed as being traumatized, but because she was said to have been behaving oddly at the hospital in Möhringen, where she was originally brought. The medical report of 16 December 1950 states that she was suffering from severe concussion with vomiting and a slow pulse, torn ligaments and joint pain, and severe bruising, contusions and cuts: 'Emotionally the patient is completely exhausted and says she thought she was going to be killed.' This perception of mortal danger, as we know better today, is what probably caused the lasting mental stress.

The doctors at the time decided to admit her to the psychiatry department because G. F. posed a risk to herself and to others. She was behaving 'in an unruly manner', demolishing objects and refusing to eat for fear of being poisoned. After consultation with the psychiatry department, however, the general hospital had to admit that the nurse treating her had not been very friendly and that the patient had not in fact destroyed anything. G. F. was discharged in January 1951.

Seven years later, the psychiatry department in Reichenau noted that her condition since the terrible experience had not improved. According to her neighbours, she still called out at night for help and mentally relived what had happened – a typical symptom of post-traumatic stress syndrome. She had not recovered her 'inner peace'. She was awarded 6,230 marks for loss of earnings and treatment costs on the basis of compensation for 'occupation damage'.[15]

The historian Svenja Goltermann has investigated the extent to which the diagnostic tools available at the time influenced doctors and psychiatrists and how society judged the returnees' experience of violence. These findings are also applicable to rape victims. Whether the contemporary state of psychiatric knowledge shaped the perception of the victims themselves, as Goltermann claims, is open to discussion. The question is whether the inability to express a physical experience in technical language with terms like trauma and post-traumatic disorders did in fact mean that the victims experienced the event differently. Against this constructivist view is the fact that the experience of violence created long-term physical and psychological structures that could not be formulated in words but still rose to the surface even decades later and expressed themselves in the form of symptoms. At all events, Goltermann is right in her conclusion that the belief at the time that external events could not cause mental illness prevented society from showing sympathy.[16]

THE MYTH OF FEMALE INVULNERABILITY

It was not only relatives and doctors who shared the general lack of understanding of the victims of mass rape. Given what we know today – that probably hundreds of thousands of war-related rape victims suffered long-term psychological consequences – it is difficult to understand how casually and how persistently post-war society spoke of the effects of mass rape. There is a powerful thesis from this time, and still current today, regarding individual reactions to the atrocity, stating that the experience did not particularly cause lasting damage to the victims. Not only did most of the women show no resistance and abandon themselves to their fate, they also came to terms with the experience of violence 'surprisingly quickly'. The reason cited is that they were able to interpret their individual fate as a shared experience, as a 'collective fate'.[17] Even renowned feminist scholars today still maintain that the Nazi ideology, the sense of community and the great contempt for supposedly inferior nations like the Soviets offered a possibility for resisting a trauma.[18]

This is in clear contradiction to the sources recently examined by me, in which there is little mention of resignation or a miraculous collective resilience by the victims. It is true that the women were not unprepared for the event, which had been extensively predicted by Nazi propaganda, particularly with respect to the Soviets and black colonial soldiers. It is also probably true that many women resigned themselves to their fate, because they had no other choice. But there are also numerous reports of women offering resolute resistance in spite of the armed superiority of the soldiers. We must bear in mind that the records of the rapes reflected the way such acts of violence were described and interpreted at the time and that the reporters were influenced by the gender stereotypes of the male conqueror and the passive female booty. This might help to explain why there is almost no mention of the fact that boys and men were also raped, possibly with the participation of women soldiers.[19]

Even less plausible to me is the view that rape victims coped with what had happened because they saw their suffering as women's collective fate. The most prominent advocate of this thesis was a post-war journalist. Erich Kuby was one of the first Germans to write about the credibility of eyewitnesses in a series in *Der Spiegel* and in a monograph about the mass rapes. His sometimes crude views still influence discussion today.[20]

At the time, Kuby focused only on Berlin and the Soviet Army, where women, on recognizing the danger of assault, showed incredible ingenuity in their defensive measures and tricks to avoid the impending disaster. They made themselves up to look old, disguised and disfigured themselves, pretended to be sick or carried other people's babies as a shield. Others acted in a fearless or particularly hard-nosed manner, seeking a strong protector to keep other potential rapists away. In Kuby's opinion, these women even showed something of an understanding for the soldiers and officers, who believed they had free rein in fascist Germany.[21] The Soviet soldiers were intoxicated by victory and by the experience of Western civilization and naturally eager for sex after all the joyless years on the front. In Kuby's depiction, the German rape victims became understanding mothers, who afterwards could not suppress 'a quiet, very feminine smile' about the rowdy but always potent soldiers – 'These wild boys didn't impress them that much.'[22]

When it was over, claims Kuby, the victims kept quiet about it, processing their experience of violence as a 'collective fate' and coping with it in some cases 'surprisingly quickly'. They got used to speaking in a matter-of-fact way, talking 'not of themselves, but of the basement, house, apartment block, hospital, authorities or whichever community the narrator felt comfortable with'. The wellbeing of the community was more important than the individual experience. For the men, it was completely different. They spoke of it as if the terrible things had happened to them.

A close examination of Kuby's texts quickly reveals, however, that he was not interested in the rape victims but in the Germans, or more precisely the German men, who at the end of the war had formed a group of 'passively patient and suffering' people.[23] The raped women served as a contrast; they were the vital sex offering promise for the future, distinct in the author's rhetoric from the supposedly weak and weakened male nation.

The image of the weak man is typical of the post-war period, occurring frequently in the years after 1945 as well. According to this theory, the defeat in war had ended the period of 'male hegemony' because the men had clearly failed as protectors of family, house and home.[24] The wave of rapes had contributed to this feeling, depriving the men of the last vestige of their legitimation.[25] Until then, masculinity had been linked with honour and hence with the ability to protect a woman. The huge rise in divorces, women with supposedly lax sexual morals and the sight of men physically damaged by war additionally got in the way of the public male image. The difference between the well-nourished soldiers of the occupying forces and the wretched returnees from the war was seen as dismal and humiliating. A new image of man in society had not yet been found and only took shape gradually in the 1950s in the form of the father and family patriarch.[26]

All this is true to a certain extent, but was the weakness of the men also the strength of the women? Here are some examples of eyewitness reports collected at Heimatmuseum Charlottenburg.

E. A. saw the relationship with her husband as one of shared suffering:

> I think we were all in shock and were happy that we had it behind us and were no longer in danger. I never experienced it as a sexual act – I didn't know anything about it; I saw it simply as an assault and that I had managed to escape alive. I met my husband later in the early 1950s. He had also been a soldier and had had a terrible time in captivity, and I told him – but only him – about my past, and he was very gentle.

C. S. also spoke principally with her husband and her family about her rape, not least because there were no experts like psychiatrists or psychotherapists at the time to whom she could have spoken about her experiences.

G. C. attempted first to talk with her father about what had happened to her: 'I told him everything. He was extremely embarrassed and helpless and didn't know what to do or say. I felt very sorry for him. Neither of us could find the right words. I still regret having tormented him so much.' Then she turned to her teacher, whom she had admired as a child: 'I found him in his unheated apartment, lying in bed in a coat, scarf and hat. I told him what had happened as well. He stroked my head and said I should try to believe that it had all happened not to me but to someone else. I felt a little better, but I couldn't imagine that it hadn't happened to me.' She finally found a friendly ear in a married couple: 'They had known me since childhood. I also told them, but this time it was completely different. They found some of it so ridiculous that they began to laugh. We couldn't stop, and I kept thinking of other funny moments, until I was exhausted from laughing. That's how I managed to get over it.'[27]

Naturally, the rape of their wives was also a problem for the husbands, one of the many disappointments as couples reunited after the war. Both partners had ambitious expectations, which were almost impossible to fulfil. Women no longer wanted to return without further ado to their role as homemakers, and men could no longer take up their role as breadwinners again. In the years on their own, women had become more independent, but were also tired, overwhelmed and in need of affection, while the men were often merely a shadow of their former selves. Their emaciated and haggard external appearance did not fit in with the fantasies that the men had cherished about their wives for years. The years of separation had also destroyed the intimacy between couples.[28] Men were unsure of their wives' fidelity, and the women had good grounds for believing that their husbands had also abused women during the war.

Interviews with eyewitnesses reveal the existence of insurmountable conflicts on account of the rapes. 'Some of our interviewees couldn't come to terms with it and remained sexually frigid for years. Some men even demanded divorce', recount Sibylle Meyer and Eva Schulze.[29] The news of sexual competition came upon the men at a time when they were in any case feeling particularly vulnerable after the defeat in war. Added to that was the absence of familiar orientations such as society, family and jobs. The men had lost their political ideals, a good deal of their authority over wives and children, their health was compromised, some of them needed nursing and were reliant on their wives. The women, on the other hand, had better contact with their children than their husbands and experienced their return as a disruption to this relationship and an additional chore. 'There was an ambivalence between men's dependence on the women's strength and their need to adapt to this situation and the women's awareness of their own strength and their disappointment at the lack of assistance provided by their husbands but also the need to act pragmatically.'[30]

Gisela Koch, born 1920 and married in 1939 to Philipp Koch, experienced her husband's return in 1946 as completely alienating.

> We had barely seen each other for six years. When he returned, we of course tried at first to warm to one another. I told him everything that had happened to me while he had been away, including that fact that I had been raped several times in Pomerania at the end of the war. It was very difficult for me to speak about it again, but I thought that he needed to know. I asked him if he still wanted to live with me. He was so shocked about what I had told him that he asked for time to think about it. He didn't know how he would decide.[31]

Only after the men got back to work and could concentrate on their careers and on being the breadwinners did relationships 'normalize', at least to the extent of accepting with greater or lesser enthusiasm the constraints of the patriarchal single-breadwinner marriage.

Nevertheless, I don't share the view that with the return of the prisoners of war and the 'remasculinization' of German society the subject of rape was taken over by men, with the recollection of the deeds being replaced by a metaphor of the raped nation, implying that the collapse should be understood as an attack on Western civilization by a brutal Soviet or Asiatic culture.[32] Read this way, German male society instructed women to keep quiet about their personal experience of rape or suggested that they should stylize themselves as the helpless victims of enemy soldiers and emphasize their vulnerability.[33]

It is correct that, under the Nazis, women were assigned the role of reproducers and comrades and men the role of the hard fighters. This made it difficult for the two sides to become reconciled after the war. If the men nevertheless brought the subject of war-related rape out into the open and supported women as they attempted to obtain compensation, it was possibly less out of sympathy than as a form of dual calculation. On the one hand they wanted to restore the honour of their women (above all to distinguish them from the immoral 'Veronika Dankeschöns'); on the other hand, they were certainly attracted by the prospect of maintenance payments and compensation for pain and suffering. The possibility of morally offsetting their own war crimes might also have played a role. The story of the brutal rape of German women by Allied soldiers was an ideal counterbalance to the crimes of the Wehrmacht. More than anything, however, the men were interested in regaining their old position as *pater familias*.

The woman as silent sufferer

Kuby, whose time-bound statements have been discussed here in such detail because they impinge even today on research into this subject and influence the popular view of these events, describes the women of the time using the Christian-tinged idea of women as silent sufferers, and the ideal of self-sacrifice that was a fixed component of the image of femininity in the 1950s and 1960s. It was this image that gave rise to the myth of the *Trümmerfrauen* (rubble women'), those remarkably long-suffering and robust women who got down to work right after the war and began to clear up the mess – literally and metaphorically.

Kuby's women in the post-war period helped with the reconstruction and were important as consumers for the *Wirtschaftswunder* ('economic miracle'), but their principal role was that of mothers and in the family that had been buffeted so much by war. If she was to emerge at all from the children's nursery, kitchen or church, then it was as the 'spiritual mother' making use of her female caring skills.[34] The ideal woman in Kuby's time was thus one who managed the household, raised the children and contributed to the family's social advancement, standing patiently and quietly at the side of her working husband without attracting attention to herself.

These social norms were not mere fantasy but norms that offered possibilities for women to identify with. It is not therefore surprising that women also styled themselves like this at times. The myth of the comrade and *Trümmerfrau* who kept bravely quiet about her suffering thus slotted smoothly into place. It influenced the collective attitude to the rape trauma and at the same time prevented individual women from coping with it.[35]

Rape as collective experience?

According to the historian Regina Mühlhäuser, the rapes did not necessarily produce feelings of shame. They could also be seen as a confirmation of the cultural superiority of the Germans compared with the 'Central Asian brute' and perhaps even as a justification for the crimes committed by the Germans against their enemies.[36] They would also have relativized other and much worse things experienced by the women at the time. For example, a rape was considered less significant than the loss of a child.

This attitude is conceivable, and we can indeed find confirmation in the sources – as we can for almost anything we want to assert. I am, however, sceptical about this thesis. First, there is plenty of evidence to the contrary in the sources, above all in regions other than Berlin. The idea of a collective experience might have been helpful for women who were able in this way to find a narrative mode in the nationwide discussion of the expulsion from the Eastern territories and its perception as a crime, but for many others this explanation was not applicable. Given the differing circumstances and places where the mass rape took place in Germany, it seems more likely to me that the fact of being raped in a Berlin basement, a remote farm while fleeing or in a mountain hut in Upper Bavaria will have impacted on the victims differently – not to mention other factors such as the victims' personal character, attitude to sexuality, political self-awareness and values, and the reactions of those around her.

The example of Gabi Köpp described earlier, for example, in no way confirms the supposed collective resilience of the rape victims. The idea of a community of victims did not apply at all in her case; on the contrary, she had to deal with isolation within a group of people who were doing everything to save their own skins and nothing to help one another. Many women, apart from Gabi Köpp, experienced their rape as a claustrophobic and captive situation, betrayed by other women, in fear of their lives and misunderstood by those around them. This is not a good basis for 'coping with' what happened. As modern trauma research shows, the thesis that the experiences of horror balance each out is also very shaky. On the contrary, today it is believed that cumulative trauma is more likely.

It is obviously not sufficient to seek out isolated examples to support or refute the thesis of the collective invulnerability of the raped women. The problem is in the source material itself. There is autobiographical literature that does indeed refer laconically to the experience: 'I was on my way to get sugar at G. when two men came along and dragged me into a doorway. Lie down, up with your skirt! It wasn't pleasant but it was to be expected.'[37] But these texts have to be read between the lines as descriptions that also say the opposite.

The victims' future life and question of balance might also have been influenced by the severity of the consequences of the rape. One particularly impressive example of a terrible experience giving meaning is the case of Eva Ebner, quoted at the beginning of this chapter. The actress and assistant director was born in Danzig in 1922. After the group rape, she had the opportunity of ensuring that her assailants were severely punished. A military superior organized a line-up and she realized that she had the power to sentence the perpetrators to death: 'I looked from one to the other, recognized them all, including the small fat one who had been particularly mean. I looked them all in the eyes, and in their eyes I saw only one thing: fear. I said to myself: 'It's not worth it for even a single life to be lost on your account and on account of the disgrace they've brought upon you. Eva, you'll get over it. Pull yourself together. Forget revenge.' I looked at them again and said to the officer: 'It wasn't any of them . . .'.[38]

We don't know whether Eva Ebner was particularly resilient, but at all events her subsequent interpretation of her action as a good deed that prevented further injustice no doubt helped her. There were indeed women who decided not to take the matter so seriously. Apart from personal rationalizations, good reasons for keeping silent, the possibility of identifying with the received image of femininity and the inability to speak about their inner feelings, there were probably also victims who remained untouched by the events. But these women were the exception.

It didn't help that the raped women were quite low down in the hierarchy of victims. First of all, the heroic male victim was seen as more important than the suffering female victim, as Frank Biess noted.[39] Furthermore, a gender order that made a marriage of comrades the ideal, a society that valued indifference to pain and the suppression of feelings of attachment, and a moral culture that attached greater importance to the feared immorality of women than to the destruction of civilization by the Nazis reduced the possibilities for rape victims to speak about what had happened to them.

We must, of course, resist the temptation to paint an anachronistic picture of the post-war world. It is only the mass rapes during the wars in Yugoslavia that have raised our awareness of war-related sexual violence. And there is still a great discrepancy between the improved international legal framework and the specific possibilities for a victim to obtain recognition of her rights. Monika Hauser from the medica mondiale aid organization, which provides support for victims of war-related sexual violence throughout the world, complains that sexual violence is still rarely considered a war crime. Instead, rape is regarded as collateral damage and the incidents hushed up, leading to post-stress trauma that extends to future generations.[40]

'ANONYMOUS' AND THE CENSORSHIP OF MEMORY

The most famous personal testimony of the mass rapes at the end of the Second World War is the diary of 'Anonymous', entitled *A Woman in Berlin*. The story of this book gives a good idea of the way war-related rape was viewed in the late 1950s. The diary was published in the mid-1950s in seven languages with great success, but the German edition in 1959 failed to attract much attention. Then it disappeared for almost half a century from the market, until it was republished in 2003. This time it remained for eight weeks at the top of the *Spiegel* bestseller list – and once again met with resistance. What upset people so much about this book? Was it because of the work itself?

After the German version was published for the first time, the supposed immorality of the Berlin author, who wished to remain anonymous, was used against her in the late 1950s and early 1960s. She was accused of 'capitalizing in a questionable manner' on the national catastrophe, including the mass rape. *Der Spiegel* defended her, writing that the text was great-hearted and described events, figures and feelings 'from the Russian era with understanding and a sense of reality'. The horror, numbness that took over after so many rapes, and the defeatist 'rape humour' were typical of those days in Berlin, said the magazine. The diary might not be literature, but it should not be dismissed as cheap sensationalism either.[41] *Telegraf*, a Berlin newspaper, patronizingly praised the woman in Berlin for reporting 'without hysteria' about a collective fate of German women.[42]

Most reactions were negative, however. *Tagesspiegel* was typical: only the high sales figures abroad (294,000 copies in the USA, 210,000 in the UK, 120,000 in the Netherlands, 30,000 in Sweden, 7,000 in Norway, 5,000 in Denmark and 4,500 in Italy) had forced the reviewer to look at the book in detail. She was irritated by the explicit description of what were just 'episodes'. The way the women friends discussed the subject was so repulsive to her that it was impossible for her to back up her judgement with quotes from the book. *Tagesspiegel* readers would thus have to content themselves with the message that the book was salacious and defamed all women who had been in that situation.[43]

Thus, it was not the subject itself that was the problem when the book was first published. Nor was it a breach of taboo, since the major newspapers had already reported on it, and there was a large documentation project on flight and expulsion, which contained hundreds of reports of rape. It is true that the documentation was written by men who had scientific licence to 'expose' the suffering of the women and shed light on it in the interests of the German question and the East–West conflict. There was no secrecy in the 1950s about what had taken place, as is often claimed, but rather certain rules about who should remember what and how. The way in which 'Anonymous' described these days in Berlin apparently broke these rules.

Other victims also found that speaking about the rapes in the 1950s put them in an ambivalent position. They were accused of having fraternized all too quickly with the Soviets, or that it was their nature. They found it impossible to talk about their emotional state. E. A. had such an experience: 'People thought that I was probably not completely blameless, so it was better not to say anything. It had such a negative image that people kept it to themselves.' C. S. also experienced mostly negative reactions:

> They would look me up and down, wag their finger at me. Or I have even heard people say, she's having a Russian brat, or things like that. It affected me, but I thought I won't show that I'm upset, I'll just ignore it. You have to have a thick skin. And when I started to show, I was proud to cross the courtyard. We lived in the back of a long building. People could see me plainly from the window, and I would sometimes hear dirty remarks, you and your Russian brat, and I would raise my dress and tell them to kiss my ass. It was my Russian brat not theirs. Do you think it was any different for women who were with Americans or English? It was just the same. Not to mention those who had been with Africans, and then a little half-caste came out. You can imagine what that was like. There were some who didn't care, but mostly people wouldn't look you in the eye.[44]

Even in Berlin, therefore, where so many victims lived, it was not possible for them to show their emotional damage publicly. Society expected them to bite the bullet, and the women probably expected that that was what they should do as well. The book by 'Anonymous' flew in the face of the needs of society at the time, which wanted to look to the future rather than the past.

Under suspicion again

After almost fifty years of hibernation, *A Woman in Berlin* was reissued in German in 2003 and, according to Wikipedia, was the bestseller of the season.[45] The book was 'unique' and 'deserved the greatest attention', wrote the *Frankfurter Allgemeine Zeitung*.[46] But, once again, there were serious reservations. In particular, Jens Bisky, writing for the *Süddeutsche Zeitung*, described the book as 'worthless'. It had been sloppily edited, he said, and probably not even written by 'Anonymous' herself.[47] The question of authenticity was only a pretext, however. It was not the credibility of the source, but rather of the author and hence of the historical events, that was questioned.

The diary by 'Anonymous' offers a personal view with almost nonchalant self-assurance. As we now know, the author was 'outed' against her will and turned out to have been a journalist in her early thirties, well-travelled and familiar with different languages and cultures, including the Soviet culture. She had led an independent life, turned her back on the traditional church, studied art and history at the Sorbonne and worked as a freelance journalist – anything but the normal life of a woman of her generation. 'Anonymous' (as the author wished to remain anonymous, we shall retain the name here) realized that she belonged to an elite. She wanted to distance herself from the 'herd instinct, a mechanism for preservation of the species', and that is why she hated going down to the air raid shelter.[48] Her vitality was boosted by every threat to her life, and she was burning more fiercely than before the air raids because she was aware that she was experiencing history at first hand: 'Each new day of life is a day of triumph. You've survived once again. You're defiant.'[49]

But even she didn't escape the rapists. After the first two assaults, she went to the commandant and complained. Then she describes very precisely how she tried to dissociate herself from what she had experienced: 'My true self simply leaving my body behind, my poor, besmirched, abused body. Breaking away and floating off, unblemished, into the white beyond. It can't be me this is happening to.'[50] In this way she appeared to relativize the rapes: 'It sounds like the absolute worst, the end of everything – but it's not.' The next time she would close her eyes and clench her teeth. It was only when one of the perpetrators dropped a gob of spit into her mouth that she sank to the ground in disgust.[51] It was then that she decided: 'I have to find a single wolf to keep away the pack. An officer, as high-ranking as possible, a commandant, a general, whatever I can manage. After all, what are my brains for, my little knowledge of the enemy's language?' Now she felt better because she was doing and planning something and was no longer a silent prey but had tamed one of the wolves, 'the strongest in the pack'.[52]

Her image of Russians is coloured by contemporary stereotypes: the Red Army soldiers were either round-headed peasants, childlike, uncivilized, fond of schnapps, occasionally also goodhearted and easy to manipulate, or highly educated, musical, melancholy aristocrats. The image 'Anonymous' has of herself is one of an anti-bourgeois woman dating from the 1920s that was cultivated during the Nazi era and lived on in the 1950s. She was sensible, pragmatic, opportunistic, concerned only with what was most important, vital and always looking to manage her life – in the spirit of 'what doesn't kill me makes me stronger'.[53] After having passed through various hands, 'Anonymous' ultimately ends up with a major, who feeds and protects her and is comparatively friendly because he is interested not only in sex but in female conversation. She wonders to herself (and to the reader) if she should feel like a prostitute, but she pushes her scruples aside, arguing that it is a matter of survival. At some point, she even sees herself as an emancipated woman: 'A German man always wants to be smarter, always wants to be in a position to teach his little woman. But that's something Soviet men don't know about – the idea of the little woman tending her cosy home.'[54]

It is true that, even today, this is an ambivalent book, with its stereotypical Russians, the unshakeable national pride and claim to superiority, its Darwinian worldview, the rustic female ideal. It is hardly surprising that it was unpopular in the 1950s, when people sought salvation in the bourgeois pre-war idea of the family. Added to this was the frank discussion of sex. 'Anonymous' spoke of the limited sexual expertise of the Red Army soldiers ('when it comes to matters erotic they're still with Adam and Eve'),[55] but also about her own sexuality, how she had been earlier, how she had become frigid through all the forced intercourse, how she also developed warm feelings for her 'Russian' and was sad when her protector was sent back to the Soviet Union.

A Woman in Berlin goes through all the shades of grey, from the most brutal sexual assault to calculated sex as a favour, prostitution and consensual sex; it deals with venereal diseases and abortion and ultimately the hurt pride of the returning men who don't allow the women's fate to touch them: 'You've all turned into a bunch of shameless bitches, every one of you in the building. Don't you realize that?' asks Gerd, the morally superior soldier returning from the front, of the 'immoral' Berlin survivor.[56] This is what 'Anonymous' and the other rape victims could expect as the attitude to their experiences in the 1950s: a depressing climate in which the woman suffers in silence for the sake of her family and marriage.

But what about the reproach that the diary is a dubious historical source, as Jens Bisky states in his review of the book? 'Anonymous' initially jotted down notes on events between 20 April and 22 June 1945 in school exercise books. After the war she typed them up and gave them to her friend, the popular author C. W. Ceram, who arranged for their publication. The first edition in English in 1954 was followed by further translations until finally, in 1959, a small publisher in Geneva published the book in German.

Jens Bisky complained that the various stages in the development of the text of the reissue, which was published in 2003 as part of Hans Magnus Enzenberger's 'Andere Bibliothek', had not been made sufficiently transparent, and it was for that reason that the book was 'worthless as a historical document' and was indication only of the efforts by the publisher, whose true motive was to present a distorted picture of the Communists. *A Woman in Berlin* was not a historical document, he said, and it was possible that the author didn't even exist.[57]

When Bisky followed up his suspicion with detective zeal, he discovered a journalist born in 1911 in Bielefeld. She had initially flirted with Communism, had then become a member of the youth section of the National Socialist Women's League and worked 'as a minor advocate of the Third Reich' by writing about spun rayon, the navy and the Reich autobahn. Bisky speculates about her attitude to Nazism: 'Like most people she will have found fault here and there, but will have welcomed the activism, modernity and sense of belonging.'[58]

Bisky refused to accept the diary as a historical source and saw it rather as a literary work of non-fiction in which it is impossible to know what was written by the author and what by others. It is quite possible, he says, that it was Ceram who turned the manuscript into a book. An objective appraisal was not possible, which also meant that what the author wrote about her experience of mass rape in Berlin could well be completely fictional.

Bisky is right to examine the text and question how it was written, but his implicit assumption that a historically authentic diary can ever be beyond suspicion as a historical source is illogical. Diaries are always subject to a whole series of editing and publication processes and are never a true reflection of the historical reality.[59]

The well-known diaries on the mass rape in Berlin that are repeatedly used as a basis for a historical reconstruction of the events, for example the book by 'Anonymous' but also Margret Boveri's *Tage des Überlebens*, have been revised several times and adapted for publication. Even if the diaries or reminiscences were not necessarily written on behalf of an exiles' association or other interest groups, there were many other reasons for their publication that went beyond direct narration towards an attempt to cope with what had happened. Diaries and similar notebooks served for crisis management, and are indeed the crisis genre per se. They address the enforced silence and offer the possibility of confronting the shocks to personal identity. They are always aimed at least at one person – in the case of raped women often their own husbands – to whom the writer opens herself. The writing involves self-justification, reflection on the future, and also adaptation of the experience to socially accepted standards. Typical motives include elevating the individual testimony into an event of 'world historical import' or advancing the notion of having made a personal 'sacrifice for Germany'.[60]

The narration strategy in many accounts of the conquest of Berlin is highly structured and clearly written for an outside audience. The experiences of personal violence and powerlessness are designed to illustrate what happened to the Germans as a whole – namely a humiliating defeat by a despised enemy. The authors' feelings are difficult to differentiate from the assumptions as to how society expects such a narration to be. In brief, diaries such as these cannot be read purely as sources of recalled facts. They are rather documents of the way raped women wished themselves and what they had suffered to be regarded by others.

For all the limitations of autobiographical testimony (and other sources, for that matter), it is remarkable in the case of 'Anonymous' that fifty years after the mass rape by Allied troops the credibility of an eyewitness could be questioned on the basis of the minor philological problems it raises. Even in 2003, it still appeared provocative that women not only regarded the entry into Berlin of the Red Army as an exhilarating 'spring of liberation' (Bisky) but were also at least ambivalent, if not prejudiced in their political judgements and undecided in their feelings and needs. The forced revelation of her identity, the investigation of her political background and the men around her indicate that the political implications of the rape at the end of the war are still a highly sensitive issue today. It is regrettable for the coherence of our own worldview that doubts should be cast on the reputation of the author and publishers – a tried and tested method for eliminating an undesirable truth.

DUTIES OF LOYALTY

Apart from the mental and psycho-historical conditions in the post-war era, at the political level it was the power constellations after 1945 that for a long time stood in the way of gradual awareness-raising of the mass rape. After all, the armies of the perpetrators were also the armies of the liberators and the new allies. In the Soviet occupied zone and later East Germany, the behaviour of the Red Army as it advanced towards Germany was justified early on by citing the 'original guilt' of the Germans.[61] The liberation of the German people from fascism by the Soviets was an axiomatic truth in East Germany and nipped any complaint about mass rape in the bud. Some, as Konrad Jarausch writes, also honestly believed that the Communists had brought the most effective break with the Nazi past, reason enough to overlook the mistakes by this occupying power.[62]

The liberation myth affected the way people dealt with one another;

the Soviets and East Germans explained away their victims by claiming it was the price to pay for victory over fascism and inferred from it a sense of cohesion and loyalty to one another. In a congratulatory telegram on the founding of East Germany in 1949, Stalin stated that both peoples had made great sacrifices in the war and shown the greatest potential 'for performing great acts of global importance', which made them the victors of history.[63] The people of East Germany were barely able to escape the idea of the global significance of the victory of the Red Army: it was part of their everyday life, anchored in rituals, not only on 8 May but also in monuments, school textbooks and political education. The monumental statue of the Red Army soldier with a child in his arms in Treptower Park quite literally overshadows the less heroic personal experiences of people with the Soviet soldiers. There was therefore no chance that the idea of 'big brother' would be revised in East Germany.

In the Soviet occupied zone and in East Germany, there was not even the cynicism prevalent in the West, whereby women had either been victims of the 'Red beasts' or behaved like immoral Yank lovers. The act itself – the countless assaults by the Red Army – was not even open to discussion in the non-democratic East German society. On account of the course of the fighting in the East, there were few indicators regarding assaults by Western soldiers. Nothing was said in East Germany about the Western allies acting in the same way as the marauding and raping Red Army soldiers. The subjugation of Germany as a heroic victory against fascism was enough of a *raison d'être*.

According to Silke Satjukow, the SED crudely stifled the few attempts to talk in public about the experiences of the women victims. As a functionary in the Ministry of Culture put it:

> In many cases there was no 'rape'; the German women, who had been destabilized by the war, 'threw themselves' at the soldiers in order to obtain food. The odd incident and the occasional child were quickly forgotten. . . . to those who insisted in 1945/46, we argued, perhaps a little harshly, that making children, even if not quite voluntarily, was better than killing them.[64]

There is an analogy here with the judgement of women in the West as 'Yank lovers', in which the nuances of violence, need and consent are ignored. Evidently, sexual contact with one's own allies, one's own 'big brother', was always particularly reprehensible. Jarausch interprets this, the sexual contact with the 'liberators', as a particularly painful symptom of the loss of power.[65]

As mentioned earlier, the cases of rape by the Western allies did not cause any great indignation in West Germany either. The Cold War demanded of both sides, the West Germans and the East Germans, 'an unequivocal domestic and foreign policy statement in favour either of the "free world" or of Socialism'.[66] The Western politicians mostly passed on complaints about assaults as polite requests, which they justified as being in the interests of the occupiers and the reputation of the Western occupying troops in the joint project of democratization and allying Germany with the West. This was an argument that would make sense to the Americans, British and French, who had undertaken to re-educate and democratize Germany.

In the 1950s, there were at best quiet mutterings, as was the case with Werner Friedmann, who wrote in the *Süddeutsche Zeitung* in January 1952 in connection with the assaults by American soldiers that the recently increasing numbers of US soldiers coming to Bavaria were now being called defence forces rather than occupying forces, which was intended to assuage misgivings within the population. At the same time the number of assaults by soldiers on Germans was rising. For that reason, a dark shadow had been cast recently on life together with the 'ambassadors of American defensive preparedness', so much so that it was unclear

> whether these soldiers were indeed here to protect us or whether we might sometimes need to protect ourselves against them. Assaults on taxi drivers, women on their own and citizens are going up throughout the country. Acts of violence and brutality are being reported daily. In Munich alone there were 222 serious incidents in 1951, including eighty assaults, not counting minor episodes.

Even if these figures were considered impartially, he continued, with account taken of the fact that soldiers are coarse types who spend their free time with alcohol and dubious women, there was still an urgent need for something to be done. This was not, incidentally, to ignore the helpfulness and genuine friendship frequently encountered in members of the occupying forces.[67]

Friedmann and other contemporary commentators performed bizarre contortions to understand the acts of the GIs. An explanation such as the fact that men in the USA were used only to 'diluted' alcohol and were bored in Germany was already plausible enough for them. In October of the same year, following the rape of two women by two US servicemen in a doctor's surgery in Hohenlinden near Munich, the *Süddeutsche Zeitung* (*SZ*) commented wryly that it was unfortunately a fact that

> young soldiers of all nationalities . . . seek some kind of physical compensation after completion of their more or less righteous war work. But this romanticism stops with the reading of the daily police reports: taxi drivers robbed, passers-by deliberately run over, women raped. And so forth. Could it be because the soldiers from overseas come here with the wrong ideas about us? It is possible that some of them arrive from the Texas hinterland with the notion that we are still living in 1945 and that they are least likely to draw attention to themselves with their glib cowboy act. They are wrong! They should . . . rather teach the occupying troops and if possible not send out-and-out footpads and bushwhackers.[68]

The midnight curfew introduced at the end of 1953 for American soldiers did nothing to change the situation in Munich. This prompted the renowned *SZ* journalist Ernst Müller-Meiningen junior to describe the Americans as a 'tribe of savages': 'Tensed up by their historical fate and their own guilt, Germans require an object lesson – based on the values and not the absence of values of the great American people. . . . The situation to date has not been ideal: the GIs, who had too much leisure time and money, whose huge cars and cigarettes were readily for sale, the inexpensive "Veronikas" and the entertaining bars offering a glittering life – compared with their private situation – were particularly conducive to excesses.'[69]

This has the tone of an anti-Americanism that was later to be voiced not only in East Germany but also increasingly in the West. Criticism of the hegemonial policy, the supposed lack of culture and the materialism had already been heard in the discussion of fraternizing German women and was at least one of the underlying issues in German–American relations, along with the great admiration for the American way of life. The rapes by US soldiers were seen as the typical features of a nation of boorish philistines, undisciplined, licentious and ignorant, and often arrogant in their attitude to the German population.[70] In this way, trivializing gender stereotypes were combined with stereotypical images of the Americans.

Towards the end of the 1950s, public criticism of breaches of the peace by the American forces became more vocal. The acquittal of a soldier accused of raping a 12-year-old girl produced a flood of indignant letters in the *Münchner Merkur*.[71] On this occasion, the newspaper also reported on a rumoured recruitment poster in the USA aimed specifically at black men. As soldiers, said the poster, they could travel abroad and earn more than the local population, with the result that white girls in Germany and Britain were queuing up for black GIs. The rumour was taken so seriously that members of parliament and church leaders wrote to the Ministry of Foreign Affairs asking the American people to change this form of recruitment for the sake of the safety of German women and girls. The Ministry replied that posters of this type had never existed and they were merely Communist and Nazi propaganda.[72] Even if it is true in this case, we now know that a potential war premium in the form of a European woman was indeed used as a recruitment argument by the US Army. But the time was not ripe for a conflict with 'big brother', neither in the East nor in the West.

FIRST FEMINIST PROTESTS

The subject of rape in general, and in war in particular, did not attract any great attention until the 1970s, at a time when the need was perceived to discuss the connection between the two problems, gender roles and war. The new attitude resulted from the recent feminist movement in the USA. The journalist Susan Brownmiller published the standard reference, *Against Our Will*, in 1975, in which she discussed the significance of rape in upholding the patriarchal society.[73] She backed her thesis with historical events, including the mass rape during and after the Second World War. It was this pioneering feminist work that first made it possible to put the phenomenon of rape in a historical perspective – in other words, to remove it from its biological and quasi-natural framework and to link it with a particular form of rule, namely patriarchy.

Brownmiller described sexual violence as one of the earliest forms of male bonding, and gang rape as men's basic weapon of force, the principal agent of his will and her fear:

> His forcible entry into her body, despite her physical protestations and struggle, became the vehicle of his victorious conquest over her being, the ultimate test of his superior strength, the triumph of his manhood. Man's discovery that his genitalia could serve as a weapon to generate fear must rank as one of the most important discoveries of prehistoric times, along with the use of fire and the first crude stone axe.[74]

War provided men with the perfect psychological backdrop for giving vent to their contempt for women. The very maleness of the military, the brute power of weaponry exclusive to their hands, the spiritual bonding of men at arms, the manly discipline of orders given and orders obeyed, confirmed to them that women were peripheral: 'A simple rule of thumb in war is that the winning side is the side that does the raping.'[75] This also sends a message to the conquered country that the rape of 'their' women is the ultimate humiliation.[76]

Surprisingly, Brownmiller already mentioned the rapes by US soldiers in the Second World War and occupation period as a historical example and criticized the paltry standard excuse by the army that more rapes take place during an occupation because the soldiers have lots of free time. Her attempt to explain rape as a form of female conditioning was also innovative. The mere learning of the word 'rape' by children, she claims, made them aware of the gender power structure.[77]

It is interesting that the feminist discussion of sexual violence, which is one of the marks of the New Women's Movement in Germany, failed to draw public attention to the war-related rape. Although the relevant publications and leading figures like Alice Schwarzer repeatedly bring up the topic of sexual violence, the focus is on civilian rape, and particularly sexual abuse among friends and in marriage. This needs to be explained, particularly given the fact that Schwarzer, the leading German feminist, writes in her biography that her mother narrowly escaped being raped by a US soldier.[78] Thus, if the old feminists of the 1970s had just asked their own mothers – quite literally – they would have had enough grounds for indignation and empathy. But for a variety of reasons, it was not possible for them at the time to address this obvious issue.

The rape question took a private turn because the thesis that all men were potential rapists and all women potential victims provided an explanation for female oppression and the massive recruitment of women for the feminist project. In addition, the war-related rape was seen in Germany primarily as a problem of the Red Army and hence part of the East–West conflict. The New Women's Movement was a product of the New Left, however, and could not or did not want to burn its fingers by touching on this theme. It is in this way that the 1970s feminists lost the opportunity to address the largest mass rape in history, of which their own mothers had been the victims.[79]

HELKE SANDER'S 'BEFREIER' AND THE GERMAN VICTIM DEBATE

It was to be almost another twenty-five years before a German feminist finally took the bull by the horns. Helke Sander had already drawn attention to herself in September 1968, when she appeared at a meeting of the Sozialistisches Deutsches Studentenbund [Socialist German Student Union (SDS)] in Frankfurt as co-founder of Aktionsrat zur Befreiung der Frauen [Action Committee for the Liberation of Women] and announced its manifesto. Women could not wait until after the revolution and the transformation of economic and political circumstances to achieve equality, she said to the hardly enthusiastic students. It was time to abandon in-fighting and place private and political difficulties in the right context: 'Why do you speak here of class struggle and at home about orgasm problems? Isn't that something of interest to the SDS as well?'[80] When her speech did not produce the hoped-for effect, one of Sander's comrades-in-arms threw tomatoes at the next speaker. This act became the symbolic initial spark for the New Women's Movement in Germany.[81]

Her documentary and accompanying book *BeFreier und Befreite* in 1992 finally triggered discussion of the post-war rapes. The dispute she provoked emphasizes the importance of her pioneering act. She and her fellow researchers had attempted to reconstruct the main aspects of the events in minute detail, to deliver initial statistics, to interview not only the German victims but also Russian men and to fit what had happened into a contemporary feminist discourse on violence. As mentioned earlier, Sander probably exaggerated the numbers involved, but this does nothing to minimize the significance of her project. It was rather her exclusive focus on Berlin and the Red Army that made her treatment of the topic lopsided.

Surprisingly, however, this one-sided approach was never held against her. On the contrary, she was criticized for the way she dealt with the testimony, which she presented without commentary, including the crude statements by one interviewee, who compared the events with the Holocaust. She was particularly censured because she had allowed a Jewish victim to speak and in doing so, it was said, relativized the crimes of the Germans against the Jews by comparing them with the crimes of (Soviet) men against women.[82]

The American historian Atina Grossmann referred to earlier was particularly critical of Sander's work. She accused her of wilfully calculating the number of victims so as to relativize the Holocaust and also countered Sander's project with her own interpretation, whereby the women who had been raped and subsequently terminated their pregnancies had all been racists. In doing so she replaced the accusation of historical relativization with a relativization of her own. By assigning a Nazi ideology to the victims, she turned the women into perpetrators, who therefore deserved no sympathy. Once again, it is the credibility of the victims that was at stake.

Compared with the excessive criticism, the impact of the first large-scale systematic study of the war-related rape of German women was of short duration. Norman M. Naimark reckons that the controversy surrounding Sander's work possibly did less to shed light on the mass raping than it did to address the complicity of women in the crimes of the Nazis, which were indeed subsequently studied more widely (a debate known as the 'women historians' dispute').[83]

Grossmann's criticism of Sander's study of the mass rape can be understood only in the context of the left-wing liberal problems with the German 'victim discourse'. The concept of 'victim discourse' recalls that, after the war and until the 1950s, the Germans initially also styled themselves as victims of Nazis and the war and not as the perpetrators of the suffering, whose consequences they were now obliged to bear.[84] It was quite common after 1945 to invert cause and effect and to offset the German losses against those of the enemy, the extermination of the Jews, Sinti and Roma and other minorities, and the war crimes of the Wehrmacht and SS. To cite just one example, Cardinal Josef Faulhaber said in the year of capitulation that the liberated concentration camps were certainly not a pleasant sight, but neither was Munich after the enemy air raids.

This post-war 'victim discourse' continues to give rise to suspicion today. The Germans are suspected of still emphasizing their own suffering merely to divert attention from their historical responsibility for the often much greater suffering they brought to half of the world. Critics of the 'victim discourse' claim that all talk of German suffering is ultimately revisionist, that books like *Der Brand* by Jörg Friedrich (2002) about the bombing of German cities, popular films like *Die Gustloff* (2008) about the sinking of a ship loaded with German refugees from the East with the loss of 9,000 people, or *March of Millions* (2007) about flight from the German territories in the East, or novels like Günter Grass' *Crabwalk* (2002) were intended to relativize German guilt.

They make a connection in time between German unity, a dangerous recrudescence of national pride and a new version of the 'victim discourse'. After a phase of ignorance directly after the war and 'coming to terms with the past' through (meaningless) remembrance rituals under the slogan 'never again Auschwitz', the subject of German war victims, say the critics, is now being used to 'cast off the fetters of inherent guilt', as the psychoanalyst and historian Gudrun Brockhaus puts it.[85] The social psychologist Harald Welzer considered even the new interest in 'war childhood' merely as an invention and evasion by the 1968 generation, who just wanted to make themselves appear important.[86] Ultimately, he feared, everyone somehow regarded themselves as victims, thereby neutralizing the enormous suffering that the Germans had inflicted on the world.

Pre-emptive self-accusation

To counter this suspicion, it has become customary for the few historians who have studied the mass rape of German women at all to precede their commentaries by long digressions on the similar crimes of the Wehrmacht, the army brothels and the forced prostitution in concentration camps.[87] Only after the misdeeds of the Germans have been spoken about at length is it allowed to discuss German victims. This rhetoric is comprehensible and sympathetic, although it is based on what I believe to be a problematic causality – the German women were raped because the Germans had caused so much devastation hitherto. This cause-and-effect argumentation falls short because the American and Canadian soldiers had no reason to take revenge on Germany in the form of rape, and in any case the logical connection must first of all be demonstrated. The Wehrmacht soldiers had not sexually assaulted the women on the other side of the Atlantic. And besides, one crime does not legitimize another. It is simply not 'natural' to act out rage against the enemy by assaulting women sexually.

The American historian Grossmann chose another way of distancing herself from the 'victim discourse'. She relativizes what happened by saying that the raped German women were not ideologically without guilt. Her incorrect claim that women who had become pregnant through rape had aborted the offspring of 'subhumans' for racist reasons, namely on account of their abiding belief in the Nazi ideology, naturally blocks any sympathy whatsoever for the victims. It deprives the women of the moral right to consider themselves as victims. Grossmann's basic assumption is already questionable, as we have seen above. But even if we accept the unlikely premise that the rape victims were all committed Nazis, what then?

To put it bluntly, a reversal of the perpetrator–victim perspective would be inadmissible and above all impossible. Since the 1990s, it has been no secret that German women and children were not only victims. Most of them espoused the Nazi ideology and were in the worst cases actively involved in the persecution and extermination policy. Without the countless denunciations by women, for example, the registration of the Jewish population and the looting, persecution and extermination would not have been possible. They were not slow in making supposedly inferior women and nations aware of the premise that German women were important for the survival of the Aryan race. There were women concentration camp guards, colonizers of the occupied. territories, agitators, collaborators, profiteers and, at the very least, passive observers of the Nazi crimes.

Women who did not voluntarily perform war service, for example in the armaments factories, 'stabilized the "home front" through their "functions" in the home, their energies within the family beyond requirements and their endurance until the end'.[88]

Even supposedly apolitical housewives believed in the superiority of the German people and the justification for war, hoped for the final victory and kept the war machinery running. They sent packages and letters to the front and made it easier for the soldiers through their endurance: 'On the one hand they would have preferred to hide their sons and husbands in the hinterland, on the other hand they didn't want any "weaklings" or "shirkers" and regarded the fight as a "character-building matter" that "strengthened the soul".'[89] German women promoted a military masculine ideal, which they unfortunately became prey to through defeat.

Women at the time were just as persuaded as men by the toughening ideology, the need for objectivity and distance, and they brought up their children accordingly. We must assume that the average German women knew or could have known about the extermination of the Jews and the atrocities committed by the Wehrmacht. It was apparent everywhere: the persecution of dissidents and political opponents, the harassment and deportation of the Jews, the burning synagogues. They had contact with slave labourers and prisoners of war; they lived perhaps close to concentration camps or witnessed euthanasia actions and death marches and they read letters from the front.

It is evident that many rape victims were at least potential perpetrators. Even children were not always innocent, having participated in the harassment of slave labourers, mobbed Jewish schoolchildren and regarded themselves as members of a master race. Neither women nor children were 'just silent and traumatized witnesses of this war nor simply its innocent victims', as Nicholas Stargardt points out.[90] But again, what does that have to do with their parallel status as victims? The answer is that, seventy years after the war, we must find a way of accommodating this ambiguity. We cannot avoid the pitfalls of revisionism by regarding the victims not as Germans but primarily as women, and hence supposedly innocent. This strategy led a few feminist historians astray in the 1990s. But we cannot either deny the German rape victims their status as victims because they belonged to the aggressor nation.

An empathic approach to the mass rapes requires that the categories of gender and ethnicity be seen together. The idea that the raped women stand as representatives of the 'defiled' nation is a product of the nineteenth-century nationalist thinking and no longer applies. We know that women from all of the warring and occupied nations were subject to sexual violence. They experienced rape as women and Germans, as the defeated and weaker nation. The story being told here is not a specifically German one. We are looking at the German chapter of this story only to examine how our society (or more exactly the German societies in the East and West) dealt with it, and what that says about a culture and its influence on subsequent generations.

The sexual violence at the end of the war was not a 'collective experience' for the victims, as some contemporary witnesses, and researchers even today, would like to claim. The women who were raped could not rationalize their suffering because they had been raped as *German* women. Even if this interpretation was helpful for some people in the West during the climate of East–West rivalry in the 1950s and 1960s, by the 1980s at the latest it had lost all significance as an exonerating strategy. This rhetoric was in any case unavailable to East German women.

THE PAST TODAY

There are some indications at least that the ability and willingness of Germans to face up to their own war suffering has changed since the millennium. This is reflected in the collective memory but also in personal therapeutic work.

The psychoanalyst Uwe Langendorf, to take just one example, made the publication of *Crabwalk* by Günter Grass in February 2002 and the series 'Die Flucht' in *Der Spiegel* a month later a point of reference for his own sudden realization that certain observations in the twenty years of his psychotherapy practice could have something to do with a collective war trauma. A few months later, a conference in Berlin of the Deutsche Gesellschaft für psychohistorische Forschung dealt with the same topic.[91] It only struck Langendorf now that over a third of his patients had a refugee background, either through their own childhood experience or from having grown up in a refugee family. In many cases, the trauma was cumulative: loss of home and property and the associated loss of status, mistreatment and rape during flight and expulsion, rejection and contempt from the people where they settled, feelings of guilt at having survived and leaving behind the homes and graves of ancestors. A frequent family constellation among his patients were the numbed and depressive mother and the physically or emotionally absent and weak father. As adults, the patients were then frequently over-ambitious, unwilling to form relationships, restless and uprooted.[92]

In the meantime, public attention has been drawn to the transgenerational consequences of war experiences for children, and even for grandchildren. To date, however, these recollections have been male-dominated. Much of the early systematic study of 'war childhood' and 'growing up without a father' has been conducted by men. By contrast, there has been little said about the collective female experience of mass rape and its possible long-term consequences. Remember, we are talking here about at least 860,000 victims of sexual violence and even more families of their descendants.

Researchers agree today that collective trauma can be lasting and cumulative over several generations: 'It is the result of unconsciously residual psychological processes and fosters dissociated perception and recollection and hence numerous psychological and psychosomatic symptoms.'[93] It is thought that children and grandchildren assimilate unprocessed feelings and hence also the characteristic personality features of their parents and grandparents and unknowingly attempt to solve the problems for them – for example the grief, reconciliation, recovery of loss and defence against powerlessness.[94]

This does not occur without conflicts and collisions with the present-day reality, however, leading to feelings of guilt by descendants about having been able to grow up in a better time than their traumatized parents and grandparents. The psychiatrist and psychoanalyst

Bertram von der Stein describes the case of a 50-year-old single woman whose mother was raped by a soldier while her eldest sister was shot by another soldier. The patient denied her own sexuality and repressed her aggression 'as a defence against transgenerationally communicated trauma'. She found aggression and sexuality to be life-threatening.[95]

The passing on of familial stress, such as that resulting from war-related rape, does not occur in the form of a simple transfer from top to bottom. The older and younger generations both participate in the transfer, which is more in the form of an exchange, in which the significance and assumption of the cultural heritage are negotiated.[96] Thus, later descendants have an influence on the processing of bad historical experiences in their family. Psychologists believe that the confrontation with painful memories is vital in this process. The trauma of the past must be faced up to, the personal family history reconstructed and the unconscious destructive consequences dealt with therapeutically. The aim is to distinguish between fantasy and reality in the collective history of earlier generations and to learn to stop identifying with the suffering – even today. This makes the history of mass rape after the war of continuing relevance. Only through knowledge can the 'society of survivors' recover from the suffering experienced at the time.

Knowledge of the events after 1945 is also still important for the few survivors. For that reason, the geriatric carer and dream therapist Martina Böhmer travels through the country to visit old people's and dementia homes. She has repeatedly seen how rape victims are traumatized again by rough treatment, the banging of doors in the corridor, insensitive remembrance rituals in the homes and even through chance meetings with Polish nursing staff, for example. She told me of the case of a resident of an old people's home who refused to allow herself to be undressed and washed, particularly by male carers. She had been raped after the war. In another case, an old woman had panic attacks because her roommate had an American husband and her language catapulted her back to the long-past rape by a GI. This follow-up trauma, says Böhmer, is often misdiagnosed as dementia and incorrectly treated with drugs. In only a few institutes, such as the Henry and Emma Budge Foundation near Frankfurt, which has Jewish and non-Jewish residents, are the psychologists routinely trained to deal sensitively with this history. It would be useful if this were the case in all care homes in Germany.

We can only speculate on more general after-effects of the mass rape by occupying troops. How has the unprocessed experience impacted in general on the relationship of the sexes to one another and on the handling of sexual violence in Germany? This is a subject requiring further study. One thing is certain: German feminists, as discussed earlier, are notable throughout the world for having difficulty in abandoning the perpetrator–victim scheme of the 1970s and their one-sided approach to the subject of sexual violence and abuse. Is there an unprocessed historical connecting line here? And there is another possibly striking symptom: just before this book was published, a long-overdue problem was once again placed on the political agenda in Berlin – namely, the fact that courts still regard only non-consensual sex with the threat of violence as rape. A new possible revision of the law on sexual offences is now addressing the problem of testimony by victims. Is it a coincidence that this badly needed reform is going to be implemented at a moment when a large number of refugees are entering the country – including many dark-skinned men who conjure up old fears of sexual violence?

After having read hundreds of reports that in a few compressed lines describe the course of the rapes all over Germany in more or less the same terms, I am forced to ask whether these incidents have not almost inevitably cast a long shadow on the sense of security, especially in the case of women. In rural communities and small towns, the danger for a child or women of being dragged from the street into a car in broad daylight, and more especially at night, and taken to a field or wood to be attacked by one or more soldiers was omnipresent. Certain places and areas, particularly close to barracks and later to military training areas, were particularly hazardous. There was not usually any possibility of resisting or of having the perpetrators punished afterwards. I remember how I myself was also warned in the 1970s of all kinds of dangers that, as a teenager, I found implausible – in particular, of course, bars, which were known as hang-outs of the occupying soldiers.

While working on this book, I was constantly reminded of the generations before me who imagined a potential murderer or rapist round every corner and who, even in the 1970s, collected newspaper cuttings of such incidents as proof of the supposedly omnipresent threat of male violence. In my psychologist family, strange behaviour of this type – for example, that of my anxious grandmother from Freiburg – was treated as the 'sexual phobia' of a war widow who after her husband's early death, to the regret of those around her, never again sought intimate contact with a man. Today I recall that when the French occupying troops arrived, she was a young single woman. I realize now that she must have known what could befall women and children anywhere and at any time. Is it possible that this had no influence on her life and that of her descendants?

Notes

Introduction

1 See Atina Grossmann, 'A Question of Silence: The Rape of German Women by Occupation Soldiers', in: Robert G. Moeller (ed.), *West Germany under Construction: Politics, Society, and Culture in the Adenauer Era* (Michigan 1997), pp. 33–52.

2 Laurel Cohen-Pfister, 'Rape, War, and Outrage: Changing Perceptions on German Victimhood in the Period of Post-Unification', in: Cohen-Pfister and Dagmar Weinröder-Skinner (eds.), *Victims and Perpetrators: 1933–1945, (Re)Presenting the Past in Post-Unification Culture* (Berlin, New York 2006), pp. 316–36, here p. 318.

3 Jens Bisky, 'Wenn Jungen Weltgeschichte spielen, haben Mädchen stumme Rollen: Wer war die Anonyma in Berlin? Frauen, Fakten und Fiktionen – Anmerkungen zu einem grossen Bucherfolg dieses Sommers' in: *Süddeutsche Zeitung*, 24 September 2003, p. 16.

4 Martina Böhmer, *Erfahrungen sexualisierter Gewalt in der Lebensgeschichte alter Frauen: Ansätze für eine frauenorientierte Altenarbeit* (Frankfurt 2011).

1 Seventy years too late

1 Rudolf Albart, *Die letzten und die ersten Tage: Bambergs Kriegstagebuch 1944/46* (Bamberg 1953), p. 91.

2 Dieter Hildebrandt and Felix Kuballa (eds.), *Mein Kriegsende: Erinnerungen an die Stunde Null* (Berlin 2012), p. 221.

3 The subject of sexual aggression by the German Wehrmacht has been studied increasingly in recent years. One of the latest articles is Regina Mühlhäuser, 'Eine Frage der Ehre: Anmerkungen zur Sexualität deutscher Soldaten während des Zweiten Weltkriegs', in: Wolfgang Bialas and Lothar Fritze (eds.), *Ideologie und Moral im Nationalsozialismus* (Göttingen 2014), pp. 153–74.

4 In the former local cemetery in Neukölln is a hidden memorial stone with the inscription: 'Against war and violence. In memory of the victims of expulsion, deportation, rape and slave labour. Innocent children and mothers, women and young girls. Their suffering in the turmoil of the Second World War should not be forgotten, so as to prevent future suffering.' Information on the feminist women's rights organization at www.medicamondiale. org.

5 Frank Biess, 'Moral Panic in Postwar Germany: The Abduction of Young Germans into the Foreign Legion and French Colonialism in the 1950s', in: *Journal of Modern History* 84, 4 (2012), 789–832.

6 Walter Ziegler, 'Bayern im Übergang: Vom Kriegsende zur Besatzung 1945', in: Peter Pfister (ed.), *Das Ende des Zweiten Weltkriegs im Erzbistum München und Freising* (Regensburg 2005), pp. 33–104, here p. 102.

7 Robert G. Moeller, 'Deutsche Opfer, Opfer der Deutschen: Kriegsgefangene, Vertriebene, NS-Verfolgte – Opferausgleich also Indentitätspolitik', in: Klaus Naumann (ed.), *Nachkrieg in Deutschland* (Hamburg 2001), pp. 29–58, here p. 32.

8 Biess, 'Moral Panic', pp. 792–3.

9 See Ruth Seifert, 'Krieg und Vergewaltigung: Ansätze zu einer Analyse', Working Paper (Munich 1993), p. 19.

10 An early interest in the fatherless male generation was shown at a congress in April 2005 in Frankfurt. See Lu Seegers, 'Die Generation der Kriegskinder und ihre Botschaft für Europa

sechzig Jahre nach Kriegsende', in: *H-Soz-u-Kult*, 1 May 2005. Other studies from the male point of view followed, e.g. Hermann Schulz, Harmut Radebold and Jürgen Reulecke, *Söhne ohne Väter: Erfahrungen der Kriegsgeneration* (Berlin 2004). The cover shows a boy in the Nazi era with a model aeroplane in his hand and a mother figure in the background.

11 Burkhard Asmuss (ed.), *1945 – Der Krieg und seine Folgen*, book accompanying the exhibition 'Kriegsende und Vergangenheits-politik in Deutschland' (Berlin 2005).

12 The research group led by Philipp Kuwert has studied the psy-chotraumatic consequences, above all of victims of rape by Red Army soldiers. Its findings are published in Svenja Eichhorn and Philipp Kuwert, *Das Geheimnis unserer Grossmütter: Eine empirische Studie über sexualisierte Kriegsgewalt um 1945* (Giessen 2011).

13 The occupation statute was in force from September 1949 until the Paris Agreements of May 1955 and determined the legal authority and responsibilities of the Western powers in the Federal Republic. The rights of the Allies did not end until the reunification and the Two Plus Four Treaty of March 1991, which restored the Federal Republic's full sovereignty.

14 See the archive items not seen by me in the Hamburg State Archive under 354–5 II (Jugendbehörde II) no. 240 Uneheliche Kinder von Besatzungssoldaten; 354–5 II (Jugendbehörde II) no. 239 Vormundschaft für Kinder aus Vergewaltigungen durch Angehörige der Besatzungsmächte; 131–1 II (Senatskanzlei) no. 2810 Übergriffe von Angehörigen der Besatzungsmacht 1946–1965; 131–11 (Personalamt) no. 1697 Schadensersatzansprüche gegen die Besatzungsmacht 1946–1952; 131–5 (Senatskanzlei – Verwaltungsbeschwerden) no. 234 Besatzungsschäden durch Straftaten britischer Soldaten 1949; 132–5/11 (Hamburgische Ver-tretung beim Bund in Bonn) no. A391 Unterhaltsverpflichtungen für uneheliche Kinder von Besatzungsangehörigen 1950–1953.

15 The American and Soviet occupied zones comprised 17.2 million citizens in 1946, the British 22 million, and the French 5 million.

16 Willy Klapproth, *Kriegschronik 1945 der Stadt Soltau und Umgebung, mit Beiträgen zur Kriegsgeschichte 1945 der Süd- und Mittelheide* (Soltau 1955), p. 205.

17 Clive Emsley, *Solder, Sailor, Beggarman, Thief: Crime and the British Armed Services since 1914* (Oxford 2013), pp. 128–30, 131.

18 On the changing role of the US Army, see Hans Joachim Harder, 'Guarantors of Peace and Freedom: The US Forces in Germany, 1945–1990', in: Thomas Maulucci and Detlev Junker (eds.), *GIs in Germany: The Social, Economic, Cultural, and Political History of the American Military Presence* (Cambridge 2013), pp. 37–54. On the crime rate of GIs, see Gerhard Fürmetz, 'Insolent Occupiers, Aggressive Protectors', in: Maulucci and Junker (eds.), *GIs in Germany*, pp. 189–211.

19 Rainer Schulze, 'A Difficult Interlude: Relations between British Military Government and the German Population and their Effects for the Constitution of a Democratic Society', in: Alan Bance (ed.), *The Cultural Legacy of the British Occupation in Germany: The London Symposium* (Stuttgart 1997), pp. 67–109.

20 I retain the term 'sexual aggression'. All other forms of 'sexualized aggression' were not perceived as such at the time. I also believe for political reasons that an understandable everyday expression is more important than academically differentiated objectivization, which risks excluding the people concerned.

21 The figures for Austria also fluctuate considerably. According to contemporary sources, there were between 70,000 and 100,000 cases in Vienna; see Barbara Stelzl-Marx, *Stalins Soldaten in Österreich: Die Innensicht der sowjetischen Besatzung 1945–1955* (Vienna 2012), p. 411.

22 According to eyewitness Cornelius Ryan, *The Last Battle* (London 1966).

23 The pregnancy rate following rape is currently 5 per cent in the USA and approx. 15 per cent in Mexico, see Susanne Heynen, 'Erzwungene Schwangerschaft und Mutterschaft durch eine Vergewaltigung', in: *Kindesmisshandlung und -vernachlässigung* (DGgKV) 6, no. 1/2 (2003), pp. 98–125. Barbara Johr assumes a 20 per cent rate for pregnancies following rape. In my opinion, she arrives at this high figure from hospital records. It is not clear, however, which women attended clinics at the time after being raped. I believe it was, above all, women who feared that they must be pregnant. Helke Sander and Barbara Johr also assume an

abortion rate of 90 per cent, see Barbar Johr, 'Die Ereignisse in Zahlen', in: Helke Sander and Barbara Johr (eds.), *BeFreier und Befreite: Krieg, Vergewaltigungen, Kinder* (Munich 1992), pp. 46–73.

24 Bayerisches Hauptstaatsarchiv (BayHStA) MInn 80207 betreff Besatzungsmacht, Ereignisse und Sicherheitsstörungen, Bericht des Landeserkennungsamt Bayern of 28 June 1946.

25 Bundesarchiv (BA) Koblenz B/126/28038.

26 Ibid., B 153/342.

27 National Archives, Headquarters XX Corps Office of the Provost Marshal, Reply to questions on rape, file no. 70, 5 June 1945: Rape of German women by American soldiers (National Archives ID 6081861).

28 Ulrich Herbert, *Geschichte Deutschlands im 20. Jahrhundert* (Munich 2014), p. 534, with reference to Regina Mühlhäuser, 'Vergewaltigungen in Deutschland: Nationaler Opferdiskurs und individuelles Erinnern betroffener Frauen', in: Naumann, *Nachkrieg in Deutschland*, pp. 384–408, which in turn is based on figures by Helke Sander and Ingrid Schmidt-Harzbach. The high figure for Austria is based on an obscure formula attributing an average of two rapes for every occupying soldier. Barbara Stelzl-Marx mentions this rule of thumb without stating whether it applies to all occupying armies or just the Soviets; see Stelzl-Marx, *Stalins Soldaten in Österreich*, p. 411.

29 Norman M. Naimark, *Die Russen in Deutschland: Die sowjetische Besatzungszone 1945 bis 1949* (Berlin 1997), p. 170.

30 J. Robert Lilly, *Taken by Force: Rape and American GIs in Europe during World War II* (Chippenham 2007, first published in French in 2003).

31 Johr, 'Die Ereignisse in Zahlen', p. 72, fn. 2.

32 See Norman M. Naimark, 'The Russians and Germans: Rape during the War and Post-Soviet Memories', in: Raphaëlle Branche and Fabrice Virgili (eds.), *Rape in Wartime: A History to Be Written* (= Genders and Sexualities in History) (Basingstoke 2012), pp. 201–19.

33 It is possible that the entire female population was erroneously used as a basis.

34 Johr, 'Die Ereignisse in Zahlen', pp. 58–65.

35 Branche and Virgile (eds.), *Rape in Wartime*.
36 Werner Sudendorf, *Verführung und Rebell: Horst Buchholz, Die Biografie* (Berlin 2013), p. 23.
37 Landeserkennungsamt Bayern, 19 June 1946, BayHStA MInn 80207, Bd. 1 betreff Besatzungsmacht, Ereignisse und Sicherheitsstörungen.
38 Stadtpolizei Bad Kissingen on 7 December 1951 to Regierung von Unterfranken, BayHStA MInn 80208.
39 Staatsarchiv Freiburg Einzelfälle D 5/1 11.6.30/5537.
40 The Deutscher Tagebucharchiv in Emmendingen has several dozen sources that await analysis.

2 Berlin and the East – chronicle of a calamity foretold

1 Sammlung Sterz, Feldpostbriefe, Bibliothek für Zeitgeschichte, Stuttgart, quoted in Ian Kershaw, *The End: Hitler's Germany, 1944–45* (London 2011), p. 312.
2 Hildebrandt and Kuballa, *Mein Kriegsende*, p. 221.
3 Wladimir Gelfand, *Deutschland-Tagebuch 1945–1946: Aufzeichnungen eines Rotarmisten* (Berlin 2008), p. 112.
4 Christian Goeschel, *Selbstmord im Dritten Reich* (Berlin 2011), p. 242; more generally, Kershaw, *The End*, pp. 112–15, 188.
5 Max Domarus (ed.), *Hitler: Reden und Proklamationen, kommentiert von einem deutschen Zeitgenossen*, vol. II/2 (Leonberg 1988), pp. 2204–5.
6 Elke Fröhlich (ed.), *Die Tagebücher von Joseph Goebbels, Teil I, Aufzeichnungen*, vol. 4 (Munich 1987), p. 696.
7 Christel Panzig and Klaus-Alexander Panzig, "'Die Russen kommen!" Deutsche Erinnerungen an Begegnungen mit "Russen" bei Kriegsende 1945 in Dörfern und Kleinstädten Mitteldeutschlands und Mecklenburg-Vorpommerns', in: Elke Scherstjanoi (ed.), *Rotarmisten schreiben aus Deutschland: Briefe von der Front (1945) und historische Analysen* (= *Texte und Materialien zur Zeitgeschichte* 14, published by the Institut für Zeitgeschichte) (Munich 2004), pp. 340–68.
8 *Kriegsende und Neubeginn in Landkreis Eichsfeld 1945/1946* (Heiligenstadt 2003), p. 267.
9 The rumours at the time went in both directions. The

colonial soldiers were said to lust violently after German women, and German women to fraternize immorally with the enemy; see Christian Koller, 'Feind – Bilder: Rassen und Geschlechterstereotype in der Kolonialtruppendiskussion Deutschlands und Frankreichs, 1914–1923', in: Karen Hagemann, Ralf Pröve and Stefanie Schüler-Springorum (eds.), *Heimat-Front: Militär und Geschlechterverhältnisse im Zeitalter der Weltkriege* (Frankfurt 2002), pp. 150–67.

10 Kurt Redmer, *Die letzten und die ersten Tage: Dokumentation über Geschehnisse in Mecklenburg im 2. Weltkrieg und danach* (Schwerin 2007), pp. 121–8.

11 Goeschel, *Selbstmord im Dritten Reich*, p. 241.

12 Ibid.

13 Albin Segmüller, *Über reactive Selbstmorde und Selbstmordversuche in der Nachkriegszeit* (Nuremberg 1949).

14 Bundesministerium für Vertriebene (ed.), *Dokumentation der Vertreibung der Deutschen aus Ost-Mitteleuropa*, vol. I/1 (Bonn 1954–6), p. 226.

15 Goeschel, *Selbstmord im Dritten Reich*.

16 See Kershaw, *The End*, pp. 114–17, 120, 122.

17 Margret Boveri, *Tage des Überlebens: Berlin 1945* (Munich 1985), p. 43.

18 See Heinrich Schwendemann, 'Das Kriegsende im Ostpreussen und in Südbaden in Vergleich', in: Bernd Martin (ed.), *Der Zweite Weltkrieg und seine Folgen, Ereignisse, Auswirkungen, Reflexionen* (Berlin 2006), pp. 91–112.

19 Bundesministerium für Vertriebene (ed.), *Dokumentation der Vertreibung der Deutschen*, vol. I/1, pp. 28–31, 106.

20 Bärbel Gafert, 'Kinder der Flucht – Kinder der Vertreibung 1945–1948', in: *Deutschland-Archiv* 40, 4/6 (2007), pp. 833–5.

21 Leonie Biallas, *Komm, Frau, raboti: Ich war Kriegsbeute* (Leverkusen 2010), pp. 17–18.

22 Ibid., pp. 19–20.

23 Ingeborg Jacobs, *Freiwild: Das Schicksal deutscher Frauen 1945* (Berlin 2008), pp. 72–4.

24 Albrecht Lehmann, *Im Fremden ungewollt zuhaus: Flüchtlinge und Vertriebene in Westdeutschland 1945–1990* (Munich 1993).

25 Bundesministerium für Vertriebene (ed.), *Dokumentation der Vertreibung der Deutschen*, vol. I/1, p. 23.

26 Mathias Beer, 'Die Dokumentation der Vertreibung der Deutschen aus Ost-Mitteleuropa (1953–1962): Ein Seismograph bundesdeutscher Erinnerungskultur', in Jörg-Dieter Gauger and Manfred Kittel (eds.), *Die Vertreibung der Deutschen aus dem Osten in der Erinnerungskultur*, Eine Veröffentlichung der Konrad-Adenauer-Stiftung e.V. und des Instituts für Zeitgeschichte (Sankt Augustin 2004) pp. 17–37; for discussion on the victims, see pp. 17–31, here pp. 21–2.

27 For discussion of the documentation, see Robert G. Moeller, *War Stories: The Search for a Usable Past in the Federal Republic of Germany* (Berkeley 2001), pp. 51–87.

28 All names have been abbreviated in this book, even if they are named in the sources. In cases from very small villages or ones that are easily identifiable for other reasons, I have also changed the initials. I only give full names when the victims have published their stories under their own names.

29 Bundesministerium für Vertriebene (ed.), *Dokumentation der Vertreibung der*, vol. I/1, pp. 28–31.

30 Ibid., pp. 59–61.

31 Ibid., pp. 63–4.

32 Ibid., p. 101.

33 Ibid., p. 181.

34 Ibid., p. 196.

35 Ibid., p. 198.

36 Ibid., p. 223.

37 Ibid., p. 265.

38 Ibid., p. 268.

39 Ibid., p. 274.

40 Gela Volkmann-Steinhardt, *Eine Stimme aus der pommerschen Passion: Erlebnisse aus dem deutschen Zusammenbruch 1945* (Freiburg i. Brsg. 1993), p. 128.

41 Ibid., p. 135.

42 Gabi Köpp, *Warum war ich bloss ein Mädchen? Das Trauma einer Flucht 1945* (Munich 2010), pp. 78–9.

43 A. A. Smirnov, head of the IIIrd Section of the People's

Commissariat for Foreign Affairs of the USSR on 21 March 1945 on the situation in the German territories occupied by the Red Army, quoted in Scherstjanoi, *Rotarmisten schreiben aus Deutschland*, p. 121.

44 Ryan, *The Last Battle*, p. 328.

45 Ibid., p. 329.

46 Ibid., pp. 362–3.

47 Ibid., p. 363.

48 Ibid., p. 382.

49 Ibid., p. 383.

50 Ibid., p. 352.

51 Ruth Andreas-Friedrich, *Schauplatz Berlin: Ein deutsches Tagebuch* (Berlin 1964 [1946]), p. 193.

52 BA Koblenz B 126/28038 Berliner Finanzsenator on 28 March 1957.

53 Andreas-Friedrich, *Schauplatz Berlin*, pp. 215–16.

54 Landesarchiv Berlin C Rep. 118/398.

55 Regine Nohejl, 'Einführung: Nation und Gender in der russischen Kultur', in: Nohejl, Olga Gorfinkel, Friederike Carl and Elisabeth Cheauré (eds.), *Genderdiskurse und nationale Identität in Russland: Sowjetische und postsowjetische Zeit* (Munich 2013), pp. 7–16.

56 Naimark, *Die Russen in Deutschland*, p. 93.

57 See Erich Kuby, *Die Russen in Berlin* (Munich 1965), p. 304.

58 Kurt Arlt, '"Nach Berlin" – Der Kriegsverlauf an der Ostfront und seine Auswirkungen auf Motivationen und Stimmungen in der Roten Armee', in: Elke Scherstjanoi, *Rotarmisten schreiben aus Deutschland*, pp. 28–9.

59 Elke Scherstjanoi, 'Sowjetische Feldpostbriefe vom Ende des Grossen Vaterländischen Krieges als Quelle für historische Forschung', in: Scherstjanoi, *Rotarmisten schreiben aus Deutschland*, pp. 28–9.

60 Vladimir Gelfand, *Deutschland-Tagebuch*, pp. 13–14.

61 Ibid., p. 31.

62 Ibid., p. 44.

63 Ibid., pp. 79–80.

64 Ibid., p. 89.

65 Catherine Merridale, *Ivan's War: The Red Army, 1939–1945* (London 2005), p. 272.

66 Ibid.

67 For some years, attention has been paid in the Soviet Union as well to the situation in the last months of the war, and the treatment of the civilian population in the countries the advancing army battled through, although the subject of mass rape is still one that has not been studied to any great extent. All the same, there is now a good research basis on the Soviet view of the war and the German aggressor. The Department of Modern History in Munich, for example, compiles the research and publications of German and Soviet scholars and makes possible the publication of studies on the history of the mutual perceptions and attitudes of the Red Army and German civilians during the conquest and occupation of German territory.

These studies help us to understand the thinking of the Red Army soldiers, who are still seen as primarily responsible for the mass rape of German women. Elke Scherstjanoi has compiled a selection of 161 letters by Russian soldiers in the last months of the war, relating their attitudes and experiences in Germany. See Scherstjanoi, 'Sowjetische Feldpostbriefe', in: Scherstjanoi, *Rotarmisten schreiben aus Deutschland*, pp. 3–193.

68 Ibid., p. 31.

69 Ibid., p. 36.

70 Ibid., p. 39.

71 Ibid., p. 41.

72 Ibid., p. 42.

73 Ibid., p. 46.

74 Ibid., p. 52.

75 Aleksandr V. Perepelicyn and Natalya P. Timofeeva, *Das Deutschen-Bild in der sowjetischen Militärpropaganda während des Grossen Vaterländischen Krieges* (Munich, 2004), pp. 267–86.

76 Carola Tischler, 'Die Vereinfachungen des Genossen Ehrenburg: Eine Endkriegs- und eine Nachkriegskontroverse', in: Scherstjanoi, *Rotarmisten schreiben aus Deutschland*, pp. 326–39, here pp. 330–3.

77 Scherstjanoi, pp. 60–1.

78 Ibid., p. 114.
79 Ibid., p. 145.
80 Ibid., p. 132.
81 Ibid., p. 151.
82 Ibid., p. 160.
83 The motive of revenge is convincingly discussed by Norman M. Naimark, most recently in 'The Russians and Germans: Rape during the War and Post-Soviet Memories', in: Branche and Virgile (eds.), *Rape in Wartime*, pp. 201–19.
84 Merridale, *Ivan's War*, p. 263.
85 See Richard Bessel, *Germany 1945: From War to Peace* (London 2009), pp. 148–68.

3 South Germany – who will protect us from the Americans?

1 Stephan Hebel (ed.), *Alltag in Trümmern: Zeitzeugen berichten über das Kriegsende 1945* (Berlin 2005), p. 137.
2 Günter Sagan, *Kriegsende 1945: Die dramatischen Wochen vor und nach der Kapitulation* (Petersberg 2008).
3 Pfister, *Das Ende des Zweiten Weltkriegs*, pp. 844–5.
4 Ibid., pp. 842–53.
5 Ibid.
6 Ibid., p. 994.
7 Ibid., p. 1326.
8 Ibid., p. 1010.
9 Lilly, *Taken by Force*, p. 120.
10 Pfister, *Das Ende des Zweiten Weltkriegs*, p. 835.
11 Lilly, *Taken by Force*, p. 120.
12 This does not mean that GIs raped women of this age with greater frequency but rather that the perpetrators in these cases were more often brought to trial.
13 Lilly, *Taken by Force*, p. 144.
14 Pfister, *Das Ende des Zweiten Weltkriegs*, p. 571.
15 Ibid., p. 323.
16 Ibid., pp. 1386–7.
17 Ibid., p. 1130.
18 Ibid., p. 1167.
19 Ibid., p. 1317.

20 See Anthony D. Kauders, *Democratisation and the Jews: Munich 1945–1965* (Lincoln, NE 2004).
21 Pfister, *Das Ende des Zweiten Weltkriegs*, p. 626.
22 Ibid., p. 502.
23 Ibid., p. 563.
24 Ibid., p. 489.
25 Ibid., p. 491.
26 Ibid., p. 437.
27 Ibid., p. 556.
28 Ibid., p. 568.
29 Ibid., p. 585.
30 Ibid., p. 328.
31 We have precise figures for victims from the following places: one from Helfendorf, four from Haag an der Amper (including 'an unblemished girl of sixteen, one married and one single woman'), six in the parish of Litzdorf (four peasant girls, one evacuee and one army helper), three in Tuntenhausen, five to ten in Dorfen, eight in the parish of Ramsau, ten in Schwindkirchen ('virtuous women and girls'), eight 'serious cases' in Taufkirchen an der Vils, one in Trudering, two married women in Hörgersdorf, one 63-year-old woman in Kirchasch, one in Alling, three in Gerlinden bei Maisach, one in Inkofen, one 17-year-old in Ensdorf, one married woman and three girls in Grossholzhausen, one in Mailling, three in Pfarrenhofen am Inn, one near-rape in Böbing ('a 15-year-old had a narrow escape'), one in Obermarbach, one 7-year-old girl in Scheyern, who was infected with gonorrhoea, one in Frasdorf, two in Zaisering, one in Osterwarngau, one mother of four children in Steingau/Otterfing, one married woman and two girls in Petting, two in Teisendorf, two in Otting, six to eight in Siegsdorf, two in Vachendorf, two in Lohkirchen, one in Niedertaufkirchen, eight in Oberbergkirchen, one in Oberwarngau, six or seven in Ranoldsberg, two in Schönberg, four in Stefanskirchen (including a 69-year-old woman), two in Baierbach, five in Hohenpolding, one in Pauluszell, one in Babensham, one in Fürholzen, one in Langenbach, and three in Lengries.
32 Pfister, *Das Ende des Zweiten Weltkriegs*, p. 1087.
33 Ibid., pp. 1193–4.

34 Ibid., p. 1252.
35 Ibid., p. 1260.
36 Lilly, *Taken by Force*, p. 163; see also Mary Louise Roberts, *What Soldiers Do: Sex and the American GI in World War II France* (Chicago 2013), pp. 222–4.
37 Pfister, *Das Ende des Zweiten Weltkriegs*, p. 1352.
38 National Archives, Headquarters XX Corps Office of the Provost Marshal, Reply to questions on rape, file no. 70, 5 June 1945: Rape of German Women by American Soldiers (National Archives ID: 6081861).
39 Ibid.
40 Ibid.
41 Lilly, *Taken by Force*, p. 149.
42 Erika Hoerning, 'Frauen als Kriegsbeute: Der Zwei-Fronten-Krieg, Beispiele aus Berlin', in: Lutz Niethammer and Alexander von Plato (eds.), *'Wir kriegen jetzt andere Zeiten': Auf der Suche nach der Erfahrung des Volkes in nachfaschistischen Ländern* (Bonn 1985), pp. 327–44, here p. 334.
43 Lilly, *Taken by Force*, p. 146.
44 Ibid., pp. 151–2.
45 Andreas Reckwitz, 'Umkämpfte Maskulinität: Zur historischen Kultursoziologie männlicher Subjektformen und ihrer Affektivitäten vom Zeitalter der Empfindsamkeit bis zur Postmoderne', in: Borutta and Verheyen (eds.), *Die Präsenz der Gefühle*, pp. 57–80, here p. 67.
46 *Meyers Grosses Konversationslexikon* of 1905 states: 'The nervous system in general is more irritable in the female sex . . . There are also mental gender differences; in women feelings and emotions have the upper hand, in men intelligence and reason; women have a more lively imagination than men but it rarely achieves the same heights and boldness as in men.' Quoted in Angelika Schaser, *Frauenbewegung in Deutschland: 1848 bis 1933* (Dortmund 2006), p. 69.
47 Women were enlisted into fighting units in the Red Army and fought alongside their male colleagues. After the invasion by Nazi Germany, it was the patriotic duty of both men and women to defend their homeland. Some 800,000 women served in the army,

navy and air force or on the home front, and from 1942 they were trained in special facilities as snipers, pilots or military officers. The ideal, as in Germany, was nevertheless a strong and independent woman on the home front to take the place of the men and at the same time to keep the home fires burning for the returning troops.

48 Reckwitz, 'Umkämpfte Maskulinität'.

49 Frank Werner, '"Noch härter, noch kälter, noch mitleidloser": Soldatische Männlichkeit im deutschen Vernichtungskrieg 1941–1944', in: Anette Dietrich and Ljiljana Heise (eds.), *Männlichkeitskonstruktionen im Nationalsozialismus* (Frankfurt 2003), pp. 45–63, 51.

50 See Sonya O. Rose, 'Temperate Heroes: Concepts of Masculinity in Second World War Britain', in: Stefan Dudink, Karen Hagemann and John Tosh, *Masculinities in Politics and War: Gendering Modern History* (Manchester 2004), pp. 177–95.

51 Thomas Kühne, 'Zärtlichkeit und Zynismus: Militärische Vergemeinschaftung 1918–1945', in: Borutta and Verheyen (eds.), *Die Präsenz der Gefühle*, pp. 179–202, here p. 183.

52 Ibid., p. 191.

53 Merridale, *Ivan's War*, p. 267.

54 Ibid., p. 268.

55 Gaby Zipfel, 'Ausnahmezustand Krieg?', in: Insa Eschebach and Regina Mühlhäuser (eds.), *Krieg und Geschlect: Sexuelle Gewalt im Krieg und Sex-Zwangsarbeit in NS-Konzentrationslagern* (Berlin 2008), pp. 55–74; see also Miranda Alison, 'Sexuelle Gewalt in Zeiten des Kriegs: Menschenrechte für Frauen und Vorstellungen von Männlichkeit', in: Eschebach and Mühlhäuser (eds.), *Krieg und Geschlect*, pp. 35–54.

56 John Horne, 'Masculinity in Politics and War in the Age of Nation-States and World Wars, 1850–1950', in: Dudink et al., *Masculinities*, p. 33.

57 Angela Koch, 'Die Verletzung der Gemeinschaft: Zur Relation der Wort- und Ideengeschichte von "Vergewaltigung"', in: *Österreichische Zeitschrift für Geschichtswissenschaft* 15, 1 (2004), pp. 37–56, here p. 46.

58 Roberts, *What Soldiers Do*, pp. 62–3.

59 Ibid., p. 7.
60 Ibid., p. 9.
61 This is still disproportionate to the percentage of African American soldiers in the military: ibid., p. 196.
62 Petra Goedde, *GIs and Germans: Culture, Gender, and Foreign Relations 1945–1949* (New Haven and London 2003), p. 83.
63 Karen Hagemann, 'Heimat-Front: Militär, Gewalt und Geschlechterverhältnisse im Zeitalter der Weltkriege', in: Hageman et al. (eds.), *Heimat-Front*, pp. 13–52, here p. 40.
64 Quoted in Goedde, *GIs and Germans*, p. 84.
65 Ibid., pp. 220–1.
66 Staatsarchiv München, Zur Sicherheitslage, Wochenbericht Bürgermeister von Bad Wiessee an den Landrat Miesbach, Wochenbericht 23–29 July 1945, LRA 148574.
67 See Christian T. Müller, *US-Truppen und Sowjetarmee in Deutschland: Erfahrungen, Beziehungen, Konflikte im Vergleich* (Paderborn 2011).
68 Ibid., pp. 220–1.
69 Staatsarchiv München, LRA 214430 Traunstein 16 May 1946.
70 Staatsarchiv München, LRA 148575.
71 Staatsarchiv München, LRA 148576.
72 Federal Minister of Justice to the German Child Protection League on 21 September 1946.
73 BayHStaA, MInn 91951, Sicherheitsstörungen ausländischer Streitkräfte allg. 1959–1961.
74 *Der Spiegel*, 45 (1963); online archive www.spiegel.de/spiegel/print/d-46172639.html.
75 Polizeidirektion Würzburg, 13 April 1952, BayHStA, MInn 80209.
76 BayHStA, MInn 80209, letter of 28 December 1951.
77 Bavarian President to Oron J. Hale on 11 January 1952, BayHStA, MInn 80209.
78 Sicherheitsstörungen durch Angehörige der Besatzungsmacht, Bayerisches Innenministerium on 30 January 1953, BayHStA, MInn 80209.
79 Innenministerium to Bayer. Staatskanzlei on 17 October 1953, BayHStA, Minn 80209.

4 Pregnant, sick, ostracized – approaches to the victims

1 Köpp, *Warum war ich bloss ein Mädchen?*, p. 137.
2 Margret S. on 12 December 1958 to the Federal Minister for Social Affairs, BA Koblenz B/126/5548.
3 BA Koblenz B/126/5548, petition to the Federal Ministry of the Interior of 12 June 1951, allowance for children resulting from enemy rape.
4 Landesarchiv Nordrhein-Westfalen, Amt für Verteidigungslasten Düsseldorf, BR 2076 No. 412.
5 Pfister, *Das Ende des Zweiten Weltkriegs*, p. 923; see also Susanne zur Nieden, 'Erotische Fraternisierung: Der Mythos von der schnellen Kapitulation der deutschen Frauen im May 1945', in: Hagemann et al. (eds.), *Heimat-Front*, pp. 313–25.
6 Klaus-Dietmar Henke, *Die amerikanische Besatzung Deutschlands* (Munich 1996), p. 188.
7 See Petra Goedde, 'From Villains to Victims: Fraternization and the Feminization of Germany, 1945–1947', in: *Diplomatic History* 23, 1 (winter 1999), pp. 1–20.
8 The Bodleian Library (ed.), *Instructions for British Servicemen in Germany*, issued by The Foreign Office, London, pp. 42–3, 63.
9 See Maria Höhn, *GIs and Fräuleins: The German–American Encounter in 1950s West Germany* (Chapel Hill and London 2002), particularly pp. 126–54.
10 *Fränkischer Tag* of 21 September 1945, quoted in Peter Zorn, '"Ami-Liebchen" and "Veronika Dankeschön" – Bamberg 1945–1952: Deutsche Frauen und amerikanische Soldaten', in: *Geschichte quer* 11 (2003), pp. 39–42, here p. 41.
11 See also Barbara Willenbacher, 'Zerrüttung und Bewährung der Nachkriegsfamilie', in: Martin Broszat, Klaus-Dietmar Henke, Hans Woller et al. (eds.), *Von Stalingrad zur Währungsreform: zur Sozialgeschichte des Umbruchs in Deutschland* (Munich 1990), pp. 595–614.
12 Almuth Roelfs, '"Ami-Liebchen" und "Berufsbräute": Prostitution, Geschlechtskrankheiten und Besatzung in der Nachkriegszeit', in: Günter Kronenbitter et al. (eds.), *Besatzung, Funktion und Gestalt militärischer Fremdherrschaft von der Antike bis zum 20. Jahrhundert* (Paderborn et al. 2006), pp. 201–10, here p. 205.

13 Pfister, *Das Ende des Zweiten Weltkriegs*, p. 668.

14 Ibid., p. 832.

15 Henke, *Die amerikanische Besatzung Deutschlands*, particularly pp. 190–6.

16 Sagan, *Kriegsende 1945*.

17 Even if there were a large number of unreported cases, this was 'not a lot given the fact that, for example, 900 people were convicted of rape in 1939 or that in 1950 the police in Bavaria alone investigated over 500 German citizens on charges of rape. These figures are a clear indication of the relative lack of violence by the US army towards the civilian population during the occupation of Germany.' The comparison is false, of course. For one thing, the author uses area as a parameter (instead of the male population), which makes no sense because the Americans were not stationed all over Germany. In addition, the cases of rape reported to the police before and after the war cannot be compared with the documented cases at the end of the war, because it was almost impossible for German civilians to report crimes. See Henke, *Die amerikanische Besatzung Deutschlands*, pp. 1038–9.

18 Ibid., p. 44.

19 Dietrich Güstrow, *In jenen Jahren: Aufzeichnungen eines 'befreiten' Deutschen* (Munich 1983), p. 34.

20 Letter from a soldier in the Field Artillery Battalion of the 99th Infantry Division, quoted in Henke, *Die amerikanische Besatzung Deutschlands*, p. 195.

21 Thus, in my opinion, the assumption that there were few cases of rape among the American occupiers, but rather consensual sexual relationships, is based on extremely unclear sources. Testimony at the time was almost always given by biased witnesses: by men who had been defeated in battle and transformed their military defeat into a moral defeat by their women, or by soldiers in the conquering army flaunting their heroic sexual exploits. The reports of allegedly consensual sexual contacts also come from soldiers who had been infected with venereal diseases and had to endure highly embarrassing questions from doctors, or – another often cited source – from clerical or other authorities (for example, the American anti-prostitution feminists, representatives of the

American 'social purity movement'), who also had their own moral agenda.

22 Konrad Jarausch, *Die Umkehr: Deutsche Wandlungen 1945–1995* (Munich 2004), p. 141.

23 Jennifer V. Evans, 'Protection from the Protector, Court-Martial Cases and the Lawlessness of Occupation in American-Controlled Berlin', in: Maulucci and Junker, *GIs in Germany*, pp. 212–33, here p. 233.

24 See Sybille Steinbacher, *Wie der Sex nach Deutschland kam: Der Kampf um Sittlichkeit und Anstand in der frühen Bundesrepublik* (Munich 2011), pp. 21–134; Eva-Maria Silies, *Liebe, Lust und Last: Die Pille als weibliche Generationserfahrung in der Bundesrepublik 1960–1980* (Göttingen 2010), pp. 37–61.

25 See Höhn, *GIs and Fräuleins*, pp. 153–4.

26 See Jens Hacke, *Philosophie der Bürgerlichkeit: Die liberalkon-servative Gründung der Bundesrepublik* (Göttingen 2006), pp. 14–15, 36. On the desire for inner stability, see also Ulrich Herbert, 'Liberalisierung als Lernprozess: Die Bundesrepublik in der deutschen Geschichte – eine Skizze', in: Herbert (ed.), *Wandlungsprozesse in Westdeutschland: Belastung, Integration, Liberalisierung 1945–1980* (Göttingen 2003), pp. 7–49.

27 Pfister, *Das Ende des Zweiten Weltkriegs*, pp. 602–3.

28 Expositus Georg Pfister on 19 July 1945 in Pfister, *Das Ende des Zweiten Weltkriegs*, p. 465.

29 See Elizabeth Heineman, 'The Hour of the Woman: Memories of Germany's "Crisis Years" and West German National Identity', in: *The American Historical Review*, 101, 2 (April 1966), pp. 354–95.

30 Quoted in Eva Gehltomholt and Sabine Hering, *Das verwahrloste Kind: Diagnostik and Fürsorge in der Jugendhilfe zwischen Kriegsende und Reform (1945–1965)* (Opladen 2005), pp. 174–5.

31 'Die Bedeutung der Kriegs- und Nachkriegszeit für die Entwicklung des Kindes, Referat von Werner Villinger (Marburg/L.)', in: *Monatsschrift für Kinderheilkunde* 103, 2 (January 1955), Verhandlung der 54. Ordentlichen Versammlung der Deutschen Gesellschaft für Kinderheilkunde in Essen 1954, pp. 65–72.

32 Gehltomholt and Hering, *Das verwahrloste Kind*, p. 123.

33 Ibid., p. 41.

34 Staatsarchiv München RA 77674.

35 Ibid.

36 Staatsarchiv München, LRA Traunstein, Kriminalpolizei, Sicherheitszustand im Land Bayern, Lagebericht für November 1946.

37 *Kreiegsende und Neubeginn im Landkreis Eichsfeld 1945/46: Eine zeitgenössische Documentation – im Auftrag des Landkreises Eichsfeld, der Stadt Heilbad Heiligenstadt und des Bischöflichen Geistlichen Kommissariates Heiligenstadt* (Eichsfeld 2003), p. 210.

38 Landesarchiv Berlin, DQ/1/1027.

39 Bundesarchiv Lichterfeld DQ1 No. 1610, Bekämpfung von Geschlechtskrankheiten.

40 Elizabeth D. Heineman, *What Difference Does A Husband Make? Women and Marital Status in Nazi and Postwar Germany* (Berkeley 1999), p. 102.

41 Bundesarchiv Lichterfeld DQ1 No. 1610.

42 Goedde, *GIs and Germans*, p. 92.

43 Bundesarchiv Lichterfeld DQ1 No. 1610.

44 Bundesarchiv Lichterfeld DQ1 No. 16, Zur Mitarbeit der Ärzteschaft im Kampf gegen die Geschlechtskrankheiten by Dr. Teller, 7 September 1946.

45 Stefan Grüner, 'Nachkriegszeit 1945–1957: Alltag, Besatzung, politischer und wirtschaftlicher Neuaufbau', in: Volker Dotterweich and Karl Filser (eds.), *Landsberg in der Zeitgeschichte, Zeitgeschichte in Landsberg* (Munich 2010), pp. 351–400.

46 Landesarchiv Berlin, Ministerium des Innern, Bestand Nr. 9, Der Polizeipräsident in Berlin, Ereignismeldungen – Meldungen an die Präsidialabteilung über wichtige Ereignisse aus den Inspektionsbereichen, 9/0284 an den Polizeipräsidenten von Berlin.

47 Else Baumann-Meyer, *'Manches vergisst man eben nie' – Aus dem Leben einer Arbeiterin* (Oldenburg 2000), pp. 53–6.

48 In the Soviet occupied zone, there were not only medical and ethical indications but also social ones. For the health authorities, the social situation of the pregnant woman was the determining factor in their decision whether to approve an abortion; see Silke Satjukov, '"Besatzungskinder": Nachkommen deutscher Frauen

und alliierter Soldaten seit 1945', in: *Geschichte und Gesellschaft* 37 (2011), pp. 1–33, here p. 6.

49 Jacobs, *Freiwild*, pp. 72–4.

50 See Kirsten Poutrous, 'Von den Massenvergewaltigungen zum Mutterschutzgesetz: Abtreibungspolitik und Abtreibungspraxis in Ostdeutschland, 1945–1950', in Richard Bessel and Ralph Jessen (eds.), *Die Grenzen der Diktatur: Staat und Gesellschaft in der DDR* (Göttingen 1996), pp. 170–98.

51 Grossmann, *A Question of Silence*, pp. 44–5.

52 See Poutrous, 'Von den Massenvergewaltigungen zum Mutterschützgesetz'.

53 Ibid.

54 My research also disagrees in this regard with Satjukow, 'Besatzungskinder', in terms both of numbers and of the frequency of abortions and institutionalization.

55 Karl-Heinz Mehlan, *Die Problematik der Schwangerschaftsunter-brechung auf Grund der sozialen Indikation* (Berlin 1956), pp. 131–2. For the legal situation in the Soviet occupied zone and in East Germany, see Poutrous, 'Von den Massenvergewaltigungen zum Mutterschutzgesetz'.

56 Fritz Naton, 'Schwangerschaftsunterbrechung nach Sittlich-keitsverbrechen', diss., Ludwig Maximilian University of Munich, 5 April 1952.

57 Satjukow, 'Besatzungskinder', p. 6.

58 State Health Department of Garmisch-Partenkirchen on 6 December 1945 to Military Government, BayHStA5086a, Bavarian State Ministry of the Interior regarding pregnancy ter-mination, abortion, premature births and miscarriages.

59 Hauptstaatsarchiv Stuttgart OMGUS 12/27–1–9/5, internal memo of 6 April 1946, quoted in Satjukow, 'Besatzungskinder', p. 6.

60 K. S. to Military Government in Munich on 18 September 1946, BayHStA 5086a.

61 Medical Council of Bavaria to Bavarian Ministry of the Interior on 18 October 1945, BayHStA 5086a, Bavarian State Ministry of the Interior regarding pregnancy termination, abortion, premature births and miscarriages.

62 Ibid., I. O. to American Military Government on 1 October 1945.

63 Ibid., letter of 17 December 1946.

64 Ibid., Bavarian Ministry of Justice on 19 December 1946 to the Public Prosecutors in Munich, Nuremberg and Bamberg.

65 Letter from a doctor to the head of the State Health Department of 22 January 1948.

66 All of the following cases: Landesarchiv Berlin, Neukölln Department of Health, affidavits, Rep. 214 no. 94.

67 BayHStaA MInn 81091 6726 – Processing of child maintenance claims against members of foreign armed forces 1958–60.

68 BayHStaA MInn 81091 – Report of juvenile departments in 1953, supplement to 6726.

69 Of 100 white and half-caste illegitimate occupation children in Bavaria, in 1954 70 and 61, respectively, lived with their mothers, 16 and 10 with relatives, 9 and 14 with distant relatives, and 5 and 15 in homes. Thus 95 per cent and 85 per cent respectively lived with close relatives. The records explicitly point out that the placement of half-caste children in foster families 'in general did not meet with the resistance that had originally been feared': BayHStA MInn 81094, supp. no. 3 to 67261.

70 BA Koblenz B 153/342.

71 Ibid.

72 Bavarian State Ministry of Justice on 23 April 1956 to the Federal Minister of Justice, BayHStA MInn 81087.

73 Satjukow, 'Besatzungskinder', p. 11.

74 Ibid., p. 14.

75 See Naimark, *The Russians and Germans*, p. 205.

76 *G. and E. v. H.* in a letter to the Petition Committee of the German Bundestag on 24 February 1958, BA Koblenz B/126/5548.

77 BA Koblenz B/126/5548, Applications to the Federal Ministry of Finance to grant compensation for rapes before 1 August and outside the federal territory; letter of 5 March 1951.

78 BA Koblenz B/126/5548, Application to the Federal Ministry of the Interior of 12 June 1951, maintenance for children resulting from rape by the enemy.

79 BA Koblenz B/126/5548, letter of 27 April 1951.

80 SPD press service, August 1856. Nadig was a member of the

Committee for the British Occupation Zone. She was appointed to the Parliamentary Council in 1948 and worked on the Basic Law. She was one of the women responsible for Article 3 (Equality before the law) and she fought, albeit without success, for equal pay for men and women for equal work and for equality before the law for illegitimate children.

81 To the Petition Committee of the German Bundestag, 27 July 1956, Occupation Damage, application by Paul Skriewe, Heroldsberg bei Nürnberg of 22 November 1955, BHStaA MInn 81085.

82 BayHStA MInn, 81085, suppl. no. 1 to 6726.

83 BayHStA MInn 81085.

84 BA Koblenz B 126/28038, Berlin Senator for Finance, 28 March 1957.

85 Federal Ministry of the Interior to Federal Ministry of Finance of 28 August 1956; BA Koblenz B 126/28038.

86 Letter from the Federal Ministry of the Interior on 5 July 1960.

87 BayHStA MInn 81086, 26 March 1954, Federal Minister of the Interior to the Bavarian State Ministry.

88 BayHSta MInn 81086.

89 Ibid.

90 See Bernd Serger, Karin-Anne Böttcher and Gerd R. Ueberschär (eds.), *Südbaden unter Hakenkreuz und Trikolore: Zeitzeugen berichten über das Kriegsende und die französische Besetzung 1945* (Freiburg 2006).

91 BA Koblenz 153/342, Statistisches Landesamt Baden-Württemberg, census of illegitimate occupation children of 30 May 1955.

92 Quoted in Edgar Wolfrum, 'Das Bild der "düsteren Franzosenzeit": Alltagsnot, Meinungsklima und Demokratisierungspolitik in der französischen Besatzungszone nach 1945', in: Stefan Martens (ed.), *Vom 'Erbfeind' zum 'Erneuerer': Aspekte und Motive der französischen Deutschlandpolitik nach dem Zweiten Weltkrieg* (suppl. to *Francia* 27, edited by Deutsches Historisches Institut Paris) (Sigmaringen 1993), pp. 87–113.

93 Marc Hillel, *L'occupation française en Allemagne, 1945–49* (Saint-Armand-Montrand 1983), pp. 83, 108–11, quoted in Perry

Biddiscombe, 'Dangerous Liaisons: The Anti-Fraternization Movement in the US Occupation Zones of Germany and Austria, 1945–1948', in: *Journal of Social History* 34, 3 (2001), p. 635.

94 Serger et al., *Südbaden unter Hakenkreuz*, p. 311.

95 Schwendemann, 'Das Kriegsende in Ostpreussen', p. 105.

96 Quoted in ibid., p. 106.

97 In view of the fact that some of the villages and hamlets are very small, I have changed the initials of the victims. The following cases come from the Landesarchiv Baden-Württemberg / Staatsarchiv Freiburg, Bestand D 5/1 Einzelfälle.

98 Staatsarchiv Freiburg, compensation court, individual cases; letters from welfare worker of 12 December 1948, 17 April 1951, D 5/1 5295.

99 Ibid., D 5/1 5387.

100 Ibid., D 5/1 5606.

101 Ibid., D 5/1 5228.

102 Ibid.

103 Ibid., D 5/1 5421.

104 Ibid., D 5/1 5408.

105 Ibid., D 5/1 5517.

106 Ibid., D 5/1 4925.

107 BA Koblenz B/126/28038.

108 H. R. to the Federal Minister of Finance on 14 January 1959, BA Koblenz.

109 I. D. on 19 July 1957 to the Federal Minister of Finance, BA Koblenz B/126/5548.

110 H. S. on 25 July 1959 to the Federal Chancellor, BA Koblenz B/126/5548.

111 Letter to Federal Minister for Family Affairs Franz-Josef Wuermeling, BA Koblenz B/126/5548.

112 Satjukow, 'Besatzungskinder', p. 10.

113 To Federal President Heuss, BA Koblenz 28 November 1957, BA Koblenz B/126/5548.

114 Staatsarchiv Freiburg, compensation court, individual cases, D 5/1 5047.

115 Ibid., D 5/1 5325.

116 Ibid., D 5/1 5312.

5 *The long shadow*

1 Eva Ebner, assistant director, who worked with Fritz Lang and Rainer Werner Fassbinder, was born in 1922 in Danzig/Gdansk to a Jewish mother. At the end of the war she fled and hid in a portside barracks, where she was found by Red Army soldiers and raped for over two hours. She passed up the opportunity to identify the perpetrators in a line-up and have them punished, which in retrospect she realized was the best thing she had done in her life because in doing so she had prevented further senseless killing (Hildebrandt and Kuballa (eds.), *Mein Kriegsende*, pp. 31–2).

2 Staatsarchiv Frankfurt, compensation court, individual cases, D 5/1 3889.

3 This comment was made during a discussion with Wolf Jobst Siedler and Martin Walser in *Die Zeit* entitled: 'Können wir uns einen Ilja Ehrenburg leisten?', quoted in Tischler, 'Die Vereinfachungen des Genossen Ehrenburg', pp. 326–39.

4 Segmüller, *Über reactive Selbstmorde und Selbstmordversuche*.

5 Ibid., p. 37.

6 Svenja Eichhorn et al., 'Bewältigungsstrategien und wahrgenommene soziale Unterstützung bei deutschen Langzeitüberlebenden der Verwaltigungen am Ende des II. Weltkriegs', in: *Psychiatrische Praxis* 39 (2012), pp. 169–73, here p. 169; see also Eichhorn and Kuwert, *Das Geheimnis der Grossmütter*.

7 Eichhorn and Kuwert, *Das Geheimnis der Grossmütter*, p. 94.

8 See Miriam Gebhardt, *Die Angst vor dem kindlichen Tyrannen: Eine Geschichte der Erziehung im 20. Jahrhundert* (Munich 2009).

9 Vera Neumann, 'Kampf um Anerkennung: Die westdeutsche Kriegsfolgengesellschaft im Spiegel der Versorgungsämter', in: Naumann, *Nachkrieg in Deutschland*, pp. 364–83.

10 'GItrace' (www.gitrace.org), the platform 'Children born of the war' (www.bowin.eu) and the Boltzmann Institute (www.bim.lbg.ac.at). In Russia there is a television programme entitled *Zhdi menya* ('Wait for me') for those seeking relatives.

11 Köpp, *Warum war ich bloss ein Mädchen?* p. 9.

12 See Svenja Goltermann, *Die Gesellschaft der Überlebenden: Deutsche Kriegsheimkehrer und ihre Gewalterfahrungen im Zweiten Weltkrieg* (Munich 2009).

13 The popularity of the concept of trauma and its inflationary position today, also in the humanities and in popular discourse, began in the 1970s. For the critical relationship between the concept of clinical trauma and its appropriation by the humanities, see Harald Weilnböck, '"Das Trauma muss dem Gedächtnis unverfügbar bleiben": Trauma-Ontologie und anderer Miss-/Brauch von Traumakonzepten in geisteswissenschaftlichen Diskursen', in: *Mittelweg* 36, Zeitschrift des Hamburger Instituts für Sozialforschung (April 2007), pp. 2–64.

14 Staatsarchiv Freiburg, compensation court, individual cases, 3889; name abbreviated to protect the patient.

15 Ibid.

16 Svenja Goltermann, 'Im Wahn der Gewalt: Massentod, Opferdiskurs und Psychiatrie 1945–1956', in: Naumann, *Nachkrieg in Deutschland*, pp. 343–63, here pp. 358–9.

17 Some formulations recur in current research literature, particularly the thesis by Kuby of the women's 'surprisingly rapid' convalescence; see Naimark, *Die Russen in Deutschland*, pp. 162–3; Sibylle Meyer and Eva Schulze, 'Als wir wieder zusammen waren, ging der Krieg im Kleinen weiter', in: Niethammer and Plato (eds.), *Wir kriegen jetzt andere Zeiten*, pp. 305–26.

18 Regina Mühlhäuser, 'Massenvergewaltigungen in Berlin 1945 im Gedächtnis betroffener Frauen: Zur Verwobenheit von nationalistischen, rassistischen und geschlechtsspezifischen Diskursen', in: Veronika Aegerter et al. (eds.), *Geschlecht hat Methode: Ansätze und Perspektiven in der Frauen- und Geschlechtergeschichte* (contribution to the Ninth Swiss Historians' Conference 1988) (Zurich 1999), pp. 235–46, here p. 239; see also Mühlhäuser, *Vergewaltigungen in Deutschland 1945*, p. 389; Atina Grossmann, 'Eine Frage des Schweigens: Die Vergewaltigung deutscher Frauen durch Besatzungssoldaten – Zum historischen Hintergrund von Helke Sanders Film BeFreier und Befreite', in: *Frauen und Film* 54/55 (1994), pp. 14–28, here pp. 19, 21; Grossmann, 'A Question of Silence'; Hsu-Ming Teo, 'The Continuum of Sexual Violence in Occupied Germany, 1945–1949', in: *Women's History Review* 5, 2 (1996), pp. 191–218, here p. 193; Sibylle Meyer and Eva Schulze, *Wie wir das alles geschafft haben: Alleinstehende Frauen berichten über*

ihr Leben nach 1945 (Munich 1993), p. 64; also sceptical of the resilience thesis: Naimark, *Die Russen in Deutschland*, pp. 162–3.

19 Pauline Nyiramasuhuko, the former Minister for Family Affairs, who organized massacres and encouraged sexual assaults on Tutsi women. There were also women soldiers in the Red Army who were at least approving bystanders. In civilian life, women are also instigators, accomplices and perpetrators of sexual violence against women and men. In a group rape in Munich in 2014, two teenage girls lulled their two female victims into a false sense of security before abusing them sexually and then handing them over to male rapists.

20 Erich Kuby, 'Die Russen in Berlin', in: *Der Spiegel* 19/1965–24/1965; Kuby, *Die Russen in Berlin*.

21 Kuby, *Die Russen in Berlin*, p. 213.

22 Ibid., pp. 314–15.

23 Ibid., p. 308.

24 Richard Bessel, 'Was bleibt vom Krieg? Deutsche Nachkriegs-geschichte(n) aus geschlechtergeschichtlicher Perspektive: Eine Einführung', in: *Militärgeschichtliche Zeitschrift* 60 (2001), pp. 297–305, here p. 298.

25 Naimark, *Die Russen in Deutschland*, p. 300.

26 Robert G. Moeller, 'Heimkehr ins Vaterland: Die Remaskulinisierung Westdeutschlands in den fünfziger Jahren', in: *Militärgeschichtliche Zeitschrift* 60 (2001), pp. 403–36.

27 Heimatmuseum Charlottenburg, exhibition 'Worüber kaum gesprochen wurde: Frauen und allierte Soldaten', 3–15 October 1995.

28 Meyer and Schulze, 'Als wir wieder zusammen waren', p. 313.

29 Ibid., p. 314.

30 Ibid., p. 316.

31 Sibylle Meyer and Eva Schulze, *Von Liebe sprach damals keiner: Familienalltag in der Nachkriegszeit* (Munich 1985), p. 134.

32 Heineman, *The Hour of the Woman*, p. 370.

33 Mühlhäuser, 'Vergewaltigungen in Deutschland', pp. 390–1.

34 Maria Höhn, 'Frau im Haus and Girl im Spiegel: Discourse on Women in the Interregnum Period of 1945–1949 and the Question of German Identity', in: *Central European History* 26, 1

(1993), pp. 57–90, here p. 89; see also Annette Kuhn, 'Power and Powerlessness: Women after 1945, or Continuity of the Ideology of Femininity', in: *German History* 7, 1 (1989), pp. 35–46.

35 See also Leonie Treber, *Mythos Trümmerfrauen: Von der Trümmerbeseitigung in der Kriegs- und Nachkriegszeit und der Entstehung eines deutschen Erinnerungsortes* (Essen 2014).

36 Mühlhäuser, 'Massenvergewaltigungen in Berlin', p. 239.

37 Quoted in ibid., p. 389.

38 Quoted in Hildebrandt and Kubella (eds.), *Mein Kriegsende*, p. 32.

39 Frank Biess, 'Pioneers of a New Germany: Returning POWs from the Soviet Union and the Making of East German Citizens 1945–1950', in: *Central European History* 32 (2000), p. 166.

40 See speeches and publications on the tenth anniversary of the International Criminal Court on the medica mondiale website, www.medicamondiale.org.

41 *Der Spiegel*, 30 March 1960.

42 *Telegraf*, Berlin, 29 November 1959.

43 *Tagesspiegel*, 6 December 1959, from the newspaper cutting collection for the exhibition 'Worüber kaum gesprochen wurde: Frauen und alliierte Soldaten', in: *Material zur Ausstellung des Heimatmuseums Charlottenburg, 3.–15.10.1995.*

44 Ibid., eyewitness accounts in Museum Charlottenburg.

45 https://en.wikipedia.org/wiki/A_Woman_in_Berlin.

46 *Frankfurter Allgemeine Zeitung*, 21 June 2003, p. 44.

47 Bisky, 'Wenn Jungen Weltgeschichte spielen.

48 Anonymous, *A Woman in Berlin – Eight Weeks in the Conquered City: A Diary* (London 1982).

49 Ibid.

50 Ibid.

51 Ibid.

52 Ibid.

53 Ibid.

54 Ibid.

55 Ibid.

56 Ibid.

57 Bisky, 'Wenn Jungen Weltgeschichte spielen'.

58 Ibid.

59 For a detailed discussion of Bisky's reservations, see also Constanze Jaiser, review of *Anonyma – Eine Frau in Berlin, Tagesbuchaufzeichnungen vom 20. April bis 22. Juni 1945* (Frankfurt 2003), in: *H-Soz-u-Kult*, 5 December 2003, http://hsozkult. geschichte.hu-berlin.de/rezensionen/2003-4-128.

60 Susanne zur Nieden, *Alltag im Ausnahmezustand: Frauentagebücher im zerstörten Deutschland 1943 bis 1945* (Berlin 1993). A number of works have been published on research into personal testimony, including by the author; see, for example, 'Der Fall Clara Geissmar, oder von der Verführungskunst weiblicher Autobiographik', in: Kirsten Heinsohn and Stefanie Schüler-Springorum (eds.), *Deutsch-jüdische Geschichte als Geschlechtergeschichte: Studien zum 19. und 20. Jahrhundert* (Göttingen 2006), pp. 233–49; more generally, Dagmar Günther, 'And now for something completely different: prolegomena zur Autobiographie als Quelle der Geschichtswissenschaft', in: *Historische Zeitschrift*, 272 (2001), pp. 25–61.

61 Silke Satjukow, *Befreiung? Die Ostdeutschen und 1945* (Leipzig 2009), p. 7.

62 Jarausch, *Die Umkehr*, p. 150.

63 Ibid., pp. 15–16.

64 Egon Renztsch, head of the Literature and Book Department in the Ministry of Culture on 27 September 1961, quoted in Birgit Dahlke, '"Frau Komm!" Vergewaltigungen 1945: Zur Geschichte eines Diskurses', in: Dahlke et al. (eds.), *LiteraturGesellschaft DDR: Kanonkämpfe und ihre Geschichte(n)* (Stuttgart 2000), pp. 272–311, here p. 293.

65 Jarausch, *Die Umkehr*, p. 46.

66 Ibid., p. 159.

67 *Süddeutsche Zeitung*, 9 January 1952, BayHStaA, breaches of the peace, newspaper cuttings, MInn 80210.

68 *Süddeutsche Zeitung*, 24 October 1952, ibid.

69 'Die Amerikaner in Deutschland', Ernst Müller-Meiningen in the *Süddeutsche Zeitung*, 25/26 April 1953, ibid.

70 Müller, *US-Truppen und Sowjetarmee in Deutschland*, p. 75.

71 BayHStaA MInn 91951, breaches of the peace by foreign armed forces.

72 Müller, *US-Truppen und Sowjetarmee in Deutschland*, pp. 78–9.
73 Susan Brownmiller, *Against Our Will: Men, Women, and Rape* (New York 1975).
74 Ibid., pp. 14–15.
75 Ibid., p. 35.
76 The relevance of this view was demonstrated last year in the Gaza war, when a professor at Bar Ilan University in Tel Aviv claimed in a radio interview that the only thing that would deter Palestinians from their suicide missions would be the fear that their women would be raped by Jews in revenge; see http://forward.com/news/breaking-news/202558/israeli-professor-suggests-rape-would-serve-as-ter.
77 Brownmiller, *Against Our Will*, p. 309.
78 A drunken GI tried to drag her mother out of the house while she was visiting Stadtlauingen. For this 'attempted rape', the soldier was court-martialled and shot by the American military police. One might wonder whether an attempted abduction like this would have prompted such a reaction at the time. At all events, Schwarzer cites it as one of the reasons for her feminist position on violence: Alice Schwarzer, *Lebenslauf* (Cologne 2011), p. 31.
79 A report by a victim in a special issue of the feminist newspaper *Courage* from 1980 about the everyday life of women during the war is one of the few exceptions in this regard; Helga Born, 'Das Vergewaltigen war noch im vollem Gange', *Courage, aktuelle Frauenzeitung* special issue 2, 3 (1980), online edition of Friedrich-Ebert-Stiftung, pp. 57–61. The rape problem remains today one of the greatest feminist works in progress. The majority of incidents are still unreported because the victims' moral conduct would be shown up in court in an embarrassing manner. Until the late 1990s, the criteria for rape were extremely rigid. For a rape to be recognized at all, there had to be a considerable amount of violence involved. Within a marriage and also with prostitution, it was not considered a criminal offence if prior consent to sexual intercourse had been given: 'The restrictive interpretation of rape is particularly surprising given that rape is one of the most serious crimes in the laws governing sexual offences and signifies an

extreme emotional burden for the victim. Judicial opinion on rape has not kept up with the development of social attitudes to sexuality and sexual delinquency. It remains dominated by patriarchal structures that have begun to lose their hold only in the last few years and by a traditional condemnation of prostitutes. All told, the attitude of the courts to rape may be regarded as backward.' It was not a feminist who wrote these words about the lax interpretation of rape but a law professor at the University of Bonn: Johannes A. J. Brüggemann, *Entwicklung und Wandel des Sexualstrafrechts in der Geschichte unseres StGB: Die Reform der Sexualdelikte einst und jetzt* (Baden-Baden 2013), pp. 289–90.

80 Helke Sander's historic speech can be read on the Internet at www.hdg.de/lemo/html/dokumente/Kontinuitaet-UndWandel_redeSandersZurNeuenFrauenbewegung.

81 See Miriam Gebhardt, *Alice im Niemandsland: Wie die deutsche Frauenbewegung die Frauen verlor* (Munich 2012).

82 Natascha Drubek-Meyer, 'Griffiths und Vertovs Wiege: Dziga Vertovs Film *Kolybel'naja* (1937)', in: *Frauen und Film* 54/55 (1994), pp. 31–51.

83 Naimark, 'The Russians and Germans', p. 206.

84 See Moeller, *War Stories*.

85 Gudrun Brockhaus, 'Kontroversen um die "Kriegskindheit"', in: *Forum Psychoanalyse* no. 26 (2010), pp. 313–24, here p. 315.

86 Harald Welzer, in Hartmut Radebold, Werner Bohleber and Jürgen Zinnecker (eds.), *Transgenerationale Weitergabe kriegsbelasteter Kindheiten* (Weinheim and Munich 2009).

87 See, for example, Jeffrey Burds, 'Sexual Violence in Europe in World War II, 1935–1945', in: *Politics and Society* 37, 1 (2009), pp. 35–74.

88 Margarete Doerr, 'Mittragen – Mitverantworten? Eine Fallstudie zum Hausfrauenalltag im Zweiten Weltkrieg', in: Hagemann et al., *Heimat-Front*, pp. 275–90, here p. 283.

89 Ibid., p. 284.

90 Nicholas Stargardt, *'Maikäfer, flieg!' Hitlers Krieg und die Kinder* (Munich 2006), p. 13.

91 October 2002 in the Institut für Psychotherapie e. V., Berlin.

92 Uwe Langendorf, 'Heimatvertreibung – das stumme Trauma:

Spätfolgen von Vertreibung in der zweiten Generation', in: *Analytische Psychologie*, 136/2 (2004), pp. 207–23.

93 Bertram von der Stein, '"Flüchtlingskinder": Transgenerationale Perspektive von Spätfolgen des Zweiten Weltkrieges bei Nachkommen von Flüchtlingen aus den ehemaligen deutschen Ostgebieten', in: Radebold et al., *Transgenerationale Weitergabe*, pp. 183–91; see also Jürgen Zinnecker, 'Die "transgenerationale Weitergabe" der Erfahrung des Weltkrieges in der Familie', in: Radebold et al., *Transgenerationale Weitergabe*, pp. 141–54.

94 Stein, 'Flüchtlingskinder', p. 185.

95 Ibid., p. 187.

96 Zinnecker, 'Transgenerationale Weitergabe', p. 143.

SOURCES AND SELECTED LITERATURE

Archives

Bundesarchiv Lichterfelde
Landesarchiv Berlin
Heimatmuseum Charlottenburg
Staatsarchiv Freiburg
Staatsarchiv München
Bayerisches Hauptstaatsarchiv München
Institut für Zeitgeschichte
Landesarchiv Nordrhein-Westfalen
Bundesarchiv Koblenz
National Archives, Washington

Literature and references

Andreas-Friedrich, Ruth, *Schauplatz Berlin: Ein deutsches Tagebuch* (Berlin 1964); in English as *Berlin Underground, 1938–1945*, trans. Barrows Mussey (New York, 1947)

Anonymous, *A Woman in Berlin – Eight Weeks in the Conquered City: A Diary* (London 1982)

Beer, Mathias, 'Die Dokumentation der Vertreibung der Deutschen aus Ost-Mitteleuropa (1953–1962): Ein Seismograph bundesdeutscher

Erinnerungskultur', in Jörg-Dieter Gauger and Manfred Kittel (eds.), *Die Vertreibung der Deutschen aus dem Osten in der Erinnerungskultur*, Eine Veröffentlichung der Konrad-Adenauer-Stiftung e.V. und des Instituts für Zeitgeschichte (Sankt Augustin 2004), pp. 17–37

Bessel, Richard, *Germany 1945: From War to Peace* (London 2009)

Biallas, Leonie, *Komm, Frau, raboti: Ich war Kriegsbeute* (Leverkusen 2010)

Biess, Frank, 'Moral Panic in Postwar Germany: The Abduction of Young Germans into the Foreign Legion and French Colonialism in the 1950s', in *Journal of Modern History* 84, 4 (2012), 789–832

Biess, Frank and Moeller, Robert (eds.), *Histories of the Aftermath: The Legacies of the Second World War in Europe* (New York 2012)

Bisky, Jens, 'Wenn Jungen Weltgeschichte spielen, haben Mädchen stumme Rollen: Wer war die Anonyma in Berlin? Frauen, Fakten und Fiktionen – Anmerkungen zu einem grossen Bucherfolg dieses Sommers', in *Süddeutsche Zeitung* (24 September 2003), 16

The Bodleian Library (ed.), *Instructions for British Servicemen in Germany 1944* (Oxford 2007)

Böhmer, Martina, *Erfahrungen sexualisierter Gewalt in der Lebensgeschichte alter Frauen: Ansätze für eine frauenorientierte Altenarbeit* (Frankfurt 2011)

Boveri, Margret, *Tage des Überlebens: Berlin 1945* (Munich 1985 [1966])

Brownmiller, Susan, *Against Our Will: Men, Women, and Rape* (New York 1975)

Bundesministerium für Vertriebene (ed.), *Dokumentation der Vertreibung der Deutschen aus Ost-Mitteleuropa*, vol. I/1 (Bonn 1954–6)

Dudink, Stefan, Hagemann, Karen and Tosh, John, *Masculinities in Politics and War: Gendering Modern History* (Manchester 2004)

Eichhorn, Svenja and Kuwert, Philipp, *Das Geheimnis unserer Grossmütter: Eine empirische Studie über sexualisierte Kriegsgewalt um 1945* (Giessen 2011)

Emsley, Clive, *Soldier, Sailor, Beggarman, Thief: Crime and the British Armed Services since 1914* (Oxford 2013)

Eschebach, Insa and Mühlhäuser, Regina (eds.), *Krieg und Geschlecht: Sexuelle Gewalt im Krieg und Sex-Zwangsarbeit in NS-Konzentrationslagern* (Berlin 2008)

Fehrenbach, Heide, 'Ami-Liebchen und Mischlingskinder: Rasse,

Geschlect und Kultur in der deutsch-amerikanischen Begegnung', in Klaus Neumann (ed.), *Nachkrieg in Deutschland* (Hamburg 2001), pp. 178–205

Gebhardt, Miriam, *Alice im Niemandsland: Wie die deutsche Frauenbewegung die Frauen verlor* (Munich 2012)

Gebhardt, Miriam, *Die Angst vor dem kindlichen Tyrannen: Eine Geschichte der Erziehung im 20. Jahrhundert* (Munich 2009)

Gebhardt, Miriam, '"Frage des Schweigens"? Forschungsthesen zur Vergewaltigung deutscher Frauen nach Kriegsende', in Silke Satjukow and Barbara Stelzl-Marx (eds.), *Besatzungskinder: Die Nachkommen alliierter Soldaten in Österreich und Deutschland* (Vienna, Cologne and Weimar 2015)

Gelfand, Wladimir, *Deutschland-Tagebuch 1945–1946: Aufzeichnungen eines Rotarmisten* (Berlin 2008)

Goedde, Petra, 'From Villains to Victims: Fraternization and the Feminization of Germany, 1945–1947', in *Diplomatic History* 23, 1 (Winter 1999), 1–20

Goedde, Petra, *GIs and Germans: Die Gesellschaft der Überlebenden – Kriegsheimkehrer und ihre Gewalterfahrungen im Zweiten Weltkrieg* (Munich 2009); in English as *Gis and Germans: Culture, Gender, and Foreign Relations, 1945–1949* (Yale, 2003)

Goeschel, Christian, *Selbstmord im Dritten Reich* (Berlin 2011); in English as *Suicide in Nazi Germany* (Oxford, 2009)

Goltermann, Svenja, *Die Gesellschaft der Überlebenden: Deutsche Kriegsheimkehrer und ihre Gewalterfahrungen im Zweiten Weltkrieg* (Munich 2009)

Goltermann, Svenja, 'Im Wahn der Gewalt: Massentod, Opferdiskurs und Psychiatrie 1945–1956', in Klaus Naumann (ed.), *Nachkrieg in Deutschland* (Hamburg 2001), pp. 343–63

Grossmann, Atina, 'A Question of Silence: The Rape of German Women by Occupation Soldiers', in: *October* 72 (Spring 1995), 43–64

Hagemann, Karen and Pröve, Ralf, *Landsknechte, Soldatenfrauen und Nationalkrieger: Militär, Krieg und Geschlechterordnung im historischen Wandel* (Frankfurt 1998)

Hagemann, Karen, Pröve, Ralf and Schüler-Springorum, Stefanie (eds.), *Heimat-Front: Militär und Geschlechterverhältnisse im Zeitalter der Weltkriege* (Frankfurt 2002); in English as *Home/Front: The*

Military, War and Gender in Twentieth-century Germany (New York, 2002)

Hamburger Institut f. Sozialforschung, *200 Tage und 1 Jahrhundert: Gewalt und Destruktivität im Spiegel des Jahres 1945* (Hamburg 1995)

Heineman, Elizabeth, 'The Hour of the Woman: Memories of Germany's "Crisis Years" and West German National Identity', in *American Historical Review* 101, 2 (April 1996), 354–95

Henke, Klaus-Dietmar, *Die amerikanische Besatzung Deutschlands* (Munich 1996)

Hildebrandt, Dieter and Kuballa, Felix (eds.), *Mein Kriegsende: Erinnerungen an die Stunde Null* (Berlin 2012)

Hoerning, Erika, 'Frauen als Kriegsbeute: Der Zwei-Fronten-Krieg, Beispiele aus Berlin', in Lutz Niethammer and Alexander von Plato (eds.), *'Wir kriegen jetzt andere Zeiten': Auf der Such nach der Erfahrung des Volkes in nachfaschistischen Ländern* (Bonn 1985), pp. 327–44

Höhn, Maria, *GIs and Fräuleins: The German–American Encounter in 1950s West Germany* (Chapel Hill and London 2002)

Jacobs, Ingeborg, *Freiwild: Das Schicksal deutscher Frauen 1945* (Berlin 2008)

Jarausch, Konrad, *Die Umkehr: Deutsche Wandlungen 1945–1995* (Munich 2004)

Kauders, Anthony, *Der Freud-Komplex: Eine Geschichte der Psychoanalyse in Deutschland* (Berlin 2014)

Kershaw, Ian, *The End: Hitler's Germany, 1944–45* (London 2011)

Koop, Volker, *Besetzt: Französische Besaztungspolitik in Deutschland* (Berlin 2005)

Köpp, Gabi, *Warum war ich bloss ein Mädchen? Das Trauma einer Flucht 1945* (Munich 2010)

Kossert, Andreas, *Kalte Heimat: Die Geschichte der deutschen Vertriebenen nach 1945* (Munich 2008)

Kowalczuk, Ilko-Sascha and Wolle, Stefan, *Roter Stern über Deutschland* (Berlin 2001)

Kuby, Erich, *Die Russen in Berlin* (Munich 1965); in English as *The Russians and Berlin* (London, 1968)

Kuby, Erich, 'Die Russen in Berlin', in *Der Spiegel* 19–24 (1965)

Lilly, J. Robert, *Taken by Force: Rape and American GIs in Europe during World War II* (Chippenham 2007)

Maercker, Andreas, et al., 'Posttraumatische Belastungsstörungen in Deutschland: Ergebnisse einer gesamtdeutschen epidemiologischen Untersuchung', in *Der Nervenarzt* 79 (2008), 577–86

Maulucci, Thomas and Junker, Detlev (eds.), *GIs in Germany: The Social, Economic, Cultural, and Political History of the American Military Presence* (Cambridge 2013)

Medica mondiale e.v. and Griese, Karin (eds.), *Sexualisierte Kriegsgewalt und ihre Folgen* (Berlin 2006)

Meehah, Patricia, *A Strange Enemy People: Germans under the British 1945–1990* (London 2001)

Merridale, Catherine, *Ivan's War: The Red Army, 1939–1945* (London 2005)

Meyer, Sibylle and Schulze, Eva, *Wie wir das alles geschafft haben: Alleinstehende Frauen berichten über ihr Leben nach 1945* (Munich 1993)

Moeller, Robert G., *War Stories: The Search for a Usable Past in the Federal Republic of Germany* (Berkeley 2001)

Moeller, Robert G. (ed.), *West Germany under Construction: Politics, Society, and Culture in the Adenauer Era* (Michigan 1997)

Mühlhäuser, Regina, *Eroberungen: Sexuelle Gewalttaten und intime Beziehungen deutscher Soldaten in der Sowjetunion 1941–1945* (Hamburg 2010)

Mühlhäuser, Regina, 'Massenvergewaltigungen in Berlin 1945 im Gedächtnis betroffener Frauen: Zur Verwobenheit von national-istischen, rassistischen und geschlechtsspezifischen Diskursen', in Veronika Aegerter et al. (eds.), *Geschlecht hat Methode: Ansätze und Perspektiven in der Frauen- und Geschlechtergeschichte* (Contribution to the Ninth Swiss Historians' Conference 1988) (Zurich 1999), pp. 235–46

Mühlhäuser, Regina, 'Vergewaltigung' in Christian Gudehus and Michaela Christ (eds.), *Gewalt: Ein interdisziplinäres Handbuch* (Stuttgart 2013), pp. 164–70

Mühlhäuser, Regina, 'Vergewaltigungen in Deutschland 1945: Nationaler Opferdiskurs und individuelles Erinnern betroffener Frauen', in Klaus Naumann (ed.)., *Nachkrieg in Deutschland* (Hamburg 2001), pp. 384–408

Mühlhäuser, Regina and Eschebach, Insa, 'Sexuelle Gewalt im Krieg und Sex-Zwangsarbeit in NS-Konzentrationslagern: Deutungen,

Darstellungen, Begriffe', in Mühlhäuser and Eschebach (eds.), *Krieg und Geschlecht: Sexuelle Gewalt im Krieg und Sexwangsarbeit in NS-Konzentrationslagern* (Berlin 2008), pp. 11–32

Müller, Christian T., *US-Truppen und Sowjetarmee in Deutschland: Erfahrungen, Beziehungen, Konflikte im Vergleich* (Paderborn 2011)

Naimark, Norman, *Die Russen in Deutschland: Die Sowjetische Besatzungszone 1945 bis 1949* (Berlin 1997); in English as *The Russians in Germany: A History of the Soviet Zone of Occupation, 1945–1949* (Harvard, 1997)

Naimark, Norman, 'The Russians and Germans: Rape during the War and Post-Soviet Memories', in Raphaëlle Branche and Fabrice Virgili (eds.), *Rape in Wartime: A History to Be Written* (Basingstoke 2012), pp. 201–19

Naumann, Klaus (ed.), *Nachkrieg in Deutschland* (Hamburg 2001)

Niethammer, Lutz and Plato, Alexander von (eds.), *'Wir kriegen jetzt andere Zeiten': Auf der Suche nach der Erfahrung des Volkes in nachfaschistischen Ländern* (Bonn 1985)

Pfister, Peter (ed.), *Das Ende des Zweiten Weltkriesg im Erzbistum München und Freising* (Regensburg 2005)

Plato, Alexander von, *Alte Heimat – Neue Zeit: Füchtlinge, Umgesiedelte, Vertriebene in der Sowjetischen Besatzungszone und in der DDR* (Berlin 1991)

Poutrus, Kirsten, 'Von den Massenvergewaltigungen zum Mutterschutzgesetz: Abtreibungspolitik und Abtreibungspraxis in Ostdeutschland, 1945–1950', in Richard Bessel and Ralph Jessen (eds.), *Die Grenzen der Diktatur: Staat und Gesellschaft in der DDR* (Göttingen 1996), pp. 170–98

Radebold, Hartmut, Bohleber, Werner and Zinnecker, Jürgen (eds.), *Transgenerationale Weitergabe kriegsbelasteter Kindheiten* (Weinheim and Munich 2009)

Reckwitz, Andreas, 'Umkämpfte Maskulinität: Zur historischen Kultursoziologie männlicher Subjektformen und ihrer Affektivitäten vom Zeitalter der Empfindsamkeit bis zur Postmoderne', in Manuel Borutta and Nina Verheyen (eds.), *Die Präsenz der Gefühle: Männlichkeit und Emotion in der Moderne* (Bielefeld 2010)

Reemtsma, Jan Philipp, 'Trauma und Moral', in *Kursbuch* 126 (1996), 95–112

Roberts, Mary Louise, *What Soldiers Do: Sex and the American GI in World War II France* (Chicago 2013)

Ryan, Cornelius, *The Last Battle* (London 1966)

Sander, Helke and Johr, Barbara (eds.), *BeFreier und Befreite: Krieg, Vergewaltigungen, Kinder* (Munich 1992)

Satjukow, Silke, *Befreiung? Die Ostdeutschen und 1945* (Leipzig 2009)

Satjukow, Silke, *Besatzer: 'Die Russen' in Deutschland 1945–1994* (Göttingen 2008)

Satjukow, Silke, '"Besatzungskinder": Nachkommen deutscher Frauen und alliierter Soldaten seit 1945', in *Geschichte und Gesellschaft* 37 (2011), 1–33

Satjukow, Silke and Stelzl-Marx, Barbara (eds.), *Besatzungskinder: Die Nachkommen alliierter Soldaten in Österreich und Deutschland* (Vienna, Cologne and Weimar 2015)

Scherstjanoi, Elke (ed.), *Rotarmisten schreiben aus Deutschland: Briefe von der Front (1945) und historische Analysen* (= Texte und Materialien zur Zeitgeschichte, 14, published by Institut für Zeitgeschichte) (Munich 2004)

Schmidt-Harzbach, Ingrid, 'Doppelt besiegt: Vergewaltigung als Massenschicksal', in *Frankfurter Frauenblatt* (May 1985), 18–23

Seifert, Ruth, 'Krieg und Vergewaltigung: Ansätze zu einer Analyse', in Alexandra Stiglmayer (ed.), *Massenvergewaltigung: Krieg gegen die Frauen* (Freiburg 1993), pp. 85–108; in English as 'War and Rape: A Preliminary Analysis', in Alexandra Stiglmayer (ed.), *Mass Rape: The War against Women in Bosnia-Herzegovina* (London, 1994), 54–72.

Seifert, Ruth, 'Militär und Geschlechtsverhältnisse: Entwicklungslinien einer ambivalenten Debatte', in Christine Eifler and Ruth Seifert (eds.), *Soziale Konstruktionen – Militär und Geschlechterverhältnis* (Münster 1999), pp. 44–70

Stein, Bertram von der, '"Flüchtlingskinder": Transgenerationale Perspektive von Spätfolgen des Zweiten Weltkrieges bei Nachkommen von Flüchtlingen aus den ehemaligen deutschen Ostgebieten', in Hartmut Radebold, Werner Bohleber and Jürgen Zinnecker (eds.), *Transgenerationale Weitergabe kriegsbelasteter Kindheiten* (Weinheim and Munich 2009)

Stelzl-Marx, Barbara, *Stalins Soldaten in Österreich: Die Innensicht der sowjetischen Besatzung 1945–1955* (Vienna 2012)

Stiglmayer, Alexandra (ed.), *Massenvergewaltigung: Krieg gegen die Frauen* (Freiburg 1993); in English as *Mass Rape: The War against Women in Bosnia-Herzegovina* (London, 1994).

Volkmann-Steinhardt, Gela, *Eine Stimme aus der pommerschen Passion: Erlebnisse aus dem deutschen Zusammenbruch 1945* (Freiburg i. Brsg. 1993)

Zinnecker, Jürgen, 'Die "transgenerationale Weitergabe" der Erfahrung desWeltkrieges in der Familie', in Hartmut Radebold, Werner Bohleber and Jürgen Zinnecker (eds.), *Transgenerationale Weitergabe kriegsbelasteter Kindheiten* (Weinheim and Munich 2009), pp. 141–54

INDEX